Counselling for Grief and Bereavement

Counselling in Practice

Series editor: Windy Dryden
Associate editor: E. Thomas Dowd

Counselling in Practice is a series of books developed especially for counsellors and students of counselling, which provides practical, accessible guidelines for dealing with clients with specific, but very common, problems. Books in this series have become recognized as classic texts in their field, and include:

Career Counselling, second edition
Robert Nathan and Linda Hill

Counselling Survivors of Childhood Sexual Abuse, third edition
Claire Burke Draucker and Donna Martsolf

Counselling for Post-Traumatic Stress Disorder, third edition
Michael J. Scott and Stephen G. Stradling

Psychotherapy and Counselling for Depression, third edition
Paul Gilbert

Counselling for Eating Disorders, second edition
Sara Gilbert

Counselling for Alcohol Problems, second edition
Richard Velleman

Counselling for Anxiety Problems, second edition
Diana Sanders and Frank Wills

Counselling for Family Problems
Eddy Street

Counselling for Stress Problems
Stephen Palmer and Windy Dryden

Counselling Couples
Donald L. Bubenzer and John D. West

Counselling for Psychosomatic Problems
Diana Sanders

Counselling People on Prescribed Drugs
Diane Hammersley

Counselling for Fertility Problems
Jane Read

Counselling People with Communication Problems
Peggy Dalton

Counselling with Dreams and Nightmares
Delia Cushway and Robyn Sewell

Counselling for Grief and Bereavement

Second Edition

Geraldine M. Humphrey Ph.D. and
David G. Zimpfer Ed.D.

SAGE Publications
Los Angeles ▪ London ▪ New Delhi ▪ Singapore

First published 1996
Second edition published 2008

 SAGE Publications Ltd
1 Oliver's Yard
55 City Road
London EC1Y 1SP

SAGE Publications Inc.
2455 Teller Road
Thousand Oaks, California 91320

SAGE Publications India Pvt Ltd
B 1/I 1 Mohan Cooperative Industrial Area
Mathura Road, New Delhi 110 044

SAGE Publications Asia-Pacific Pte Ltd
33 Pekin Street #02-01
Far East Square
Singapore 048763

Library of Congress Control Number: 2007927263

British Library Cataloguing in Publication data

A catalogue record for this book is available
from the British Library

ISBN 978-1-4129-3565-4
ISBN 978-1-4129-3566-1 (pbk)

Typeset by C&M Digitals (P) Ltd., Chennai, India
Printed in Great Britain by The Cromwell Press, Trowbridge, Wiltshire
Printed on paper from sustainable resources

Contents

About the Authors   vi
Preface   vii
Acknowledgements   viii

Introduction   1

1   Loss and Grief in Life   3

2   Assessment Strategies   19

3   Grief Counselling and Grief Resolution   35

4   Family Grief   55

5   Group Counselling   80

6   Children and Grief   107

7   Anticipatory Grief   125

8   Special Issues   137

9   When Grief is Not Resolved   147

Appendix: Resources on Dying, Death and Grieving   159

References   171

Index   176

About the Authors

Geraldine M. Humphrey, PhD has worked as a counsellor in the Department of Psychology at the North Canton Medical Foundation, North Canton, Ohio for the last 20 years. She was also the director of the Grief Support and Education Center for 15 years, and a part-time instructor of counsellor education at Kent State University, Kent, Ohio and Walsh University, North Canton, Ohio. She has been certified as a Grief Therapist and Educator through the (Association for Death Education and Counselling).

David G. Zimpfer Ed.D was professor of counsellor education for over 40 years, including positions at the University of Rochester and Kent State University. He has recently retired and lives in New York. He was director of the Cancer Counselling Center of Ohio for many years. He now serves as business advisor for the Association for Counsellor Education and Supervision.

Lisa M. Humphrey, MD is currently a chief resident in pediatrics at the Children's Hospital of Philadelphia, University of Pennsylvania, Philadelphia. She has an undergraduate degree in Psychology from Columbia University, New York City, NY and has done graduate work in Early Childhood Development. She was the camp director for bereaved children sponsored by the Center for Grief Counselling and Education, North Canton, Ohio and authored the script for the video 'Camp Lost and Found'.

Preface

This book grew out of a perceived need to offer health care professionals a resource that could be utilized in programs and services that address the issues of those who are both anticipating and subsequently coping with loss and grief in their lives. Over time in our practices we have become aware that many professionals often use strategies from earlier bereavement models or general mental health interventions. While it appears that more individuals are seeking bereavement services, especially in the wake of terrorist attacks, war, and natural disasters, there is little evidence that professionals are receiving adequate training for this subspecialty.

The book is not intended to replace the need for additional training. Our intent is to offer a practical guide for a wide range of help providers, including counsellors, social workers, psychologists, nurses, clergy, educators, and volunteers in social service agencies and schools. Education programmes for these providers typically do not acknowledge the complexity of loss, nor do they commonly provide adequate skills to facilitate the process of grief. Our contribution here is intended to be introductory to the field, and offers providers the opportunity to view loss and grief as an important specialized area of counselling.

Acknowledgements

One cannot write a book that focuses on loss and grief without being reminded of what we have loved and appreciated the most in our lives. What has meant the most, upon reflection, has often been taken for granted. Writing this second edition has once again given me the opportunity to remember and appreciate my gifts of life. These gifts include my husband, children, and grandchildren. John, my husband of 40 years, has enriched my life in ways that would not have been possible without his encouragement and support. My children, whose adult friendships I now cherish, have validated my belief that life presents difficult challenges that can become opportunities of growth. And now my young grandchildren, symbols of new life and fresh energy, are reminders that despite the losses of those we love, we can and will love and live fully again.

I would like to acknowledge the North Canton Medical Foundation and staff for the support they have provided for this second edition. Finally, I want to thank the clients that I have counselled for the last 20 years. Their willingness to share their lives with me has provided necessary direction as we, together, have explored their unique journeys through grief.

Geraldine M. Humphrey

My wife and I have lost two children to untimely and tragic deaths, one very young and the other in the prime of young manhood. Our own sense of loss and the accompanying grieving have been powerful personal experiences of what bereavement feels like, what it does to one's sense of being, and how it shakes one's values and challenges meaning in one's life. Though the learning these children have offered me is quite unwelcome, I must thank them. In addition, in my work as a counsellor with persons who have life-threatening illnesses, I have dealt with loss and grief on a daily basis. My clients have been special in how they guide me on the path of helping them. Finally, I am indebted to my dear spouse, Lou, for her constant support and unfailing belief in me. Without her nothing I do would be easy; in fact, perhaps impossible. For 50 years she has been my rock.

David G. Zimpfer

Introduction

This book starts from the premise that loss and grief are normal and integral aspects of life itself. Grieving is a process, not something to 'get over'. While a good share of the contents here relate particularly to death, we maintain that death is only one kind of loss to be grieved; there are many other types of loss which one may be expected to cope with and to resolve. The materials here easily translate to a variety of losses that people experience.

Human service care providers rarely work with an individual who has not experienced some type of loss. A lifetime is an accumulation of losses; these may play upon each other as triggers or may ignite what otherwise might be considered an inappropriate or excessive grief response. In addition, losses are often ignored or not validated, and unresolved losses are often found to be at the root of later mental health problems. Any given loss is set in the context of a lifetime and cannot be seen as an isolated event.

Chapter 1: Loss and Grief in Life

Theory in human growth and development is offered as the foundation for the concepts of attachment, loss, and grief. This second edition includes more recent theories and models that provide different conceptualizations of both the grieving process and resolution. Categories of loss, perspectives involved in the grief process, and a sketch of various bereavement models provide the content base for the reader.

Chapters 2 and 3: Assessment Strategies, and Grief Counselling and Grief Resolution

These chapters, in the realm of service delivery, offer assessment and intervention strategies with many case examples. We attempt to offer concrete direction for providers to work with their clients in a manner that promotes healing and a sense of growth. Attention has been given to illustrate some of the new concepts that focus on meaning reconstruction and accommodation to new realities following events of loss.

Chapter 4: Family Grief

Every client represents and is influenced by membership of one or more families. We have considered these memberships and various underlying theories of family systems, along with attention to the unique issues of grief that each member experiences during times of loss. This second edition introduces some recent contributions to families in grief and related strategies for assessment and intervention. Concrete examples for death and non-death losses are given for consideration.

Chapter 5: Group Counselling

This chapter offers an adult 10-week structured support group that can be used with death and non-death related losses. Each session has a grief-related theme, objectives, interventions, and homework assignments. Concepts and strategies introduced in the first two chapters are incorporated throughout the sessions.

Chapter 6: Children and Grief

Because there is so little literature on specific intervention for grieving children, children's grief is often disenfranchised; thus opportunities for developing healthy coping behaviours are often missed. Difficulties with adults experiencing grief often have roots in unacknowledged childhood losses. This chapter addresses concepts of development as related to grief, grief with potential complications, and models for intervention. Based on the allowance of one chapter for this population, we believed that it was important to focus extensively on theoretical constructs and how they have been applied to existing models and programs. It is our belief that practitioners must first be grounded in sound theory; thus, we have deviated from our format of presenting case examples. The theoretical models presented in this chapter are easily adapted for professional practice. The program that is offered is a 5-day camp for children and adolescents that includes program goals, along with daily themes, objectives, and interventions. This camp program may be used as presented, adapted to fit a support group format, or used in individual counselling sessions.

The message this second edition stresses is that loss changes lives dramatically, but that life needs to be, and can be, lived with renewed meaning and purpose. The role of the professional is to offer services that empower the bereaved to heal and reconstruct their changed realities. No matter what the event of loss that has occurred, human beings must have meaning, purpose and value to their existence. Inherent in all loss is the challenge for growth.

Chapter 7: Anticipatory Grief

Although the focus of this chapter is on illness and death-related losses, anticipatory grief can refer to a process for any loss that is expected in the future. Consistent with the format of this book, theoretical constructs, programs, and interventions are discussed. This edition also includes a discussion of palliative care and the advancements that have occurred within the last 10 years in this specialty.

Chapter 8: Special Issues

Special applications in this chapter include instances of murder, suicide, AIDS, and the early loss of a child. Theoretical considerations of loss continue to be the basis of assessment and subsequent models for intervention with these populations.

Chapter 9: When Grief is Not Resolved

This chapter considers existing theories of complicated, pathological, and unresolved grief. This second edition also offers new perspectives on what previously has been considered pathological grief, and presents more current conceptualization on resolution and continued attachments. Newer thoughts do not undermine the realities of complications or pathology; rather, they offer additional perspectives that can facilitate healthier processes and accommodation to changed realities.

1 Loss and Grief in Life

Loss is an integral part of life. It is not something that happens to us as we live; rather, it is life itself. Death is not the only loss a human might experience; yet it is often the only loss that is validated as a legitimate grief experience. In our view, any event that involves change is a loss that necessitates the process of grief and transition. A loss event requires that some part of the individual be left behind and grieved for before the process of transition and rebuilding can occur.

Loss is defined as the state of being deprived of or being without something one has had, or a detriment or disadvantage from failure to keep, have, or get. Grief is the pain and suffering experienced after loss; mourning is a period of time during which signs of grief are shown; and bereavement, as discussed by Raphael (1983), is the reaction to the loss of a close relationship.

The bereavement experience includes the concept of grief, as pain and suffering must be experienced in order to heal and resolve the loss event. It also includes ideas of reaction, adaptation, and process. Reaction involves a response. The bereaved person reacts emotionally as the pain of grief is experienced, and gradually reacts cognitively and behaviourally as a new identity is formed and a life is rebuilt. Adaptation refers to the concept of letting go of that which has been lost, compromising, and gradually adjusting to and accepting a new life. And process involves the total experience. The work of bereavement is not linear; it is cyclical in nature, with many painful returns to the beginning to start the process once more. Tailspins back to an earlier stage of grief are an inherent aspect of the bereavement experience.

Effective resolution entails an active involvement. Loss, grief, and bereavement violate personal boundaries and remove a sense of security and control. The bereaved person will never have the same identity as before. He or she is no longer attached in the same way to a person, object, or activity that provided security, meaning, or purpose. Although this has the potential to be positive in terms of growth, initially a person feels a sense of aloneness and helplessness. Models of loss have evolved over time, including theories of attachment and ways to conceptualize the severing of these attachments. Current models have moved from concern with mere coping towards interventions that foster growth and self-actualization. However, despite research and insight into this human condition, grief for many remains a passive process. Grief is often perceived as something to 'get over' in a fixed period of time. Yet we will come to understand in this book that process implies more than fixed tasks. Counsellors must continuously be aware that process involves trial and error, change, and frustrating returns back to earlier experiences of grief. It demands an active response in order to restore one's sense of ability to be in control again. Moreover, loss cannot be narrowly viewed as one event. Each loss is influenced by past losses, and each loss will be affected by additional secondary losses that will occur as a result of the present loss at different times of the process.

In the discussion that follows, we will consider the evolution of models, plus the categories of loss, and the perspectives that influence a bereavement experience. These ideas provide frameworks for assessment and interventions and will be referred to throughout this book.

Evolution of Models of Loss and Bereavement

Models and theories have attempted to explain the complex process experienced after significant loss and change in our lives. Evaluating the models of bereavement over time shows more of an evolution of theory and practice than the creation of distinct models. The focus has gone from theories of attachment and loss, to concepts of acute grief, to tasks, to stages, to psychological processes and phases. There are numerous models and it is beyond the scope of this book to identify all of them or to discuss any one in detail. The intent is to identify several that have been particularly influential and useful to persons who counsel others in their loss and grief.

From Freud on there has been an emphasis on personal attachment to objects and people, and the giving up of some part of self following a loss (death or non-death) event. Attention to this loss of some aspect of self is an integral part of grief resolution; however, it is the part that is often negated and avoided today. During human history the experience of grief and its resolution has become more of a task to be accomplished, or something that must be gotten over and forgotten. The importance of healing the internal void within us, or that part of us that has been eliminated because of the loss, is not often understood as the foundation of self-restoration.

Freud offers one of the earliest models for consideration. He referred to the emotion present in melancholia as 'mourning', meaning that one is searching for an attachment that has been lost. Using the concepts of the ego and id, he discussed the need for the ego to disengage from that which has been lost and to eventually withdraw energy from the lost object. The bereaved was not grieving just one object; rather, he/she was grieving and letting go of multiple layers of attachments (stored memories and symbols) that are involved in the formation of a relationship. In a slow and arduous process, the reality of the loss is accepted by the ego and instinctual energy is withdrawn; thus the ego can accommodate the loss and search for new attachments. Although he does not provide a clear framework for operationalizing the process, his theory offers an understanding of the multiple levels of human attachment and the difficulty facing the bereaved who must undertake the task of grief work.

Lindemann's (1944) work is considered a milestone in the development of ideas about bereavement. His study was based on his interventions with 100 bereaved individuals, following the deaths of family and friends in the Coconut Grove night club fire in the Boston area in 1942. After the disaster, Lindemann provided opportunities for the bereaved survivors to work through their grief. From his interventions he gathered and studied data, which resulted in his study that offered a description of various symptoms of normal grief, with additional signs that he believed might indicate potential pathology. In the initial stages, he conceptualized acute grief as a normal part of the process. Lindemann proposed six characteristics of acute grief: somatic distress, preoccupation with thoughts/images of the deceased, guilt related to the deceased or the death event, hostile reactions, loss of function, and a tendency to assume traits of the deceased in one's behaviour. The last characteristic could indicate pathology in a later part of the process. In addition to these descriptions, Lindemann has provided a model and frame of reference that allow one to consider grief as work, with specific tasks to accomplish. His tasks included undoing emotional and psychological attachments with the deceased, readjusting to an environment without the deceased, and rebuilding new relationships.

Although Kübler-Ross was neither the first nor the last theorist in this field, her name and stage theory are still the connection that many people make today when death and grief are the topic of consideration. Her landmark contribution, *On Death and Dying* (1969), came at a time in the history of the United States when stage approaches to psychological theorizing were acceptable and death was a taboo subject. She opened the doors to discuss and acknowledge death and to address the loss experience. Her focus was on persons who were dying, not on those going through a bereavement process after a significant loss. Yet because of the simplicity of her stages, the ability to comprehend them, and the lack of other theorists in this field being as visible, hers is the theory and approach still most widely recognized today.

As a psychiatrist, Kübler-Ross acknowledged her allegiance to the psychological concepts proposed by Freud. Noteworthy among these were theories of the unconscious mind, and the belief that the psychiatrist was more capable than the layperson to understand and interpret what was occurring in the unconscious mind. This recognition of her background is important, as the tenets of her stage theory are grounded in Freudian concepts. Stephenson (1985) critiqued Kübler-Ross's contributions to this field of study. He appreciated the fact that she opened pathways to communication of a subject that had been avoided; yet her psychoanalytical orientation has been a subject of debate. Her primary intention was to understand the experience of those who had a terminal prognosis and to facilitate a supportive process of coming to terms with one's mortality. As she and her assistants listened to over 200 hospitalized patients who were terminally ill, she interpreted what she heard and subsequently identified five predictable stages of those who are dying. Through these interviews, she interpreted their actions and emotions and delineated the stages of denial, anger, bargaining, depression, and acceptance. Today these emotions and behaviours are not viewed as separate entities in a linear progression; rather, they are acknowledged as part of a larger and more cyclical process. Moreover, what is questioned today is the concept of the unconscious mind (i.e., whether or not it can control actions) and the ability of the psychiatrist to better understand the reality of the patient's experience (i.e., the patient is not in touch with an inner reality, because he or she has not been professionally trained).

Debates in the counselling profession today focus on how accurate the counsellor can be in interpreting a client's experience, diagnosing, and prescribing treatment. Emphasis is turning towards the concept of co-facilitation of a process, with the client's perspective taking the lead.

Bowlby's Attachment Theory is another important landmark in this field of study. In three volumes entitled *Attachment and Loss* (1969, 1973, 1980), he explores instinctive and attachment behaviours of humans and animals, the course of development (ontogeny) of human attachment, an ethnological approach to human fear, and the trauma of loss. In addition to his research, his clinical work with young children and adults (on issues of separation and grief) has provided a wealth of knowledge and a framework for interventions. His professional background was psychoanalytical; however, he broadened his theoretical groundwork to include cognitive psychology, developmental psychology, and ethnology. Cognitive psychology emphasizes that actions and emotions are a result of cognitions and belief systems. Developmental psychology is the framework for understanding an individual on the basis of one's progression physically, mentally, and emotionally as compared to a chronological age and the developmental expectations for a particular age. And ethnology refers to the study of the characteristics and beliefs of communities and individuals.

Bowlby (1980) believes that attachments are developed early in life and have a basis of security and survival for the individual. When these attachments are endangered or broken, there is a normal human response of anxiety and protest. He bases much of his theory on findings from his work with children separated from their mothers. Papers written from the 1950s through to the 1980s reported findings from his infant studies that reflected the similarities between the responses of human infants separated from their mothers and other high-order primates. These similarities led him to believe that these responses had a biological basis, were instinctual and adapational, and provided a basis for survival of the species.

The conceptual framework that Bowlby (1980) brought to the study of mourning differed from what had been traditionally accepted. He believed that his new paradigm allowed him to dispense with some of the abstract concepts, such as psychic energy and drive, which he had found in the course of his research to be unsatisfactory. He stated that his attachment theory facilitated a way of understanding the distress and emotional disturbance experienced by humans when affectional bonds to particular others were broken. Underlying this theory is the belief that attachment behaviour is instinctive and mediated by a behavioural system that is developed early in life. This system is goal-directed and functions to maintain attachments. Attachment behaviour has the potential to remain active throughout life, and is often observed in situations of loss and grief that force bereaved individuals to fill painful voids and make new attachments. It should not be viewed as pathological in an individual after a significant loss; however, new attachments should not be sought with the intention of avoiding other aspects of the grief and mourning processes.

Bowlby also views mourning as including a variety of psychological processes that are set into motion by the loss of a loved one. He cites four general phases: numbing, yearning and searching, disorganization and despair, and reorganization. In addition to the phases that he conceptualizes an individual progresses through, he discusses cognitive biases (cognitive structures) which filter information and serve as the mechanisms that form individual perceptions and belief systems. He hypothesized, based on his research findings of the role of attachment figures throughout life, that experiences with these early figures form cognitive biases and serve as the basis for patterns of relationship that a person makes throughout life. Moreover, he maintained that future losses would be influenced and processed by these cognitive biases.

Bowlby's interventions centre on cognitive insight and cognitive restructuring. He has emphasized the need to process information:

> For it is only when the detailed circumstances of the loss and the intimate particulars of the previous relationship, and of past relationships, are dwelt on in consciousness that the related emotions are not only aroused and experienced but become directed towards the persons and connected with the situations that originally aroused them. (Bowlby, 1980: 200)

Once insight is gained and the cognitive and emotional aspects of relationships have been explored and experienced, the bereaved progresses towards changing cognitive constructs. How one viewed his or her world and experienced it, no longer applies. Life will never be exactly the same. Life can be meaningful again; however, this necessitates the creation of a new internal template of how one will view his or her world.

Worden (2002) did not propose a new theory. His intention was to provide a practical application of established theory in counselling sessions. His book *Grief Counselling and Grief Therapy* (2002) focuses on counselling for the tasks of grief. His contribution in the area of assessment and interventions has been recognized in the field as a milestone. His tasks of grief build on Lindemann's (1944) approach that delineated three tasks and Bowlby's conceptualization of attachment and loss. He views mourning as necessary and sees counselling as a facilitative process that allows the bereaved to take action and not just passively go through the painful experience. He identifies four specific tasks of grief: to accept the reality of the loss, to work through the pain of grief, to adjust to an environment in which the deceased is missing, and to emotionally relocate the deceased and move on with life.

Rando (1993a) has proposed her conception of 'the six "R" processes of mourning'. She mainly addresses loss following a death; however, she states that her model may be generalized to other types of loss. Although there are some similarities to Worden's (2002) tasks, this model elaborates the grieving tasks and includes phases during which they might occur. Moreover, Rando broadens considerations for each task or process beyond what is implied in Worden's model, providing a more extensive base for assessment and intervention strategies:

- **Avoidance phase**: to Recognize the loss and achieve a meaningful understanding about the loss event.
- **Confrontation phase**: the bereaved must React to the separation from that which has been lost. During this phase it is also necessary to Recollect and re-experience the deceased and the relationship through reviewing and remembering. Lastly, during this phase, the bereaved must Relinquish the old attachments to the deceased and the old assumptive world.
- **Accommodation phase**: includes the processes of Readjusting to a new world without forgetting the old, and Reinvesting in meaningful life.

Since the first edition of this book there has been ongoing research and proposed concepts that facilitate greater insight into the process of grief. Continuing

Bonds (Silverman and Klass, 1996; Silverman and Nickman, 1996b), the Dual Process Model (Stroebe and Schut, 1999, 2001), and Meaning Reconstruction (Neimeyer, 2001a) are three that will be considered in this edition.

Continuing bonds challenge prevalent beliefs that successful grief resolution involves a disengagement from the deceased in order to be free to make new attachments and to construct a new identity. During the twentieth century pathological grief was often defined in terms of the need to maintain an ongoing attachment to the deceased. This model proposes 'a process of adaptation and change in the post death relationship and the construction and reconstruction of new connections' (Silverman and Klass, 1996: 18). Resolution involves holding the deceased in loving memory (often forever) and maintaining an inner representation of them. Continuing these bonds and maintaining an inner representation acknowledge that gratification in these relationships changes with death, but that new sources of gratification emerge and develop throughout the process of accommodation. The bereaved reinvest in meaningful living that may redefine them; yet, they are aware that their past is an integral part of who they are:

> The deceased are both present and not present at the same time. It is possible to be bereft and not bereft simultaneously, to have a sense of continuity and yet to know that nothing will ever be the same. The reality is that there is an inner system that continues to be centered on the person who is no longer physically present. This inner reality may encourage the mourner to carry on … The bond may shift so that it is not so central to the lives of the bereaved. The bond can take on a new form with time, but the connection is still there. (Silverman and Nickman, 1996b: 351)

The dual process model (DPM) (Stroebe and Shut, 1999, 2001) integrates previous theories and methods, proposing a model that considers other processes in addition to the grief work hypothesis. They identify shortcomings to the 'grief work' hypothesis as the lack of clarity in the definition, lack of empirical evidence to confirm that confrontation is a predictor of adaptation, lack of application to gender and cultural differences, and inadequate studies regarding the value of social settings and support.

The importance of grief work is acknowledged; however, the DPM conceptualizes a stressor-specific model of coping with bereavement that focuses on two types of stressors: loss orientation and restoration orientation. The model relies on research that has shown that the bereaved must cope both with the loss of a loved one and with major change and adjustments in their lives as a result. The DPM further defines and operationalizes Rando's concepts of accommodating to changes in one's assumptive world and coping with the secondary and symbolic losses that occur as a result of the primary loss event.

Inherent in this model are concepts of cognitive stress theory as proposed by Lazarus and Folkman (1984). The model proposes that stress is experienced when the demands of situations exceed individual resources, with the potential to endanger well-being and health. Cognitive appraisal processes then analyze events as challenging or stressful. Within this framework bereavement is a major stressor, with multiple other concurrent stressors that need appraisal and coping strategies. Utilizing these concepts of coping with the DPM provides opportunity to oscillate (a regulatory process) between loss-oriented issues (grief work) and restoration-oriented experiences (attending to life changes).

Neimeyer (2001a) focused on contemporary constructivism and narrative concepts to propose the notion that meaning reconstruction is a core process for grief resolution. He discusses the limitations of theories proposed during the twentieth century that focused on bereavement as a process of *letting go* of an attachment, *moving on*, and eventually recovering and returning to normalcy. He is part of a 'new wave' of grief theory that has been emerging since the latter part of the 1990s.

> A prominent theme in these newer models is their insistence that *symptoms have significance*, that the outward manifestations of distress associated with grieving can be understood only in terms of the struggle of bereaved people and their social domain to accommodate to a changed (inter)personal reality resulting from the loss. Viewed in its broadest terms, this suggests the gradual emergence of a new paradigm for grief theory, research, and practice, one founded on the postulate that *meaning reconstruction in response to a loss is the central process in grieving.* (Neimeyer, 1998, 2001: 4)

Neimeyer postulates that bereaved individuals search for personal narratives in order to make sense of their changed realities. He states that 'significant loss – whether of cherished persons, places, projects, or possessions – presents a challenge to one's sense of narrative coherence as well as to the sense of identity for which they were an important source of validation' (2001b: 263). This validation for one's self-identity most often came from responses from significant others (e.g., the deceased). Thus, the life story of an individual that has been changed by a loss must be reorganized and rewritten with a sense of continuity that connects the past to the future in some rational manner. Each person constructs the significance of their individual loss based on their internal realities; not on external (societal) realities.

As specialists in this field, we have relied on concepts from the above models as well as others in the field. The above theorists have successfully built upon or elaborated upon past models, using creative innovations based upon their personal efforts in research and counselling. From our past and present experiences (Humphrey as hospice program coordinator to grief counsellor and educator, and Zimpfer as cancer counsellor, researcher, and educator), we have observed that those who seek counselling support often have additional issues previously repressed. Our belief is that there is never just one loss event. There are the secondary and symbolic losses that follow; but even more significant are the past repressed losses that emerge and compound and complicate the present experience. Loss and grief must be approached from a sound basis of theory that involves an understanding of attachment and loss and the tasks of the stages of human development. But theory alone is not sufficient. Theory needs methods that provide for an in-depth understanding of the uniqueness of each bereaved individual. This book will not only explore concepts and heighten awareness of the impact of loss and grief in the lives of individuals; it will also instruct the professional in the use of various tools for assessment and intervention.

Categories of Loss

There are several types of loss. Understanding these categories provides a framework that encourages the counsellor to examine and organize the effects of prior losses: to understand the full significance of the present loss(es), and to anticipate secondary or symbolic losses that could occur as a result of the present loss. Rando (1993a) emphasizes the necessity to assess and address secondary and symbolic losses. She defines these losses as those which develop as a consequence following the first loss. This assessment is not meant to create an overwhelming situation for the bereaved individual who already feels out of control. The purpose is to help the counsellor more fully understand their present reactions and behaviours, and to gain a more accurate understanding of what this loss means to the bereaved, given a more detailed understanding of their past loss experiences. Moreover, by anticipating potential secondary losses, we can educate, prepare, and plan more effective intervention strategies for coping and grief resolution.

The following discusses each of the categories of loss and offers examples that illustrate potential losses under each category.

Relationship loss

Relationship losses include (among many possibilities) experience of death of a loved one, illness, divorce, separation, abandonment, rejection, abuse within what was expected to be a trusting relationship, moving geographically from parents or friends, and so forth. Any change in a relationship as we once knew it, perceived it to be, or experienced it, constitutes a relationship loss. Individuals experience loss in relationships in numerous ways:

> I am an adopted child. We moved sometimes twice a year, every year that I can remember. I never really had enough time to make a good friend. I have no close friend to confide in. (18-year-old male, after a suicide attempt)

> The divorce was bad enough; but then mom remarried and we moved into my step-father's house. He has two kids that I hate. He never sees what they do; I'm always the one in trouble. Now mom is siding with him. I've lost her too. (15-year-old female)

Loss of some aspect of self

We cannot experience a relationship loss without losing an integral part of and sense of who we are. If there was a relationship, we have invested some part of ourselves in it. Who we view ourselves to be comes from the feedback in the interactions/dynamics of relationships. A major component of the grief process involves letting go of a former identity, grieving that part of you which is gone forever, and rebuilding a new identity. This loss of some aspect of self not only occurs in relationships with others, but also in any situation that demands change in personal identity. In addition to the above, loss of some aspect of self is also experienced in child abuse, rape, illness, physical change, loss of hopes, dreams, and major change and disappointments. Professional burnout and professional impairment are profound losses of self. Losses of aspects of self appear in various ways:

> Biking was my life. When I wasn't biking, I was repairing cars or building something. I could never stand to see a person who was handicapped. Now I have to depend on others to wheel me around in this chair. I was just starting my life; now it's over. (26-year-old paraplegic)

Everything I do is wrong. I can't keep a job, I can't get any control in my life. Everything I touch turns to dirt. (47-year-old male who had been laid off)

Treasured objects

Objects are physical and tangible; however, their importance is intangible. A treasured object is any object that connects one in reality or memory to an important relationship or some aspect of identity. Often they are objects that have been part of a family for generations, connecting that individual to an important part of his/her past and heritage. The family home that is sold after the death of parents often represents the loss of connection to childhood. Fire and theft often deprive individuals of treasured objects that have important significance. Loss of a lifestyle is an intangible loss in this category, and often occurs after a loss in another category such as divorce or death.

His death was one matter to get through. I don't even remember the funeral. The hardest thing was having to sell the camper. I can't afford to keep it. I don't even know how to drive it. Anyway, where would I take it? That was our camper and we traveled in it for the last 14 years. I feel like I'm losing more than a camper. (67-year-old widow)

I know we were lucky to get out alive; but 23 years of my life have just disappeared. I don't have a birth certificate, a driver's license, or a social security card. Someone gave me a purse to use, but I have nothing to put in it. (50-year-old female, following a total loss of home and possessions after a fire)

Developmental losses

Developmental losses are a natural part of the life-cycle, and are often not recognizable. Growth, insight and maturation are losses because change is involved and a part of self must be relinquished. Maturing, aging, and physical changes can be very poignant losses.

Often developmental losses compound or confuse more visible losses. A 65-year-old whose job position is eliminated is also coping with developmental issues of aging and possible retirement. An adolescent being 'dumped' by a lover may also be experiencing losses inherent in that stage of development. A major loss during the adolescent period of development is to let go of carefree ways and to become responsible. And for children who lose significant others through death, the grief process may span their developmental stages. For children, at each new stage of development, the loss will be re-evaluated and new meaning will be integrated. Developmental losses can take many forms:

For 20 years I was in charge of the entire department. In the new reorganization I am part of a committee. I don't even have a private office anymore. I'm 58. I can't find a position elsewhere. I feel trapped and too old to do anything about my situation. (58-year-old female executive)

I don't know if I can handle growing up. I'm so stressed right now. I think it's only going to get worse because after I graduate I'll have to get a job and be responsible for taking care of myself. If I can't handle the stress of college, how will I ever handle being an adult? (20-year-old female)

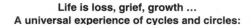

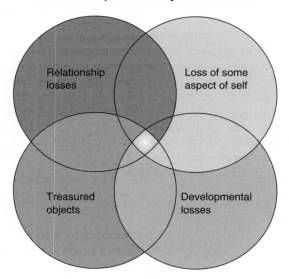

Figure 1.1   Categories of loss

The categories of loss overlap. Figure 1.1 serves as a visual aid that allows the counsellor to educate the client about losses in life that might not have been considered as contributors to the present grief experience. This matrix would first be used as an assessment device by the counsellor, as he/she listens for additional past, present, and potential future losses that will influence and impact the presenting issues of loss. Several sessions into the counselling process, it can then be used as an educational tool in assisting the client to reflect upon his or her life and gain insight about the pervasive nature of loss. Case examples throughout the book will offer additional possibilities.

Perspectives on Loss

The counsellor needs a framework to understand more fully the experiences of loss and grief. The framework becomes a holistic tool that allows one to gain fuller access into the client's private world of grief and his/her unique experience of it. It must be remembered that no two people will experience the same loss event in the same manner. Our framework comprises several perspectives, including the philosophical, spiritual, psychological, sociological/cultural, and physical.

It is important to be aware of these various perspectives and how they influence a client's frame of reference and grief experience. Not all the perspectives may emerge or be relevant at any one time. Some, however, may emerge several times during the process and be more influential. The influence exerted and the contributions from each perspective can be positive or negative.

Philosophical perspective

Philosophical issues are always a part of a grief experience. How an individual lived and previously interacted with his or her world no longer makes sense. Numerous questions about the meaning of one's existence emerge. Attention to the category of loss of some aspect of self is important here. How much of the invested self that has been lost because of this event is a pivotal issue in rebuilding? Is this individual willing and capable to look within and find new dimensions of self? This question becomes the foundation of ongoing assessment and subsequent intervention strategies. Moreover, loss of some aspect of self also brings attention to the fact that death becomes personalized and real for the survivors. One can no longer hide behind the cloak of immortality.

This perspective introduces difficulties of aloneness, meaninglessness, despair, responsibility, and existential anxieties. From a philosophical perspective, one can consider each loss event in life as part of the eventual process of coming to terms with our own mortality. Avoidance of grief after any loss or change event can be viewed as part of the difficulty humans face in reflecting upon core issues of their existence and eventual demise. Every loss involves change and letting go that needs to be processed. Theorist Ernest Becker (1973) asserts that man can live more fully and authentically when one faces this ultimate reality. He postulates that the anxiety experienced after any loss has the fear of one's own death at its core.

Spiritual perspective

Clients are influenced by their spiritual beliefs (or lack of them). As the categories of loss are explored and a number of losses identified, it is often the observation that the spiritual realm is the only emotional anchor left for survival. Belief in an afterlife often provides a reason for going on and the hope of reunion with a loved one. However, spiritual beliefs and/or the tenets of organized religions may also be the source of fear and guilt. Often individuals may believe that a loss is a sign of punishment from God for some wrong that has been committed. Believing this, additional guilt is often imposed upon the grief, and the bereaved can have a tendency to see themselves as bad and not worthy of forgiveness for past wrongs. An understanding of this perspective in a client's life is essential. During times of loss, conflicted beliefs or a lack of spirituality can become additional issues for an individual.

A lack of spirituality exerts a different kind of influence. Although guilt may not be experienced, there is often a deeper sense of meaninglessness and lack of perceived purpose in life. Those without a belief in someone or something beyond the human dimension often verbalize regrets that they have nothing to 'hang on to' or to 'fall back on' during this time of loss. Many have verbalized that they envy the strength and comfort that faith and hope provide for those who have a sense of spiritual connectedness and beliefs.

Although the philosophical and spiritual perspectives overlap, there are some differences. When considering this perspective, there is more of a focus on an individual's relationship (or the lack thereof) with God, a higher being, or some cosmic consciousness. Affiliation with an organized religion should not be the only consideration here. Many consider themselves religious or spiritual but do not participate in formal, community worship. Jackson states:

> Religion has many facets, but in the complex creations that are a part of the religious consciousness, there has always been a clear pattern of seeking to speak to the deep anxiety within man that seems to be incident to his mortality ... Anxiety usually emerges when there is a threat to man's value system. Religion seeks to provide a value system that counters that threat by making man aware of a dimension of his being that is not merely biological or chemical or mechanical, but by its very nature has about it already the element that transcends mortality by being in tune with the infinite and eternal. It does this in part by expanding man's perspective so that while he is in life, he sees beyond it. Religion seeks to give to man's life a cosmic status, so that, in the presence of things that might make him feel helpless and hopeless at one level, he can rise above those events so incident to his biological death and the existential threat to his being. (1977: 78–9)

Whereas the philosophical perspectives bring these existential questions and anxieties to the surface for an individual, the spiritual attempts to provide answers, direction, solace, and a potential opportunity for immortality (i.e., to live on in an afterlife).

Psychological perspective

The loss of some aspect of self is a core issue to be explored. If one has invested a part of his/her identity and energy, this is a loss that has to be acknowledged and grieved. Included in this perspective is the loss or compromise of meaningful roles. Contributing factors include personality, coping styles, affective and cognitive domains, present stressors, and overall mental health.

Another consideration within this perspective is the idea that relationships are not created in a linear fashion. Raphael (1983) discusses the psychological work of undoing the bonds that created the relationship. She discusses this task of undoing as an integral process of reversing all that has gone into building a relationship. The many layers that were internalized into the complex, multidimensional image of the loved one or role are now reviewed. Moreover, the emotional components that made it valuable (positive) or painful (negative) must also be reviewed. Until one can address the multiple levels of connectedness, it is difficult to address the normal tasks and processes of grief. A poignant example of this is the grief of a parent following the death of a child. The layers of a parental relationship are often complex and conflicted. There are few other relationships that demand such an investment of self and have the potential for complications following the end of a relationship. It should be noted at this point that death is not the only loss that can sever the parental relationship. Parent–child disagreements can end in broken relationships, necessitating a grief process. One mother whose adult son had been estranged from her for over ten years could only remember the young, innocent boy who played so well with others. She dwelt on these memories, would not discuss problems during his adolescence, and lived for the day that he would surely return to her. She was experiencing a tremendous loss and needed to carefully review, grieve, and reconstruct each aspect and year of their relationship. There were layers of experiences and memories that had been denied and avoided. Some layers had been too painful at the time (and continued to be); thus, more pleasant memories from the past were selected and focused upon. However, grief demands that the painful, avoided reality be reviewed, grieved, and released. Without partaking in this part of the process, she was not able cognitively and emotionally to integrate all aspects of the relationship that would facilitate an incorporation of her son in healthy memory, and foster resolution of her grief.

Included in this psychological perspective are concepts of resiliency. Resiliency has been discussed as the human capacity of all individuals to transform and change, no matter what their risks; it is an innate self-righting mechanism (Lifton, 1994). Trauma, loss, adversities, and the like present major challenges to survivors. Steven Wolin, MD and Sybil Wolin, PhD (1993) state that American society operates from a 'damage model' which tends to turn individuals into victims by having them dwell on their traumas, rather than on their potential to surmount difficulties in order to rebuild their lives. Therapy provides the opportunity to evaluate innate resiliencies and to promote new behaviours that build on existing strengths.

Coping strategies are central to the concepts of resiliency and the operationalization of the processes outlined in the DPM. Major loss taxes the ability to cope effectively. Discussion of the DPM highlights additional changes and adjustments that the bereaved must learn to cope with over the course of bereavement and restoration.

Stress is not a unitary event and coping is a complex process. Lazarus and Folkman defined and outlined strategies for effective coping. Coping is defined as 'constantly changing cognitive and behavioural efforts to manage specific external or internal demands' (1984: 141). The objectives of coping are to change the problem that caused the distress and to regulate the distressful emotions. Two main categories were suggested: problem-focused and emotion-focused. Both strategies are useful and need to be used interchangeably from the onset of the event to its resolution.

A problem-focused approach utilizes cognitive-behavioural strategies and involves taking action to resolve a distressful situation. When strategies are successful there is a renewed sense of internal locus of control and self-efficacy. The complementary strategies, emotion-focused, concentrate on ways to diminish intense and negative emotions. Healthy release of emotions and seeking emotional support from others provide respite from the distressful situation and an opportunity to rebuild internal resources.

Forgiveness, as a psychological concept, is often an integral part of the grief process and a key component in the development of resiliency. Without the ability to emotionally let go of perceived and real injustices, people remain victims and cannot resolve their losses and reconstruct meaningfulness in their lives. The very nature of some losses often leaves the survivors with intense negative emotions and an experience of being violated.

Prior to the early 1900s, concepts of forgiveness had been well discussed in fields of philosophy and religion, but not in psychology. Currently, there is not a consensus for the definition. Despite this lack of agreement, Thoresen et al. offer a working definition of forgiveness for consideration:

Interpersonal forgiveness can be seen as the decision to reduce negative thoughts, affect, and behaviour, such as blame and anger, toward an offender or hurtful situation, and begin to gain better understanding of the offense and the offender. The choice to let go of the negative affect, cognitions, and behaviours may commonly occur in the beginning phases of the forgiveness process, yet the various outcomes of forgiveness, such as reduced anger and blame, may not occur for weeks, months, or perhaps years. Furthermore, the offender is not required in this perspective of forgiveness to acknowledge the offense, seek forgiveness, or make restitution. (2000: 255–6).

Facilitating forgiveness within the grieving process enables survivors to reinterpret and reframe past and present negative experiences in order to identify pre-existing internal strengths that will promote a sense of personal empowerment in the face of current adversity. Augsburger (1981) suggests that the root meaning of the word forgiveness implies a process of *letting go*. Letting go can be seen as a journey (similar to grief) that involves incremental steps that necessitate authentically working through the anger, sorrow, betrayal, and loss of trust in order to gradually release bitterness and hostility.

Sociological/cultural perspective

This perspective greatly influences how one grieves or fails to grieve, and encompasses the impact that one's culture has on the bereaved. A culture/society establishes norms, many of which are unspoken but exert subtle (or not too subtle) pressures for conformity and prescriptions for belief systems and behaviours. Today we are influenced by past and present cultures, and as we look towards a new century, there is evidence of ideological shifts and some return to former beliefs and behaviours. There is a growing opinion that past emphasis on scientific rationality for answers in this century has created new problems that need new solutions. Within the field of loss and grief work, there is a growing awareness of the need for support systems, renewed emphasis on spirituality (a view especially held from a fundamentalist religious standpoint), and a return to the use of rituals during times of loss and transition.

In the sociological/cultural perspective it is also important to consider the nuclear family, the family of origin, support systems (real and perceived), ethnicity, socio-economic status, gender, religion, and other variables important to one's culture and frame of reference. Individuals will always refer to these factors in order to make sense out of the loss experience. Moreover, it is often the lack of support systems and the loss of religious and ethnic rituals that pose current problems for grief resolution. In the past, shared cultural backgrounds often provided the environment that not only prescribed rituals of mourning, but also fostered the process of grief within an emotionally close community of family and friends. Changing societies have altered the make-up of these communities. Individuals can cognitively refer to their roots; however, from a behavioural vantage point, there is little opportunity to enact traditional rituals without the availability of the extended family or background culture.

Lastly, societies are becoming multicultural. This is a factor that may require additional education for the counsellor in order to understand the world of the client and be effective in the process. Multicultural issues are an inherent part of many clients' experiences of loss and grief, and are often negated or disenfranchised by the counsellor who is not perceptive. Counsellor training, in the past, has reflected the norms of the dominant society; diagnoses have often been influenced by social and cultural prescriptions of that society.

Physical perspective

This perspective includes all aspects of the biology, physiology, pharmacology, and general functioning of a bereaved individual.

From a medical perspective, Engel (1961) proposes that loss and its resolution are integral aspects of homeostatic balance. He views the grief process as parallel to the process necessary for healing after a physical illness. Engel does not pathologize grief. He views it as a normal function that requires time and attention, with a distinct focus on difficult emotional tasks.

Grief can also mask itself in somatic complaints. It is always important to rule out physical problems, but the bereaved will not succeed if they try to find answers and solutions solely through physical diagnosis and medication.

The case study that follows is that of a client who initially came for counselling four months after her husband had committed suicide. At that time her goal for counselling was the well-being of her three sons. She was focused on the restorative aspects of their lives. In addition, she had been dealing with a chronic illness for over 12 years. The demands of the illness and her concerns for her family made her unaware of the impact of grief on her life over the last five years. Her journey in counselling illustrates a resilient woman, who had never been aware of her inner strengths and abilities. The case study illustrates the processes described in the DPM, meaning reconstruction, and the psychological perspective; all of which provided opportunities for effective intervention strategies.

The Journey of Ann

Ann was a 47-year-old Caucasian female who initially sought counselling, four months after her husband's suicide, for two sessions. Her initial goal for counselling was her concern regarding her three sons and their well-being. One son was married and living on his own; however, two were still at home. The sessions were primarily educational in nature, supporting her in her need to make sure that her sons grieved appropriately and resolved the suicide of their father in a healthy manner. She expressed no concerns for herself at this time and believed that she was coping effectively. Based on the DPM, Ann was choosing to focus on the restoration-oriented experiences of the loss. She chose to cope with the death at this time by focusing on the major changes and adjustments that her family would have to address.

Five years later she returned. She felt a deeper sense of loss of control than when her husband had died. Her opening statement indicated that the purpose of her return to counselling was due to her inability to control the physical symptoms and cope with the chronic, debilitating medical condition that she had effectively dealt with for the last 18 years. At this point the illness was controlling her life. Other than her ability to function within her home, she had greatly reduced her activities outside the home. She could not understand why she had lost her abilities to cope.

(Continued)

Ann asserted that she was never the 'strong one' in the marriage. Despite her husband's psychological problems and self-destructive behaviours that resulted in his suicide, she had always relied upon him for everything. She had dated him since high school and had married after graduation to escape a dysfunctional home life. Her perceived abilities resided in her role as a mother. Thus, for the years following his death she coped by focusing on the needs of her sons and assuring their well-being. Now her youngest son was soon to graduate and go away to college, and her sense of meaningfulness and purpose as a mother and homemaker was ending. At the same time, her physician had informed her that he could no longer prescribe the medication that she had relied upon for the last ten years.

After a number of sessions, Ann realized that she had never emotionally dealt with her husband's death. She had over-utilized the problem-focused strategy of coping and avoided the emotional strategies. Cognitively she was harsh and critical of herself and hadn't allowed herself the opportunity to address the loss-oriented experiences of her grief. She had never given herself permission to review aspects of her marriage and acknowledge the anger she might righteously feel for her husband's actions. Moreover, she was unaware that the increased intensity of her physical symptoms might have a potential connection to her grief.

Once the above assessments had been made, the initial plan was to make Ann aware of her strengths. In some ways Ann had been operating from the perspective of the 'damage model', as discussed by Wolin and Wolin (1993). Resiliency factors were discussed and past events throughout her lifetime were reinterpreted so that she was able to see the strengths that she had all along. This process greatly empowered Ann and it set the stage for future sessions.

Emotion-focused strategies of coping were suggested, and Ann agreed to explore these areas of her grief. This strategy brought issues of her husband's suicide into focus, demanding difficult emotional work. Realizing her strengths and acknowledging her resiliencies gave Ann the power to follow through and address intense emotions. Forgiveness concepts were discussed and issues of forgiveness were explored. There was no evidence of resentments or unfinished business that needed further resolution.

Lastly, Ann needed to create a new personal narrative to make sense of her changed world. Throughout the months of counselling, Ann realized that the validation for her identity had come from her husband. Slowly throughout the sessions she had begun to reconstruct a new identity for herself, seeing strengths and abilities within herself. This was further evidenced when she arrived one week and announced that she had handled a current crisis with a new sense of confidence and control. Moreover, she was pleased to report that she had been capable of leaving her home for longer periods of time despite the fact that she no longer had the medication. She was coming to terms with the fact that she would eventually need surgery, but chose not to have it now when she was feeling well. She commented that she hadn't felt physically well in so long that she just wanted to enjoy this period before she had to undergo surgery and cope with the after-effects of the procedure.

Ann's life story needed to be reorganized, and now it needs to be rewritten. Reconstruction of one's life with meaningfulness means that Ann will make personal sense of how she can connect her past realities to her future in some rational manner. Grief resolution is not just *letting go and moving on* (Neimeyer, 2001a).

2 Assessment Strategies

The purpose of assessment is to gain entry into the client's inner world and to understand the unique experience of grief as influenced by present and past losses and the contributions from the various perspectives. Assessment is an ongoing process and should never be considered completed simply because the initial intake has been done. Assessment and intervention go together throughout the sessions, with one paving the way for the other. Assessments allow for the next interventions to be planned for; and interventions facilitate change, which prompts new issues to emerge.

Various tools can be utilized to gather information about each client and the significant issues surrounding each loss event. These range from intake forms, to a specific line of questioning around the perspectives that include concepts of personal narratives, continuing bonds, resiliency, and coping strategies, to a psychological needs assessment, to describing a history of loss, to tests that measure depression, anxiety, quality of life, and so forth. Not every tool needs to be used with every client. Different tools are available to gain access and understanding when, in the professional judgment of the counsellor, something needs clarification or further understanding. The most important assessment and intervention tool will always be the counsellor. Without good clinical judgment and skills, external tools can be a hazard; they are often interpreted literally and at face value, misjudging the reality of an individual and his or her reactions to a loss.

Pre-Counselling Assessment

The first assessment starts with the telephone call from the client requesting counselling services. A pre-counselling intake form (Table 2.1) is used. This form identifies the type of loss; whether or not the client is presently receiving other counselling services; what the current feelings are; and if there are personal changes in habits such as eating, sleeping, or alcohol/drug use. After a significant loss many express feelings of not wanting to live any more. Thus, an initial assessment is necessary to determine if the statement is within the normal grief experience or if there is a level of lethality to the suicidal ideation. Other questions help to determine the mental and emotional status of the client and the need for immediate intervention. A question on gender preference has proven to be important, as a number of clients have suffered some type of abuse but hesitate to request a male or female. Having some of this basic information before seeing the client for the first time allows the counsellor time to reflect on potential issues and what direction to pursue during the formal intake. If the client is in a state of emotional crisis, the counsellor may decide not to do a formal intake, but to address the present needs of the client immediately.

Table 2.1   Pre-counselling intake form: to be completed during initial phone call, requesting counselling

NAME _____

PHONE NUMBER: (HOME) _____(WORK) _____

WHAT IS THE CONCERN YOU WANT ADDRESSED THROUGH COUNSELLING?_____

(For example, death, divorce, loss of job, etc.)

_____

_____

WHEN ARE YOU AVAILABLE FOR APPOINTMENTS?_____

REFERRED BY: _____

ARE YOU PRESENTLY RECEIVING COUNSELLING SERVICES?_____

ARE YOU PRESENTLY FEELING ANY OF THE FOLLOWING:

DEPRESSED   ANGRY   LONELY   SUICIDAL

Any changes in habits (e.g. sleep, eating, alchol/drug use)?

Do you have a gender preference for your counsellor?

INTAKER'S INFORMATION

CALL RECEIVED BY: _____

DATE: _____ TIME: _____

DID CALLER SEEM TO NEED COUNSELLING AS SOON AS POSSIBLE? _____

ANY DETAILS THAT YOU THINK PERTINENT:

CLIENT ASSIGNED TO:

DATE: _____ TIME: _____

COUNSELLOR'S SIGNATURE: _____

The counselling intake form (Table 2.2) is completed by the client on the first visit, but before the intake session. At times the counsellor will have to assist or clarify the information being requested. Intake forms for other types of loss are similar. The last part of the form can be changed to address the specific issues of each loss.

Perspectives on Loss

Designing questions around various perspectives on loss initiates the counsellor's process of joining with the client in order to understand more fully the totality of the individual's grief experience. Table 2.3 (see page 22) illustrates the several perspectives discussed in Chapter 1, with different loss examples given for each perspective. In an actual assessment, the counsellor takes the one loss issue presented initially by the client, and pursues the line of questioning across each perspective.

Table 2.2   Counselling intake form

BACKGROUND: DATE _____

NAME _____   BIRTHDATE _____

ADDRESS _____

PHONE: Residence _____ Work _____

AGE _____ SEX _____ OCCUPATION _____

WHO REFERRED YOU TO THIS OFFICE? _____

IN YOUR OWN WORDS, WHAT IS THE MOST DIFFICULT THING FOR YOU NOW? _____

_____

_____

WHO LIVES AT HOME WITH YOU NOW? _____

IF YOU HAVE FAMILY (NO LONGER LIVING AT HOME) PLEASE COMPLETE THE FOLLOWING:

Family Member's Name	Age	Sex	City of Residence
1.			
2.			
3.			

ARE THERE ANY OTHER PERSONS WHO ARE EMOTIONALLY SUPPORTIVE AND AVAILABLE TO YOU?

Name	Relationship
1.	
2.	
3.	

ARE YOU CURRENTLY RECEIVING MEDICAL CARE? _____

IF YES, BY WHOM? _____

ARE YOU CURRENTLY TAKING ANY MEDICATIONS? _____

ARE YOU CURRENTLY RECEIVING ANY ADDITIONAL COUNSELLING? _____

NUMBER OF YEARS THAT THERE WAS A RELATIONSHIP WITH THIS PERSON OR ACTIVITY _____

SIGNIFICANT DATES THAT HAVE THE POTENTIAL TO TRIGGER GRIEF REACTIONS
(Examples: holidays, birthdays, anniversaries, special events)

DATE THAT RELATIONSHIP ENDED _____

Philosophical

Questions should explore how this loss has affected one's outlook on life; if there is a personal philosophy that is helping at this time; what holds meaning and purpose at this time; if there is any sense of connection or relation to anyone or anything; if there have ever been similar feelings from past losses; what questions about life this loss has triggered; and what this loss has made the client more aware of? These questions are not all inclusive; rather, they suggest a starting

Table 2.3 Perspectives

Consideration of perspectives	Philosophical	Spiritual	Psychological	Sociological/ Cultural	Physical
ASSESSMENT					
A. Contributions to present loss	HIV-positive diagnosis	Death of son	Illness and loss of professional identity	Repressed trauma of a war veteran	Grief of a caregiver
	'No one really wants to hear my story ...'	'I have nothing that gives me any solace.'	'I always had control over my decisions.'	'... I lived and they died ...'	'... I don't understand why I am sick ...'
B. Contributions from past losses	Survived racial prejudice and an abusive relationship	Son had spent 10 years in prison.	Over-controlling mother. Death of father. Divorce.	Multiple death and non-death losses over time.	Seventeen years of care-giving and anticipatory loss.
C. Interventions	Narrative strategies. Listen and validate. Continue to assess for other contributing factors.	Don't challenge loss of faith. Connect with her connection of flowers to continue other aspects of spirituality.	Assess and use strategies based on resiliency and coping constructs. Assess for changes in area of psychological needs and potential areas of compromise.	Narrative strategies. Assess resiliency factors. Assess need for self-forgiveness.	Education re: disease process and the mind-body connection and utilization of both coping strategies (DPM constructs).

point. Additional assessment questions concerning this perspective will be generated by clients' responses to the counsellor's initial queries. Concepts from Neimeyer's meaning reconstruction and the use of the clients' personal narratives can be utilized at this entry point of an assessment. Early in the experience of grief, the bereaved are more aware of a sense of emptiness and meaninglessness. They do not feel connected to others, nor do they want to be. There is an overwhelming sense of being alone in their grief and a belief that no one could truly understand or feel their pain. They do not want to be told that they are similar to anyone else who has experienced a similar loss. There is a true sense of being in an existential crisis, totally disconnected from others. It is not the counsellor's role at this time to try to lift grievers from the depths of their despair; rather it is important to assess the meaning of their existential crisis and encourage their personal narrative. Validating their unique narratives facilitates connection and trust with the counsellor. Moreover, a desire to hear their story from their perspective (and not only from the counsellor's predetermined questions) provides the opportunity for richer assessments.

Illustrating the philosophical perspective and considering the use of narrative techniques, the following is an excerpt from an initial assessment with Pat, a 45-year-old female, who had recently been diagnosed as HIV-positive. Her second husband, to whom she had been married for five years, had been diagnosed with the AIDS virus. She presented herself as an independent and strong woman who had successfully conquered multiple challenges throughout her life. She had sought out a local support group; however, she was the only heterosexual female amongst a group of gay men. Five minutes into the assessment session she initiated her life narrative, which included this present crisis. She felt that no other life crisis could compare to her present situation.

Pat: I have to go back 20 years and tell you all about my life so you can understand my present situation and why I am so devastated and feel so alone. No one really wants to hear my story; they don't think it has anything to do with my present anguish.

Counsellor: Please tell me your story. That will really help me understand more about who you are and the effect that this crisis has had on you.

Pat: [After a 30-minute narrative] I rose above multiple injustices, survived an abusive marriage and was independent for ten years without a man. I dated this man for two years before I married him. He was everything I had ever wanted in a husband. One year after the marriage, he totally changed. He had become verbally abusive. We had agreed to separate, but it was at this time he became chronically ill. Testing was done as he was not responding to medical interventions. He was diagnosed with AIDS, and after I was tested I was found to be HIV-positive.

Counsellor: Your story tells me that the person you knew yourself to be has been violated. I sense that you are experiencing a death of yourself while you are still alive and are unable to use any prior strengths or skills to cope with the demands of your situation.

Pat: You are right. I never thought of this as a type of death. I tried to do this on my own and just couldn't figure out why I seemed to be losing more control.

Counsellor: It is important to understand this as a loss of who you were in the past and first allow yourself a healthy expression of grief. However, you must also

> try to believe that there are parts of you that haven't been totally destroyed by these events, and eventually we will be able to identify them and once again use them to help you rebuild inner strengths and reconstruct your life.

Pat continued to share her life story. She emphasized past difficulties and her survival techniques. Her narrative highlighted her strengths and ability to grow through hardships.

Willingness to listen to a client's story provides the groundwork for future sessions. Counsellors need to understand clients' personal histories and the depths of their character in order to appreciate their limitations and abilities to cope with their grief experience.

Spiritual

This perspective encourages questions around the client's relationship with God or a higher being. This does not necessarily mean that a client will be affiliated with an organized religion. Questions posed range from directly asking a client if he or she believes in God and an afterlife and if this loss has affected or changed their relationship with God, to indirect questions about their conception of sin and punishment, to questions about possible affiliations within a church community. For example: 'What type of support are you presently getting from your church; what would you like to get from your church; what rituals (through your church) have you used that have been meaningful and helpful; what religious beliefs sustain you the most during these times; has your religion or spiritual convictions helped you through past losses; and are you presently experiencing any personal conflicts between your thoughts and emotions and your spiritual beliefs?' Again, it is necessary to state that these questions provide a beginning for the assessment of this perspective. They are not all-inclusive.

The untimely death of a child, at any age, raises deep questions regarding the existence and the nature of a God that would allow this to occur. Karen had only one child, a 30-year-old son who had been killed in a head-on collision by an intoxicated driver shortly after Christmas. Prior to this he had served 10 years in prison, having been in the company of friends who had been arrested for breaking and entering. His friends managed to get away, and believing that one must be loyal to friends, he would not give their names. As a result he served the 10-year sentence alone. Karen and her husband had visited whenever they were allowed, and had lived for the day he would be released. At the time of his death, he had been home for 18 months. He had rebuilt his life, was employed as a landscaper, and was planning on marriage within the next six months. Karen and her husband were overwhelmed with their grief and were experiencing a significant breach of faith.

Karen: This is so hard. I have nothing that gives me any solace. Our minister's words meant nothing to us at his funeral. He kept talking about my son being in his heavenly home and at peace with God. My husband and I just wanted to scream at him. We just got him back after 10 years in prison. We don't want him with God – if there really is a God or life after death. The only thing that helped us was to retrieve the flowers from his casket.

Counsellor: I am not certain that I understand what you mean. How did getting the flowers help? I do understand that you and your son loved gardening. Did taking the flowers help you feel closer to him for a while longer?

Karen: We had decided to have the flowers preserved even before we had ordered them. We carefully chose flowers we all loved and had planted together over the years. Each flower we chose had a memory and a special significance in our relationship with our son.

Counsellor: Now I understand. Despite your overwhelming grief and loss of faith, you have initially found a way to keep your son within you.

Anger directed at God, the question of whether or not a God exists, and the beliefs that God should protect the good are common grief responses, especially after the untimely and perhaps preventable death of a child. It is important to listen and resist giving personal statements of your religious beliefs. Responses back to the client during this time period should be non-judgmental and reflective of what the client has expressed to you. The spiritual perspective goes beyond the framework of organized religion and promotes a deeper sense of a spiritual and ongoing connection to the deceased. Assessment offers the opportunity to hear early attempts to connect and facilitate ongoing bonds of attachment. Information gleaned from the above dialogue provides an opportunity in future sessions to explore concepts of continuing bonds and ways to integrate their son within them as described by Silverman and Klass (1996) and Silverman and Nickman (1996a).

Psychological

This is a pivotal perspective that continues to emerge throughout the entire grief experience. Different aspects of this perspective will demand attention at varying times, often causing the client to feel drained of energy, unable to think or function. It will be important, early in the assessment, to listen for styles and characteristics of personalities; and to assess both premorbid and present personalities of the clients. Ask the clients if they view themselves as being a different personality before the loss event. Use questions that encourage responses that provide information about clients in relationships with others and about their own sense of personal self-worth. Listen for responses that might indicate personalities that are dependent, histrionic, narcissistic, compulsive, and the like. A client's personality and how one views himself or herself are an important criterion in resolution of loss and grief.

Assessment of the affective and cognitive domains is an ongoing part of the counselling sessions. Early in the assessment determine the primary and/or current grief emotions and how the client expresses these feelings. Many admit to suppressing, avoiding, denying, negating, and rationalizing most of their feelings when they begin to emerge. Some fear total loss of emotional control if they were to allow expression of these feelings. Others operate on faulty cognitions, such as grief is a sign of weakness, emotion means self-pity, or that you should keep your feelings to yourself. Inappropriate effect (i.e., smiling as one relates a tragedy) is another clue that needs further exploration. Perhaps the client believes that it is important to maintain a certain outward countenance or perhaps the client is not in touch with his or her emotions.

The belief that one should not or cannot express emotion affects the emotional status of a client as well as one's mental abilities. Many with suppressed emotions develop more negative thoughts, lack ability to make decisions, and cannot find ways to cope with additional stress.

Concepts from the DPM can be operationalized into effective strategies, beginning with the assessment and throughout the ongoing counselling process. During assessment, an evaluation of the bereaved's current coping behaviours is essential. As indicated, many cope only with problem-focused strategies, fearing that any display of grief is a sign of weakness. Assessment is also an important time to educate regarding the necessary use of both strategies as discussed in the DPM.

Ongoing cognitive assessment is a key variable throughout the counselling sessions. Early assessment needs to determine the present status of cognitions and the ability to make decisions; moreover, a goal of assessment is to identify lifelong belief systems and possible cognitive distortions. What is the client's pattern of self-talk? What distorted or negative messages about himself or herself are continuously being reinforced? Within this cognitive assessment, it is often necessary to do a mental status exam that might identify impaired functioning, disorientation, or drug or alcohol involvement.

Psychologically, it is also important to assess the nature of the relationship that has been lost, what functions had been previously provided by this relationship, and what roles have been changed. Develop questions that bring out the stored symbols and inner images of the layers and meaning of this relationship. Symbols stored (or inner representations of how that relationship was perceived and experienced) are both those that accurately reflect the experience of the relationship, and ones that elevate a relationship to a highly idealized place. The death of an alcoholic spouse offers an example that illustrates this concept. Life with an alcoholic has many negative experiences; however, in death the deceased alcoholic is often raised to the status of sainthood. Memories only focus on the positive attributes of this 'wonderful' person. Other stored symbols that reflect the misery experienced during the deceased's lifetime are often repressed immediately following the death. Because this expression of idealization may not match the reality, later reality testing and cognitive restructuring of this relationship may be a major focus of the interventions. Early assessment will tend to elicit highly idealized memories and assess the reality. The opposite can also occur. Those who have experienced negative relationships may not be able to produce any positive memory, and it will be important to assist the client in finding at least one positive memory to balance the negative relationship.

Beginning questions can inquire about the functions provided by this relationship and what roles were involved. Clients can also be asked to tell the story about this relationship from the beginning. Relationships are not just those one has with people. They include jobs, positions of status, and other roles one has had in a variety of activities. Roles and relationships can be identified further by examining some of the functions carried out by one person with another, such as intimacy, guidance and assistance, companionship, nurturing, maintenance (fulfilling needs such as food, clothing, shelter), and security. Thus when a client exclaims in despair that everything has been destroyed by this loss, it is necessary to explore each function that this lost relationship had provided in order to determine what exactly has been lost.

Resiliency factors, a psychological construct, provide both assessment and ongoing intervention strategies. Categorizing the concept of resiliency introduced

Table 2.4   Psychological needs

Use as part of an assessment to understand the present situation, as it relates to the past. Example: Client who lost professional and personal identity after two major heart attacks and open-heart surgery.

Needs	Past	Present	Future
Affiliation			
Keep same description	Psychologist in charge of outdoor challenge programs for troubled youth. Work provided professional identity, professional and personal friends.	Teaching part-time in a 2-year college course.	
Power			
Keep same	Total control. Respected and admired by peers and youth. Won national awards.	Come alive when teaching. Good feedback from students. Lack of personal control in 90% of his life.	
Fun			
Keep same	Work was fun. Little social life outside of work and peer/professional activities.	Not much. Getting into photography. No extra money for 'fun'.	
Freedom			
Keep same	Made major work decisions and all personal decisions.	No discretionary income. Unable to see new choices for personal or professional life.	

in the first chapter, Grothberg (1995) classified the numerous features of resiliency in order to make them adaptable for research and clinical interventions. The term I HAVE is used to address *external supports*; I AM identifies *inner, personal strengths*; and I CAN is used for *social, interpersonal skills*. Assessment questions based on this format help the client and the counsellor identify the presence or lack of these important characteristics that are so necessary for resolution and reconstruction of their future identity and meaningful existence. Societies often perpetuate a victim identity for those experiencing trauma and loss. Concepts of resiliency identify strengths and present opportunities for personal growth and empowerment despite the circumstances.

Another tool that facilitates an exploration of what has been lost is the psychological needs chart (Table 2.4). This is an adaptation of Glasser's (1990) psychological needs of love and belonging, self-worth and self-esteem, fun, and freedom.

Used early in assessment, it asks the client how each of these needs had previously been met before the loss and how these needs are presently being met. It is an excellent tool that visually allows the client another, and perhaps deeper, level of understanding of his or her grief; moreover, it reflects what a client still has in each of these areas of psychological needs that will be valuable assets in rebuilding and regaining a sense of personal control after loss has taken away that which was held most dear.

Illustration of psychological needs assessment

Marie was a 46-year-old patient who was referred to counselling after two heart attacks and open heart surgery. In between the two heart attacks she had successfully completed cardiac rehabilitation and was medically stable. She had always been physically active and healthy; thus, she returned to her work as a social worker involved in working with incarcerated youth in a physically challenging outreach program. Having no medical restrictions, she fully resumed her former position, only to experience her second heart attack and subsequent surgery a few months later. Currently she was again medically stable, but felt that she had become resigned to the existence of an 80-year-old. Her current life lacked meaningfulness and purpose and her future outlook was dismal.

Marie: I have never been in this position before. I always had control over my decisions from the time I left home for college until two years ago. I was extremely successful and loved what I did in the outreach programs. Now all this is gone. I am teaching part-time, but never know if I will have a job from semester to semester.

Counsellor: You have certainly experienced a significant loss of yourself. Have you been able to realize the extent of this and grieve appropriately?

Marie: No, I didn't realize this until my primary care doctor referred me for counselling. Perhaps because I am a psychologist, my cardiologist felt that I knew this and could handle it on my own. It would have made a huge difference if I had known and anticipated this. I would have sought counselling after my first attack before returning to work.

Counsellor: Yes, counselling is important, even for professionals. You are a human being first and foremost and need support just as anyone else would. It is important to remember that you have never had to cope with a personal situation such as this one. You cannot have the same insight that you would for a client when you are immersed in a life-threatening illness and are no longer capable of functioning as you once did. Do your physicians have restrictions on you now in terms of physical exertion, work, and other activities?

Marie: No, but the fear of a third heart attack is always present. There is no guarantee that a third attack wouldn't occur. I seem to be a mystery to my doctors. I have always needed to put 110 per cent of myself into a job. When I tried to physically do that after my first attack, I failed miserably. I am now putting 110 per cent myself into teaching, but it is not the same and my part-time position is not secure.

Counsellor: It is hard to compromise. You have always identified yourself as a someone who is capable, successful, and gives more than 100 per cent. It gives me an image of a person who needs to 'drive' their life at 120 m.p.h. and now your heart is dictating a speed of 25 m.p.h. I believe compromise is necessary to protect your health and future, but you need to determine an acceptable speed to achieve a meaningful existence; 25 m.p.h. is unacceptable.

Marie: That's an interesting concept. I never thought of doing anything less than how I have always have; but the idea of finding an acceptable 'speed' gives me something to think about.

Another goal of an initial psychological assessment is to ask the client about past experiences of a similar nature. In Marie's it was important to know if she had any life experiences that had been difficult that she didn't feel in total control of. Marie was able to relate to difficult experiences growing up with a controlling mother and the ending of her marriage. Solutions for both these experiences were similar: she moved away and became fully involved in her professional life. She was always able to define and redefine her identity after various difficulties and losses in her professional roles. It was an important part of the assessment to understand this if there was to be a successful reconstruction of her life as we moved through future counselling sessions together.

Sociological/cultural

Societies and the cultures within them exert great influence over reactions to loss and ways in which their members experience grief. Multicultural issues may have to be the first issues to be addressed in an assessment in order to avoid placing the template of the dominant society over that of the client's. The culture that has shaped this client's identity and the culture that the client presently is living in provide a rich background for understanding this individual's unique and highly individualized grief experience. A client often feels torn between two worlds, and it is usually during a time when grief is the most acute that an individual will not feel that he or she belongs to either world.

In addition to the larger sociological understanding of a client's background and present world, it is important to assess additional sociological variables such as the individual's race, gender, socio-economic level, ethnicity, family of origin, nuclear family, and perceived support systems. Many losses are not visible and do not receive social support. Some are not understood as losses, such as the secondary ones that follow after death or another recognizable loss event. A secondary loss can be loss of a past lifestyle. Many have to move, stop leisure activities, or give up discretionary income. These are extremely difficult losses, but are often not visible. Many have commented that the funeral was not as difficult as the months and events that followed because they were numb initially, and there was support available.

Questions should explore how one was socialized; what were expectations because of gender, race, or ethnicity; how does one perceive himself or herself in the eyes of others at this time; what ethnic or cultural rituals have helped or hindered; and what has been perceived as losses for which no social support has been received? An additional consideration is the client's status (real or perceived) in the community, work, and other activities. Social status or the lack of it can be an important sociological factor and exert considerable influence on process and outcome. Those with a higher social status often have more financial means to acquire the needed resources during their bereavement period.

If the loss was a death, there are additional considerations within this perspective to assess. What was the type of death? Was it one that was validated as legitimate, or did it lack social support because of a stigma attached? AIDS, suicide, and murder often have issues involved that do not make them socially acceptable. These will be discussed in Chapter 8. Miscarriages and other perinatal deaths also lack social support, as potential support systems have no history with the deceased child and no memories to share about them with the bereaved parents.

These are deaths that require the parents to grieve for a wished-for child, with little frame of reference for the relationship that was lost.

Funerals and rituals also need to be explored after a death-related loss. Questions that inquire about the type of funeral and the calling hours often provide important clues for further assessment. Some view calling hours and the funeral rite as strong sources of emotional support; others have refused to have calling hours and have had a closed casket in an attempt to avoid the pain. Many clients have been denied input into the planning of the funeral and this often has negative effects on their grief process. A funeral is a ritual of transition and provides the opportunity to say goodbye and begin the process of letting go. Those bereaved who choose not to be part of this type of ritual, or who are denied participation, need to find a psychologically acceptable way to begin this process. Moreover, there are cultural difference and beliefs regarding rituals for the funeral process. For example, open caskets and the public viewing of a deceased individual are not acceptable and often incoherent to the beliefs and values of those from various cultures and religious groups. Careful assessment regarding beliefs and values is important for the client to feel respected and accepted for who they are, and not who the counsellor believes they should be.

Family and support systems can be a source of conflict or comfort. The counselling intake asks clients to indicate who lives with them now, where family members live if no longer at home, and who are the persons emotionally supportive and available. Many clients lack available support systems, and this must be assessed during the early visits. Moreover, support systems may be available, but the client may not perceive them as being available when they need them, or they may be perceived as being unhelpful. Time, effort, and additional grief can be lessened when the issue of support systems and a clearer understanding of them can be determined during early assessment times.

George was an 82-year-old veteran of World War II. He was referred for counselling by his primary care physician because of his inability to sleep for the past nine months and his increased anxiety despite medication. He did not believe in counselling, and came reluctantly. He prided himself on being a veteran and having survived the trauma of war and a life of hardships. From the time of the initial assessment and on through a year of counselling, the narrative approach proved to be the most effective strategy. Connecting with him initially by encouraging him to tell me about his life experiences quickly opened the door for an enriching professional experience and insight into traumatic memories never revealed over 60 years.

Counsellor: George, I realize that you really don't want to be here; nor do you believe that counselling could be beneficial for you.

George: You are right. My wife and doctor made me come. My wife says she is tired of hearing my old war stories and doesn't know why I just recently have brought them up again. My doctor says he won't give me any more medicine because nothing has helped me sleep over this last year.

Counsellor: It seems as though something has changed for you in the past year. Also, your wife seems surprised that you are bringing up stories from the war. Is there a reason for all of this?

George: I'm not sure. It could be a lot of things. Events from 9/11, the current war, and the last reunion that I had with area veterans could be reasons. However, what really annoys my wife is that I start crying all the time. In over 50 years of marriage she's never seen me cry. I cry because I keep remembering the day I was in the infirmary and my unit was on a mission and they were shot down. If I had been there I could have gotten them out. My position in the plane was in the rear, and I was the only one who knew how to evacuate everyone. I lived and they died. That's not right. I should have been there.

Counsellor: Have you ever shared this with anyone? You said that your wife was tired of you retelling old war stories.

George: No, I never shared this one. I decided that if I had to come and see you that I might as well be honest if you showed any willingness to hear my story. I need to do something to stop this crying. Men shouldn't cry. I never have and don't know why I am now.

Counsellor: Crying should not be a matter of what is acceptable or not acceptable. However, I do realize that American society often dictates different behaviours for men and women in terms of coping and emotional expression.

This excerpt illustrates gender issues in terms of coping with trauma and loss experiences. Moreover, it indicates that adherence to societal norms based on gender only represses trauma. Time doesn't eradicate emotional horror. Societies all over the world determine acceptable ways to cope and express emotion. Almost always there are gender-based differences. Early assessment, such as the above, identifies a client's ingrained beliefs regarding acceptable behaviours. This identification also supported a potential diagnosis of George's presenting symptoms. Ongoing assessment using the narrative techniques did not pose a threat to his view of himself as a male nor his beliefs of acceptable behaviours. The approach provided the opportunity to connect with him, validate his narrative, and move towards a reconstruction of a grief process that had been denied.

Physical

Grief often manifests itself in physical symptoms. Understanding the potential that grief has in terms of interrupting one's normal existence, it is easy to comprehend the effect it might have on one's physical health and the disruption in the effectiveness of the immune system. It is not unusual for the bereaved to complain about chronic viral infections after a major loss (death or non-death) in their lives.

Concerns with issues of morbidity and mortality, psychosomatic symptoms, psychiatric care, medications, lack of sleep, nutrition, and general areas of functioning are all priorities for early assessment. A specific question that assesses daily functioning should also be included in the initial assessment: describe a typical day; how has your routine changed; what is difficult for you now to accomplish in a day; do you have one goal each day; and other questions that promote a clearer understanding of the client's ability to function on a daily basis.

To illustrate this perspective, let us look at a 62-year-old woman who pursued counselling 18 months after the death of her husband. Katy was a nurse who was still employed at a local hospital. She had willingly and lovingly cared for her husband at home for 17 years until his death. He had been diagnosed with MS shortly after they had married and had been totally disabled for the last 17 years. Being a nurse, she was able to assume all the medical care at home in order to avoid putting him into a nursing home. This entailed years of physical lifting and turning, which became more difficult as his condition deteriorated. She claimed that it never bothered her to do this either physically or emotionally. He was an excellent patient and always grateful. In addition to caring for him, she had continued her full-time job at the hospital. She thought she had mentally and emotionally prepared herself for his death, but something wasn't working for her now, despite her careful planning. She wasn't sure what was wrong with her, but she had experienced six months of constant viral infections, severe back pain, and an inability to sleep. She initially came focusing on her physical symptoms and a need to 'fix' herself.

Katy: I am usually healthy. I don't understand this. I knew he was going to die someday. I had rehearsed and planned for this day for years. So I know that I prepared for that and grieved along the way. I just don't understand why I'm sick, my back aches, and I can't sleep. My physician has tried three different sleeping medications. None worked. Right now I am taking Prozac. It doesn't help me sleep, but it stabilizes my emotions so I can work.

Counsellor: It certainly sounds as if you had prepared yourself and that you have no regrets in terms of your willingness and ability to care for him long term. What had you anticipated (emotionally) for yourself after his death?

Katy: I'm not exactly certain, but I feel that I should be over this and not feel this way 18 months later. I don't think it is my grief, I just think I didn't have enough time to get over one illness before I caught something else. I don't see this as having much to do with his death. He died in October. In November I decided to get laser surgery to stop smoking. By December I felt healthier than I ever have and could even breathe better. Then in January all these illnesses started. It just doesn't make sense.

Counsellor: Are you aware that grief often manifests itself through physical symptoms? Despite your anticipatory grief work and preparation for your life without your husband, you are experiencing a type of death of yourself. Your caregiving role was a focal part of your identity, providing meaningfulness and purpose. Your husband's love and appreciation were valuable feedback. This has all changed. Despite your planning, your physical symptoms are letting you know that there are additional grief issues that you must attend to. I fear you tried to psychologically plan too well and your physical body is giving you a message.

Clients who present with physical problems tend to focus on their symptoms and not see the relationship to their grief. However, it is important to encourage clients to get medical evaluations. We should not assume that it is only their grief manifesting itself through physical symptoms. The literature has documented issues of morbidity and mortality following significant losses; thus it is prudent to rule out potential illnesses suggested by various symptoms. Once possible illnesses have been ruled out, a counsellor must continue to be sensitive to the client's complaints, but know when it is appropriate to change the focus. The experience and process of grief are extremely painful, and it is often more comfortable to focus on the physical symptoms in order to avoid or circumvent the other perspectives.

History of Loss

The history of loss (Table 2.5) is a tool that leads the counsellor during assessment and intervention to a greater understanding of the losses that a client has had to

Table 2.5 History of loss

Use as part of an assessment to gain understanding of the influence of past (and often unresolved) losses on the present losses and circumstances. Client is often not aware of the past losses.

Case example: Client who presented the death of her son.

Loss	Age	Experiences (feelings/behaviours)	Unanswered?	What changed? (money, residence, etc.)
Death of son	61	Devastated.	How did the car lose control? Did he know it/did he scream for help? Did he feel the car ignite and burn him?	Everything; no meaning left in life.
Broken back	60	Suffered alone. Did not want to burden family with her pain.	None.	Surgery; physical limitations.
Potential diagnosis of cancer	60	Fear. Still disagreement among physicians if cancer exists. Tries not to think about it.	Is it cancer or not?	Testing every six months.
Son sent to prison for 10 years	48	Shared deep emotional pain with husband. Coped with fear and blame. Sadness by remaining involved by telephone and monthly visits. Coped anticipating his release and return home.	Why did he have to take the … ? Why didn't one of his friends come forward?	Life focused on visits and and his return home.
Husband's accident	46	Anger. His work conditions were unsafe. Fear he was going to die.	Why did they cover up the incriminating evidence?	Did not pursue a law suit. Husband can no longer work.
Death of parents	44	Both were ill. Relieved they were no longer suffering. Missed them. Hard to lose both in one year.	None.	Care-giving activities.
Hysterectomy	35	Felt a great loss of part of self. Sad.	Why me?	No more children. Still grieving stillborn.
Stillborn child	34	Tremendous sadness. Grieved alone.	What went wrong?	Couldn't recover physically.

carry to this point in life. It provides a visual representation, not only of the actual losses, but also of the experience of each loss, the unanswered questions, and the changes in life style experienced after each loss. Often the counsellor observes a common experience, reaction, or coping style that a client relies upon after a loss (e.g., anger, guilt, suppression), learns that a client has many unanswered questions about the losses in his or her life, or sees that there have been multiple changes following losses that there have been little control over. All of these findings provide valuable material upon which to investigate further and design intervention strategies.

Psychological Tests

Other assessment tools include the use of psychological tests. Some appropriate instruments include the impact event scale (Horowitz et al., 1979), Rotter's locus of control scales (Rotter, 1966), the IPAT anxiety questionnaire (Cattell et al., 1957/1976), and Beck's depression inventory (Beck, 1978). These tests measure psychological reactions that are common after a loss experience. They facilitate a deeper understanding regarding the effects that a loss event may have had upon an individual. At the same time the counsellor should be cautioned not to rely upon a psychological test as the sole tool of diagnosis, nor to use a test to pathologize an individual. Tests should only be used to arrive at a clearer understanding of an individual and his or her personal reactions and needs after an experience of loss.

3 Grief Counselling and Grief Resolution

The process of grief is an individual journey. Although losses appear to have similar qualities, and there are universal dimensions of grief, each individual has unique issues to cope with and resolve. No two people grieve in the same manner or on the same timetable. Each individual is influenced by various perspectives at different times during the process. Thus, who comes for counselling, when, and with what issues is always idiosyncratic.

When asking the question 'who comes' for counselling, in general it appears to be those who are not able to get needed support from family or friends. This may be a result of not having family nearby, not feeling comfortable sharing deep emotions with family or friends, or the family and friends not being knowledgeable about the grief process and neglecting to provide emotional support.

Grief Counselling

Bereaved clients (no matter what the loss) may request counselling at any time during the grief process. Usually, it is during a time period of acute pain, frustration, or confusion regarding what to do to feel better. This can be during an early stage of the process or years removed from the actual event. Some clients come within six months after a loss, because they believe that they should be doing better or 'over this by now'. Others come years later, and after several major losses, because they never had the time or the permission to grieve, or because the accumulation of the affects of losses has become overwhelming.

The issues that need to be addressed and resolved vary from individual to individual. Some clients simply do not understand the grief process. Thus, education is an important component of counselling. Many come from cultural backgrounds which have negated the grieving process, and so they believe it to be a sign of personal weakness. Others come during a time of acute grief and want the counsellor to rescue and reassure. This can be a trap for caring mental health professionals whose mothering instincts would soothe the clients' grief. However, a major premise of grief counselling is to help clients experience the pain in order to heal, rather than to avoid or deny it. Still others come with chronic issues of grief. The acute phases may have subsided; now the issues are long-lasting ones of rebuilding new identities and making new choices.

Idiosyncrasy also is revealed in the characteristics that are inherent with the type of loss or the manner in which the loss occurred. If the loss was violent in nature, there may be legal complications and conflicted emotions. Often highly charged feelings, such as rage, must be addressed before the normal aspects of grief.

With regard to the counselling process for grief, there is no set number of sessions. Many come once for information about the process and validation of their grief. The majority come between four to ten sessions during the first year after their loss. Some return a year or two later to address issues that are emerging for the first time. Most of these latter issues center on the letting go and rebuilding phases. And, in our experience, a few clients have come weekly for as much as a year. Much depends upon the personalities, the type of loss, the coping abilities, and available support systems. Various issues may emerge at any time during the process. Some emerge more than once, but with different aspects and questions to be resolved. Other issues may never emerge and exert no influence on the client's experience. The influence that a perspective contributes to the loss experience can be positive or negative. Moreover, the influence has to be considered in terms of past and present loss(es). Examples will be given to illustrate.

Movement from early to middle sessions of counselling is very individual and dependent upon many factors. Close listening and continued assessment provide the best guidelines as to where a client is in the process. Counselling should be a process of joining with clients on their journey and co-facilitating the experience. Professional judgment needs to be used to evaluate the effectiveness of the sessions and interventions, and to assess the client's desire and/or ability to go through this process. Those who take the risk to fully experience their grief will guide the counsellor to the next phase of their grief work.

Early sessions are marked by acute experiences of painful grief. Clients ask whether or not they will survive this experience and question if life will ever have meaning again. Pain is felt psychologically, spiritually, cognitively, emotionally, and physically. There is a feeling of total loss of control in one's life. Grief is experienced as an overwhelming assault. The middle sessions are characterized by relapses. Perspectives re-emerge that clients felt they had already addressed. They do not understand that the perspective might be the same, but the issues and aspects of it are different. The grief is chronic, nagging, and often relentless. Issues revolve around identity and role changes, and the need to create a new 'I'. Later sessions are times of reconstructing and reinvesting in meaningful life and new narratives. The experience has been integrated and there is energy and motivation to make new choices. Clients initiate these sessions describing their plans, goals, and new achievements. Counselling has become a mutual experience between the client and the counsellor. Ivey discusses that 'dialectics involves a search for more workable answers and a search for truth. The therapist–client relationship can also be considered a dialectical, co-constructed approach to knowledge and truth' (1986: 19).

To illustrate the above concepts, case examples will be used that highlight areas of focus during early, middle, and later counselling sessions of individuals working through their grief. Using the perspectives (Tables 3.1 and 3.2) and interventions discussed in the first two chapters (Figure 1.1 and Tables 2.3 through 2.5) facilitated ongoing assessments and treatment strategies, and provided an expansion of the counsellor's awareness of the totality and depths of clients' loss experiences. These tools, with examples of their use, will be discussed in the case examples that follow.

Table 3.1   Directions for perspectives

Considerations of perspectives	Philosophical	Spiritual	Psychological	Sociological	Physical
Early counselling sessions (acute)					
A. Contributions present loss					
B. Contributions from past losses					
C Interventions					
Middle counselling sessions (chronic)					
A. Contributions to present loss					
B. Contributions from past losses					
C. Interventions					
Later counselling sessions (reinvesting and rebuilding)					
A. Contributions to present loss					
B. Contributions from past losses					
C Interventions					

Perspectives: Tools for assessment and intervention. They can exert a positive or a negative influence at any time during the experience of grief. They may also be absent or exert no influence. They may emerge differently at different times, presenting different issues.

Directions:

1. Assess where the client is in the counselling process (early, middle, later).
2. Listen for characteristics of the various perspectives which are exerting an influence.
3. Make notes on the chart that indicate where a client is at in the process (time) and perspective(s). These can be direct quotes, or your reflections of the content or observations of nonverbals.
4. As perspectives are noted, explore for past losses and possible influences (positive and negative) that each perspective might have exerted. Make notes.
5. Review chart after assessment(s) and ongoing sessions. Design interventions based on where the client is at (time frame) and the current influence of perspectives.

Early Sessions

Counselling during the early sessions entails ongoing assessment, encouragement of their personal narrative, expression of emotions, and the provision of needed support (non-judgmental listening). During the acute experiences of grief, clients initially experience an incredible sense of aloneness and meaninglessness. Many

Table 3.2 Case examples using perspectives: perspectives can contribute both positive and negative influences simultaneously

Considerations of perspectives	Philosophical	Spiritual	Psychological	Sociological/cultural	Physical
Early counselling sessions (acute): Karen: death of only child					
A. Contributions to present loss	*Can't see any future meaning in life. *Has disconnected from supportive friends.	No solace in her religion.	*Daily panic attacks. *Evidence of resiliency: I CAN. *Evidence of coping: both strategies.	*Evidence of resiliency: I HAVE (support from sister; strong marriage). *Difficulties with co-workers.	*Uncertainty re: her cancer diagnosis. *Daily functioning impaired. *Discontinued exercise. *Weight loss.
B. Contributions from past losses	At present time is aware of the influence of past losses on the present death: death of parents, her husband's disability, son's incarceration, and her own diagnosis of cancer.				
	Questioned unfairness of so much happening to her.	Faith sustained her; hope for her son's parole.	*Evidence of resiliency: I AM, I CAN. *Evidence of coping: both strategies.	Evidence of resiliency: I HAVE (friends, family).	*Exercised. *Functioned well.
C. Interventions	Narrative strategies: *Listen, validate. *Encourage repetition of the story.	Use concepts from continuing bonds. Foster an internal reality.	*Promote coping strategies *Build on resiliency factors: I AM, I CAN. *Use of categories of loss and history of loss. *Reminiscing exercise (Figure 3.6).	Build on resiliency factors: I HAVE.	*Promote proper diet and exercise. *Follow-up for medical treatment. *Medication for anxiety.

Table 3.2 (Continued)

Considerations of perspectives	Philosophical	Spiritual	Psychological	Sociological/cultural	Physical
Middle counselling: Mike: life after heart surgery					
A. Contributions to present loss	*Life has no meaning. *Dislikes people/does not want to be around them.	*Anger with God. *Church has no meaning.	*Old coping styles don't work. *No options for a new professional career. *Present relationship with mother deepens resentments.	*Aware of male gender issues. *Aware of lack of support systems.	*Afraid to do anything physically. *Lowered/ineffectual functioning. *Impaired sleep.
B. Contributions from past losses	At present is aware of the influence of the death of his father on his present 'non-death' losses of health and career.				
	Questioned life's unfairness.	Questions God for allowing this death.	*Evidence of resiliency: I AM, I CAN. *Evidence of resentments towards mother. *Evidence of problem-focused coping. *Use of categories of loss and history of loss.	Resiliency factors: I HAVE (professional peers).	*High level of functioning. *Exercised daily. *Physically fit/never ill.
C. Interventions	Narrative strategies: begin to encourage a new chapter to his life story.	None at present.	*Evaluate old coping strategies; activate new ones using both strategies. *Promote resiliency factors: I AM, I CAN. *Concepts and process of forgiveness.	Explore male gender issues related to current thoughts, emotions and life issues.	Encourage return to appropriate/safe physical exercise.

(Continued)

Table 3.2 (*Continued*)

Considerations of perspectives	Philosophical	Spiritual	Psychological	Sociological/cultural	Physical
Later counselling: Ann: suicide of husband and chronic, debilitating illness					
A. Contributions to present loss	*Uncertainty of life's meaning. *Concern for any future meaning.	Nothing at present.	*Loss of control/no sense of choice. *Ineffective coping. *Increased panic attacks. *Negative thoughts and self-defeating beliefs. *Repressed anger. *Unaware of resiliency factors (I AM, I CAN).	*Resiliency factors: I HAVE (support systems). *Daily functioning impaired. *Considering application for disability. *Ongoing weight loss. *Impaired sleep.	*Exhausted medical interventions for 18-year illness.
B. Contributions from past losses	In later sessions becomes aware of the contributions of past losses both non-death and the issues involved with her husband's suicide five years earlier.		*Emerging anger/resentments. *Evidence of awareness of resiliency factors: I AM, I CAN. *Understanding of self-defeating talk. *Awareness of dysfunctional marriage.		
C. Interventions	Narrative strategies: *Re-evaluate past personal stories of self and marriage. *Reconstruct new story ('meaning making').	Explore issues of personal spirituality.	*Educate and encourage re: resiliency: I AM, I CAN. *Foster forgiveness process. *Reconstruct faulty self-beliefs. *Develop effective coping: both strategies.	*Explore/reconstruct female (helpless) identity. *Encourage resiliency: I HAVE.	*Explore treatment options. *Medication for panic disorder. *Re-evaluate daily goals. Set realistic goals.

describe this time as feeling like they are outside of their bodies, looking in. Others experience tremendous anxiety, to the point of panic. Spiritually, they ask why God has allowed this to happen to them; and psychologically, they are 'searching for what has been lost'. This search reflects the fact that the psyche has not been able to accept the reality of the loss and tries to undo it by retrieving it. This often occurs by mentally replaying the event, looking for different endings; dreaming of what has been lost; or hearing and seeing the lost object in a crowd. Sociologically and culturally, during the early sessions, support systems or the lack of them will be identified, and influences such as gender and ethnicity will be most apparent. Lastly, physical perspectives often focus on psychosomatic complaints and diffi-culties with eating, sleeping, and overall daily functioning. These perspectives and their influence have been discussed in Chapters 1 and 2.

Along with continued assessment and early interventions, questions can be directed toward exploring the possible contributions to the present loss from these various perspectives. This can provide insight into the personal meaning of the loss for the bereaved, the nature and meaning of the attachment (relationship) to the deceased (or that 'object' that has been lost), how much of the self (identity) has been lost, what are the personality factors involved, what are the main issues that need to be addressed, what is the primary affect of the bereaved, and what has changed in their lives as a result of the loss? These questions are not all inclu-sive, but they do provide a framework for early exploration.

The Case of Karen

Karen (introduced in Chapter 2) had lost her only child, a 30-year-old son, after his car was impacted head-on by an intoxicated driver. The car went off the highway, hit a tree, and immediately exploded. He was burned beyond recognition. Two years before his death he had been released from a 10-year prison term and had returned home to rebuild his life as a young adult. Karen and her husband were devoted to their son. They had spent 10 years maintaining whatever contact they were allowed with him and lived for the day of his release. The two years they had with him were all they had anticipated, and they looked forward to their future with him.

Karen:	I don't want to be around anyone. I go to work and close myself in my office. At first people were supportive at work. Now they act like I should be doing better. I can do my job and not dwell on my son, but before and after work I am a mess. No one can ever really understand my pain.
Counsellor:	You are right. No one can ever truly understand your pain because no one had the relationship with your son that you had. Right now you are doing all you can just to function at work.
Karen:	I find myself waking up with panic attacks. I barely am able to make it to work. I force myself though, and I haven't missed a day of work in the five months since his death.
Counsellor:	Have you ever had panic attacks before your son's death?
Karen:	No, I've managed to cope well with a lot in my life. During the 10 years that he was in prison I never experienced anything like this. Eight years ago my husband had an industrial accident and became disabled. Two

(Continued)

(Continued)

years ago I was diagnosed with cancer. I don't understand why I am now having these panic attacks.

Counsellor: Despite past crises, the death of your son has rendered you more out of control than ever before. Anxiety and panic attacks are not unusual after the death of a loved one, especially a child. You are more vulnerable in the morning as you face each new day, not knowing what to expect and uncertain if you can manage the challenges of each new day.

Table 3.3   COPING STRATEGIES

PROBLEM-FOCUSED (utilizes techniques from concepts of self-efficacy, internal locus of control, and cognitive strategies):

- Rehearse a situation; visualize yourself making effective choices.
- Prioritize what is important to address; let go of the rest.
- Practice giving each situation and choice more than one assessment/perspective.
- Elicit feedback from respected support systems for their point of view and appraisal.
- Resist seeing yourself as a victim and choose behaviours based on a survivor image.
- Develop abilities to set realistic goals.
- Learn effective strategies to make and execute plans.

EMOTION-FOCUSED (focuses on expression, creativity, and support):

- Foster a healthy expression of all emotions.
- Develop stress management and relaxation techniques.
- Creatively channel stress through all art forms.
- Exercise to release the negative energy of stress.
- Foster the appropriate use of humor and the ability not to take oneself so seriously.

The above excerpt reflects the experience of the depths of aloneness, meaninglessness, and anxiety. It was evident that the philosophical and psychological perspectives were exerting the most influence during these early sessions. Currently, Karen was aware of several past losses (non-death) and realized that she had coped with them effectively. In order to understand the meaning and impact of these past losses and how they might influence the present loss, future questions can be formatted using the categories of loss (Figure 1.1, page 12) and the history of loss (Table 2.5, page 33). This approach will also provide clues to the client's sense of resiliency that has allowed a sense of mastery over prior losses and challenges.

From the psychological perspective, Karen was anxious to the point of frequent panic attacks. It is important to assess for pre-morbid personality, functioning, and coping factors at this time in order to assess the nature of the panic attacks. Anxiety is often one of the first symptoms of grief, especially after a traumatic and unexpected death. Pre-morbid assessment will either normalize the anxiety as a symptom of grief or alert us to previous psychological issues. Moreover, designing questions based on concepts of resiliency, this chapter provides a format (Table 3.4, page 46) to facilitate additional insight into pre-morbid characteristics that aid future strategies.

Counsellor: I am not sure how much you want to share about the accident with me at this time. You have told me that you and your husband keep replaying that night of the accident when he stopped by your home for some money at

2 a.m. You keep wondering if he had been drinking himself and you didn't realize it because you were both tired. You keep berating yourself that you hadn't asked him to come in or questioned him as to why he was out so late.

Karen: I can't get it out of my mind that he might still be alive if only we had insisted he come in. He seemed in such a hurry, and to the best of our abilities to remember, there was no sign that he had been drinking. He was a very cautious driver and he would never drink and drive.

Counsellor: I can understand your torment. No matter how old our children are, parents still feel a sense of responsibility to keep them safe. You are dealing with a double burden of trauma and grief. Your mind is desperate to change the outcome, so you keep replaying the last time you had together, looking for what you could have done differently.

Karen: You are right. Moreover, I have not had the courage to go to the scene of the accident. All I have is the memory and sight of him on our doorstep. I know that I have to go at some point to get past where I am. I just keep imagining the scene of the explosion and his body in flames. I can't stop wondering if he saw it coming and felt any pain.

As suggested in the above excerpt, it is important to encourage clients to tell the story of what happened. Encourage details and provide opportunity for expressions of grief as they relate their stories. This is a good opportunity to assess whether they have the correct information, lack a clear understanding of what transpired, or for some reason cannot talk about the event or person. The more they talk, the more the cognitive acceptance is integrated.

Early sessions also provide the opportunity to encourage additional stories that lead to a greater understanding of lives prior to the loss. Stories that tell us how individuals have previously constructed their lives for meaningfulness provide insight into understanding their present distress and their difficulties accommodating to changed realities. The bereaved cannot adapt to a loss without some ability to restore some coherence to the narrative of their lives. Life stories must be reorganized and rewritten (Neimeyer, 1998).

Psychologically, to accept the reality that this death (or loss event) has occurred, asking questions and encouraging repetition of the stories promote integration of the event and eventual acceptance. By talking, and as the loss is cognitively accepted, feelings will emerge. The more feelings that they can release, the more capable they are of moving forward in their grief work. Family and friends are often frightened by feelings that are similar and are openly shared; thus, they fail to validate emotions that are necessary and valid. Counsellors also need to assess the type of support that is coming from these systems. Support systems may be hindering a normal grief process if they are helping the bereaved avoid their grief. Moreover, many who form the support systems lack information about normal grief and try to rush the process. Examples of this are family and friends who encourage the bereaved to dispose of the clothing and memorabilia the day after the funeral, or who keep the bereaved person so busy that he or she has no time to think.

A primary benefit of counselling is that it provides an environment conducive to releasing these intense emotions. Counsellors need to be aware of the intensity of emotions being expressed. Sessions may have to run longer if clients are still experiencing some intensity and have not returned to some level of stability. It would not be responsible to release a client to drive home who had just gotten in touch with a high level of anger. Probe for feelings early in a session in order to allow time for both an expression and a return to some state of equilibrium. The following exchange was initiated within the first ten minutes of a session, and it required a full session to process the total experience. The client needed to share it, relive it, and become emotionally stabilized before leaving. Grief work is hard work and takes time. Do not rush the process.

> *Karen*:   I finally did it. My sister took me to the scene of the accident. I knew it would be bad, but not this bad.
>
> *Counsellor*: What motivated you to finally do this?
>
> *Karen*:   Nothing really. My sister and I were out driving and I told her to just drive to the site of the accident.
>
> *Counsellor*: So, you really hadn't prepared yourself to do this?
>
> *Karen*:   Yes and no. I have been thinking about doing this since the day he died. I wanted to do it before winter came and the snow fell, covering everything up. I was afraid that I would never find it then. But what really made it so bad was the fact that I had to find the tree he hit. I knew it was the tree because when I rubbed my hands on it, black soot came off. No other tree around had this soot. Then I began looking under the brush around the area and found burned pieces of his car. I don't know why, but I bundled up all the burned pieces that I could find and took them home with me.
>
> *Counsellor*: I think that is very understandable. Although traumatic, those pieces of your son's car are a part of him. Right now that is all you have. Some day you will know what to do with them.

Feelings of unreality and numbness, with intrusions of intense pain, are hallmarks of initial grief experiences. Psychologically, we are not ready for these assaults and do not immediately comprehend or process them. The early sessions of grief counselling also need to address regrets and feelings that something different could have been done by the survivors that would have changed the course of events. This is a normal part of the process whereby the bereaved need to replay the event, search for what has been lost, and work through feelings of guilt and anguish that they were not able to have prevented the event.

Gradually over time, with the release of emotion, permission to go back over events and feelings, and provision of a supportive environment, the bereaved will experience a lessening of the acute intensity of pain. They will realize that they are beginning to experience days with segments of time that are not painful. Hope begins to build on this new experience of freedom from pain for short periods of time. Clients are encouraged to keep journals on a daily basis in order to gain awareness of what is changing and happening within them and in their environment.

During the latter part of the early sessions, counsellors introduce the idea that grief work is multidimensional and that there is more to grieve over than just an individual; also there are all the objects and associations connected with that individual. Counsellors, from listening over a number of sessions, now have some understanding of their clients' worlds and all that needs to be grieved (i.e., from 'we to I', to lifestyle changes, to treasured objects that connected individuals to relationships). Counsellors must assess the nature of the bonds that the bereaved had to the deceased in order to guide them towards accommodation and reconstruction. Accommodation does not ignore past realities. It fosters adaptation to changed realities while maintaining a connection to the past. These past meanings become the foundations for new realities and identities. Loss resolution may require the bereaved to move on in their lives; however, it does not mean that bonds must be totally severed. Death does not end love and caring. Attachment after death is different. The past will always remain a part of who they were and will serve to connect them to who they will become. The value of continued bonds to the deceased is that they provide gratification in a new way. Death is a reality that changes relationships forever. However, bonds continued after the death of a loved one create a sense of continuity and an 'inner system that continues to be centered on the person who is no longer physically present. This inner reality may encourage the mourner to carry on' (Silverman and Nickman, 1996a).

Helping clients describe the nature of their attachments and identify important objects, places, and events makes them more aware of the multiple losses that need to be grieved in order to move towards future goals of integration, continuity, and reconstruction.

Making memory quilts for family and friends from clothing that had belonged to the deceased is an example of mourning the death while maintaining past meanings and fostering continued bonds. Clothing can become treasured objects that link the bereaved to past memories and ongoing connections. Memories are bittersweet, as they are reminders of what has been lost and will never be possible again. However, the grief eventually lessens and the memories prompted by each article of clothing in the quilt provide a sense of continuity and create an inner system that allows the mourner to focus on their loved ones for renewed gratification and inner strength to carry on.

Middle Sessions

During the middle parts of the counselling process, practitioners will hear reflections of continued pain and the torment of adjusting to and grieving an environment that is a poignant reminder of the loss. During the latter period of these middle sessions, there is some evidence of willingness and ability to accommodate to changed realities. Once past the acute phases, where more emotional support is necessary, bereaved individuals move into new realms that need exploration and intervention. Perspectives emerge and re-emerge, often centering on the psychological and sociological ones. Psychologically, the bereaved feel more in control of their emotions. They have begun to make new decisions and take small risks in an effort to rebuild their lives. With encouragement and guidance from the counsellor, coping efforts (Table 3.3, page 42) become more effective. Characteristics of resiliency assessed during earlier sessions can be incorporated into treatment strategies (Table 3.4, see below).

Considering the bereaved from a psychological perspective, it is now important to assess unarticulated resentments that require forgiveness and a process of letting go (Table 3.5, see below). Inability or unwillingness to let go creates a victim position for the bereaved, preventing reconstruction of meaningfulness in the future. Loss violates a sense of personal control. Effective interventions re-establish an internal locus of control and, in addition, facilitate positive effects on the neuroendocrine and immune systems which are often compromised during the experience of grief.

From a sociological/cultural perspective, they gain understanding into the influence of their cultural backgrounds and often discard some of the negative messages that had previously influenced them. An example of this is the fact that

Table 3.4   Categorization of resiliency factors (adapted from Grotberg, 1995)

I HAVE (external supports):

- People around me that I trust and who love me.
- People who act as role models when life lacks purpose and meaning.
- People who support me by letting me know when my behaviours are potentially unhealthy.
- People who believe I can learn to make new choices and live a meaningful life again.

I AM (inner, personal strengths):

- A unique individual that people can like and love.
- Someone who cares about others and can show my concern.
- Respectful of myself and others.
- Willing to be responsible for what I do.
- A person with hope and the belief that life can be 'good' again.

I CAN (social, interpersonal skills):

- Find supportive people to talk to about my difficulties.
- Find ways to solve problems that I face.
- Control myself when I feel like doing something that is potentially dangerous or harmful.
- Know when I need to take action on a situation that I face.
- Know my limits and get help when I need it.

Table 3.5   Processes involved in interpersonal forgiveness

- Examination of psychological defenses prohibiting forgiveness or a process of 'letting go' of hurts and resentments.
- Confrontation of anger: the goal is to embrace, re-experience deep pain, and release festering emotions.
- Admit feelings of shame that may be connected to the event and the individual's part in it.
- Develop an awareness of the amount of personal energy that is being invested into past hurts; as a result, energy is lacking for current investment into relationships and activities.
- Realization that one might be permanently and negatively changed by the injurious event or action by another.
- Insight and acceptance of a perspective that life is not fair.
- Finding new meaning in the suffering and the forgiveness process: a transformation that promotes healing.
- Realization that you might have a new purpose as a result of what has happened: transformation to a new identity and renewed purpose and meaning in life.
- Forgiveness is a gift that you give yourself: it is an opportunity to move on and do better things with your life.

men in white, middle-class society are often socialized not to have emotions. Moreover, many Americans and Britons have been indoctrinated with the belief that expressing grief is a sign of weakness.

This perspective also fosters attention to the category of resiliency that identifies external supports (I HAVE) in an individual's life. Prior to this time in their grief they felt more disconnected from the world around them and perhaps could not appreciate the benefits of being connected to those who were willing to be supportive. Previously, the focus had been more on what one no longer had and the intense pain of aloneness.

Table 3.6   Reminiscing

In addition to sharing pictures, items, and favourite stories about your loved one, the following questions offer an opportunity for personal reflections and sharing about the meaning and purpose of a loved one's life.

What will you never forget about ———?
What did you like most about ———?
What was unusual or out of character for———?
What was the favourite expression of ———?
What was a favourite song or type of music of ———?
What was ——— favourite way of doing things?
What qualities of ——— would you like to have?
What do you hope that others will always remember about ———?
If ——— were face to face with you now, what would you say or do?
How would you describe ——— to a stranger?

Philosophically, many bereaved clients have found support from other bereaved individuals and no longer experience existential aloneness and meaninglessness. Moreover, support is often experienced as friends and family share memories of deceased loved ones. Sharing memories often elicits renewed emotional pain; however, the process also promotes integration of a loved one's life into mourners' inner realities. Remembering can be daily, spontaneous, or even structured. Some individuals like to plan special occasions and invite family and friends to come prepared to share memories that highlight special characteristics of the deceased. Table 3.6 is a tool that encourages participation in this type of ritual. As clients address philosophical issues that emerge during this time and begin to feel a desire to connect with others, they also begin the process of asking and finding answers to the changed meanings of their lives. Use of narrative techniques and strategies that promote reconstruction continues to be a valuable tool throughout the sessions.

Spiritual perspectives often arise during this time, even for those who do not have spiritual backgrounds. During the earlier sessions, this perspective often emerged with intense anger directed towards God for allowing a loss to occur. Now there broader questions with an exploration of religious beliefs in order to arrive at a sense of spiritual wholeness and peacefulness. Many begin to question an afterlife and wonder where their loved one is. Some develop a more mature relationship with God, realizing that they had never grown past their childhood views. And others, who had never considered this perspective as important, begin to develop a sense of spirituality and respect for life around them.

Lastly, physical perspectives can continue to exert influence and create additional stress during this time period. Counsellors must continue to pay attention to this aspect of their clients' lives, as it is pivotal in the healing process.

During these middle sessions it is important to assess prior losses as they pertain to and influence the perspectives (Table 3.2, pages 38–40). Prior losses are assessed through the history of loss, which is introduced (at least verbally) during the intake. The use of the chart on perspectives facilitates questioning into past losses and how possible contributions (from the past) might be affecting the present loss. For example, for a person who has experienced a major loss in the past and has healed because of his or her spirituality, it is quite possible for this past experience to exert positive influence in the present loss. This tool offers a basis for investigation and treatment planning. During these middle sessions, counsellors should explore each perspective and build treatment plans on the findings.

The Case of Marie

Marie was discussed in Chapter 2. She was a social worker, referred by her primary care physician, following two heart attacks and surgery. She had not been able to reconstruct new meaningful realities either in her personal or her professional life. Early in the middle sessions, her narrative began to reflect more than a fear of her physical condition as her reason for not finding new opportunities and getting on with her life. Using the perspectives and encouraging her narrative, with an emphasis on the present influence of past losses, emotions of anger and resentment emerged. It was easy to understand her present bitterness and feelings of unfairness for the major loss and interruption in her life; however, the intensity of her emotions was indicative for something deeper. Earlier she had mentioned his dislike of her mother's control and her negativity. At 18 she had successfully removed herself from her control by moving far away and gradually establishing herself as a respected professional in the field of social work. Now she was back in her presence, unable to leave as she had in the past. Issues she thought she had resolved when she had left home had not been. Until insight achieved during a counselling session, she had never realized the impact of her deep resentments towards her mother. Emotionally she had never differentiated from her control over her, and in addition she now realized that she held her mother responsible for her father's death several years ago.

Marie: I had a hard weekend trying to cope with my mother's demands. It has always been about her. My father lived his life trying to make her happy. He tried so hard that I think it killed him. Nothing was ever good enough for her. Now that I am back here she thinks it's my role to cater to her every need.

Counsellor: I know that you were not close to your mother, but I am hearing something new today. You came in here looking very angry, and now I hear a bitterness that I haven't heard before.

Marie: When my dad was alive, he protected me from her. Every time she tried to control me or cut me down, dad made it better for me. I went to dad for everything. I always called him and shared my life's work with him. He validated me. Mom always diminished every award I received in my field. Now I am ill, stuck here, and stuck with her. I can barely stand the sight of her.

Towards the latter part of the middle sessions the bereaved become more aware of the necessity to leave behind former identities and to begin the search for new aspects of themselves not yet emerged. If resentments emerge, as in the above example, counsellors must facilitate forgiveness and a letting go of the past. New identities and roles cannot be constructed if the client remains in a victim position harboring resentments.

The middle sessions gradually move from an emphasis on expressing painful emotions to more effective coping and to making new choices. Counsellors facilitate this transition by assisting clients in the use of strategies of coping, decision-making, and exploring new options in their lives. We cannot change what has happened and eventually clients need to adapt, move beyond grief, and accommodate new realities. The ability to cope more effectively and to make decisions reawakens personal feelings of being in control. Loss and grief destroy a sense of personal control. Counselling must address regaining control both within oneself and in the external environment. Attig (1992) terms this task *relearning the world*. The bereaved are no longer the same and cannot try to live in their worlds as they once had. All have some potential to relearn and live life differently, yet meaningfully. Counselling has the potential to offer a major contribution in this regard.

Later Sessions

Later sessions do not declare that grief work has ended completely. There is no single right way to grieve and there is no set timetable for the specific experiences. There is some agreement in the field that at least two years is needed. However, even this time can vary, depending upon the loss; and this does not mean that counselling is needed for two years. Some may only need one professional visit, but will, on their own, take a full two years to experience their grief and begin to rebuild their lives. The basic guideline for assessment and treatment is to be aware of potential problems associated with personalities, pre-morbid functioning, and complications after loss; and also to reserve judgment on an individual's manner of grieving and the amount of time he or she takes to go through the process.

A major part of these later sessions addresses the experience of letting go of former roles and identities and making new choices to initiate new life narratives. Reinvestment does not mean replacement. Simply stated, it is the willingness and the ability to integrate the past into an inner reality and to invest mental and emotional energy into the reconstruction of a meaningful life. Since grief is considered to be a cyclical process, it is possible for many of the earlier experiences to re-emerge, in much the same way as the perspectives do. Often holidays, anniversary dates, and other special events trigger emotions and create reversions back to earlier experiences. The perspectives will indicate a process of integration of the loss and signs of future growth. Philosophically, the bereaved find meaning and purpose again in life. They feel connected to others and a larger system beyond themselves. They are aware that life is not fair, but they can appreciate the goodness of it. Spiritually, many who have been angry at God have seen past their anger and have reestablished their relationship with God or a higher being. Many experience growth in their spirituality and realize that even as adults they may have had childish views and expectations of God. Psychologically, they have made many new decisions and choices and understand the concepts of role realignment and new identities. Many have had to change their belief systems and accept new ways of thinking, such as the reality that bad things do happen to good people. Continued efforts to promote effective coping strategies and characteristics of resiliency provide opportunities for empowerment and growth despite significant loss and upheaval.

Table 3.7   Instructions for psychological needs

Needs	Past	Present	Future
Love: Those whom I can trust and love me, and I can love in return (family, friends, etc.).			
Belonging: List what you belong to/what you feel comfortable with/feel a part of and contribute to.			
Worth: What do I do or like about myself, that makes me feel good about myself?			
Recognition: Who appreciates me and gives me recognition? What do I do that I feel is worthwhile and important to me?			
Fun: What did I do for fun - alone/with others? How much does it cost? How much of my fun is free?			
Freedom: What does freedom mean to me? Time, money, what I eat, activities, choices, what I say.			

Directions:

1. Instruct clients to fill out how each need was met before the change (loss), illness, or death.
2. Write down (present) how these same needs are being met, or not being met, have changed or have been compromised in some way.
3. Facilitate clients to think about new ways/choices to meet these needs in the near future.

During these final sessions an adaptation of Glasser's (1990) psychological needs (Table 3.7) can provide a framework for exploration and rebuilding based upon specific needs. This is a worksheet, presented in Chapter 2 as an assessment tool, that identifies basic needs of love, belonging, power, self-worth, fun, and freedom. Clients identify how these needs were met in the past, what has changed in the present, and possible steps to take to meet these needs again. In a graphic way, it facilitates awareness of changes that have occurred because of loss, and encourages the search for new choices that will satisfy each need. New goals should be simple, realistic, concrete, and attainable in the near future. Longer-term goals can be set once there is a firmer foundation to build upon.

From a sociological/cultural perspective, many have new-found friends, new activities, and new support systems. Environments have changed somewhat, so the former ones no longer have the potential to exert such painful influence. Many have had to rethink their cultural backgrounds and accept different ways of coping with their grief. Some men have joined with their wives in counselling to be supportive, and later acknowledge (sheepishly) that they are there for themselves also. Many have been raised in families that are very stoic, where grief is seen as selfish or a sign of weakness.

Finally, from a physical perspective during the later sessions, symptoms diminish that once aggravated the grief during the early and middle sessions. Clients have learned the interaction between the various perspectives of grief and their physical symptoms. They have incorporated healthier lifestyles into their routines. Results are seen in their outward appearances, their changed attitudes, and their abilities to laugh again and show a renewed interest in life.

The Case of Ann

Ann was introduced in Chapter 1, 'The Journey of Ann'. As the vignette suggested, by the later sessions Ann showed evidence of being a client who had successfully progressed through her journey of grief. Although her motivation for counselling was to regain control in her life that was currently debilitated by chronic illness, she slowly learned and accepted the fact that she had never addressed issues in her marriage or her husband's suicide five years ago. She showed courage, character, and ability as she painfully went back over her dysfunctional family of origin, marriage at a young age to escape her family, total reliance on an addictive husband, her 18-year illness (that was currently debilitating), and the suicide of her husband. Her view of herself as a female was based on stereotypes of female helplessness. She never questioned her husband, although she suspected that he was not psychologically healthy. Until after his death she had no idea that his addictions not only destroyed him but also left a legacy of financial ruin for her and the four children. For the intervening five years she had coped by doing whatever was intervening necessary for the well-being of the children. Ongoing bankruptcy and legal issues of back taxes, her declining health, and most recently her father's heart problems were powerful motivators for personal counselling.

Ann: Once I stopped putting so many demands on myself to keep everything *normal* and perfect for the children, I began to think more about the questions you were asking me about my marriage. For the first time I felt a real anger towards Jake. I never had before because I felt I owed him so much for marrying me. He was the only boy I ever dated in high school. I never knew that a marriage should have been different. My parents were certainly not good role models. I think I have a lot of anger that's just beginning to surface. The other night I was looking at his picture and all I could say was 'Damn you'.

Counsellor: I know this is difficult for you. Not only are you experiencing painful emotions that you are uncomfortable with, you are also being challenged to re-evaluate and change basic assumptions about yourself.

Three weeks later:

Ann: Last week I was 20 miles from home and I got a call that my dad was having heart problems and was being rushed to the hospital. I didn't panic as I usually do; rather, I calmly drove to the hospital. This made me think that perhaps you have been right telling me that I have a lot of inner strengths and resiliencies that I never realized I had. All these years I never thought I could manage or make a decision on my own. I am the person that you see. You will never know what your words have done for me.

(Continued)

(Continued)

Counsellor: I realized your strengths the first time I met you. I felt confident then that I could safely guide you back to your past. Without a broader awareness of your life and a full expression of grief, you would not be capable of appreciating your strengths and reconstructing a renewed sense of your full potential.

One month later:

Ann: I went to the Mayo Clinic for a surgical evaluation of my illness. The surgery is new and has multiple risks. The surgeon assured me that I was a good candidate for it and that I should have it immediately because I am feeling good right now and my symptoms aren't active. He was domineering and he made me feel that I had to accept his opinions. But then I caught myself and firmly asserted that I needed time to think it over. This was the first time in two years that I was feeling good and doing things outside the house. It will be summer soon and that is my favorite time of year. I don't want to miss being able to enjoy it. I felt good saying this to him – like I wasn't allowing someone to further control me. My illness is not life threatening, so putting the surgery off is not harmful. I had to remind myself that I only went to him for an opinion so I could better evaluate my options.

Counsellor: You have really taken ownership of your life. Over the past few months I have seen you grow in many ways. Your new life is just beginning.

Resolution and Growth

Within the broader considerations of resolution there is an understanding and an acceptance that life will never be the same again and that certain realities and assumptions must be relinquished in order to survive the pain, to integrate the experience, and to rebuild a future existence. Resolution, like reinvestment, is not replacement. This notion may be difficult for a client to comprehend. Many modern societies are based upon the replacement of objects and relationships. Often grief counselling must address current philosophies of the society/culture of the bereaved. Nothing, whether it was a relationship or an activity (e.g., job), that was lost is ever replaced. A meaningful part of an identity and investment of time is never replaced; it is reorganized after grief and incorporated in memory in a manner that has potential to console and be growth-producing. That which has been lost is integrated within, and is always a part of the human spirit. Grief has the potential to be a growth experience.

Along with the above considerations regarding resolution, the question is often asked: 'When is grief work ended'? This question cannot be clearly or definitively answered. Individual timetables, anniversary reactions, personality, and the influence of various perspectives are some of the factors that make it a unique experience for each individual. Moreover, the concept of ended grief work implies that the grief will never again have to be addressed. 'Grief resolution' seems to be a more accurate term, and complements the concept of grief as a process. However, even considering a broader view, there is no accepted concept of grief resolution. The differences of opinion are in terms of what resolution is and what it is not. Some believe resolution means getting over the loss and forgetting. Others believe that one never entirely gets over a loss; rather, the larger process to is learn to cope, live with it, and integrate that which has been lost in healthy memory.

Newer concepts discussed regarding continuing bonds and maintaining inner representations of the deceased broaden conceptualizations of resolution. Rubin defined resolution as 'the process that supplements and continues beyond adaptation and/or coping with loss. The connections to the representations of the deceased and to the memories of the relationship to the deceased continue on across the life cycle' (1996: 220). Silverman and Nickman (1996b) further state that the process of accommodation and adaptation is the manner in which the bereaved reorganize their lives and a sense of themselves in a way that fosters living in the present time, while experiencing the acute pain created by the loss:

> An ongoing construction of a deceased person is propelled by the sense of the deceased that is embedded in the mourner from the relationship before the death. The construction of the new relationship uses some different elements. All this takes place over time at speeds determined by individual circumstances and history. There is no fixed formula, no one way at arriving at a resolution. (1996b: 353)

Grief holds the possibilities for tremendous growth. However, it is premature to mention this possibility during early sessions. In the early and middle sessions clients primarily need a trusting environment that validates their normal grief reactions. The latter part of the middle sessions and the later sessions cautiously (and on the clients' timetables) move them towards new choices and the viewpoint that grief has not only a negative value, but it can also be a challenge and an opportunity.

The pain, experience, and resolution of grief take place on two levels: within oneself and within one's environment. They involve many changes and reflect many dimensions. How the world has been previously viewed and various personal belief systems may need revision. Many have been raised according to certain religious, philosophical, and ethical principles. The art of counselling involves becoming involved in existential crises: e.g., 'I have been a good person and this is not fair. Is anything worth it?' The world can be a cruel place, and life is not fair; but counselling can assist the client through this crisis. What does a client have left after this experience of loss? Resolution entails taking an assessment of psychological needs, evaluating what is still intact, and determining how life can be rebuilt. Resolution involves a process of acting upon the world again, making decisions, and choosing effective behaviours. It can be compared to learning how to walk again: take small steps, consistently; fall, get up, and try again. Resolution is a choice; however, it may be the hardest task individuals have to face. It also involves hope and a belief that life will get better and that the pain will subside. Without this, it is difficult to set goals, to trust, to take risks.

Resolution does not mean forgetting. Some may tenaciously hold onto their grief for fear of forgetting a relationship that was so much a part of their lives. The more that others tell the bereaved to stop talking and to continue on with their lives, the more the process is retarded. Resolution does mean making new choices; thus, to talk about nothing else or to grieve without breaks is not healthy either. Resolution implies an eventual letting go of past realities; however, more importantly, it necessitates an integration of the deceased into the survivor's life in a different way – a way that promotes future growth and meaningfulness. Silverman and Klass (1996) do not emphasize a 'letting go'; rather they promote a focus on negotiating and renegotiating the meaning of loss over time. Death is unchanging and permanent; but the process involved is continuous. Further, they state that the meaning of grief resolution 'is tied to the meaning of our bonds with significant people in our lives, the meaning of membership in family and community, and the meaning we ascribe to our individual lives in the face of absolute proof of our own mortality' (1996: 22).

4 Family Grief

This chapter discusses various aspects of family grief, with consideration of issues that will be different for each family member. It will illustrate family case examples, but will also ask the reader to keep the individual in mind as a separate entity since most counsellors see clients individually (independent of the family unit) and their bereavement is addressed within that individual context.

Every client represents and is influenced by membership in one or more families. These memberships need to be assessed and understood as one deals with the individual. Issues of grief that currently affect the bereaved are often rooted in unresolved, multigenerational family relationships, norms, and patterns of communication. Understanding an individual's loss from a systems perspective provides valuable insight into potential complications in the process.

From a systemic view, the family is understood as an 'entity maintained by the mutual interaction of its parts' (Davidson, 1983: 26). What happens in one part will affect the others. Although patterns in families are undergoing change, Zimmerman (1992) proposes that the fundamental concept of family is that it represents distinct types of close relationships that continue to have meaning and importance for the individual and larger society. The family historically has provided the framework of a fundamental social unit that produces and raises children, cares for the elderly and the disabled, and socializes its members in the basic values of individual character development and in general responsibilities of citizenship (Wisensale, 1992). Sprenkle and Piercy, considering the current influence of constructivism upon postmodern thought, proposed the following as a criterion for a healthy family:

> … a healthy family is a kinship group whose primary functions include providing for the physical well-being of its members, the nurturing socialization of children, and the meeting of basic emotional needs for unconditional love … Families should empower persons to become capable of living both loving and productive lives. Family members should relate to one another in ways that are nonexploitive and encourage a similar attitude toward the broader community. Family values should include the belief that all humans have equal opportunity regardless of gender, race, creed, sexual preferences, or age (independent of maturity and training). (1992: 406)

This definition allows one to consider a variety of different types of families and to understand an individual in the context of the unique type of family membership that has shaped and influenced his or her identity. Previously, many societies had proposed two parents and their children as the norm for the definition of family. Today, there is a growing awareness and acceptance that there are different configurations of 'family': one-parent families with children, couples without children, blended families from remarriages, grandparents parenting children, foster families, and couples of the same sex raising children are all current examples.

Current models of interventions must include strategies that adequately address the uniqueness of these family configurations that are growing statistically and becoming more prevalent than the past norm of two parents and their children.

When working with individuals or families some background in family theory and therapy will provide important guidelines for assessment and interventions.

Basic Family Tasks

Although there is evidence of new norms in family configurations, these changes do not negate the belief that a family is expected to function as a basic social unit and provide fundamental necessities for its members, especially those who are not capable of meeting their own basic needs. Who the members are in this group and who should assume responsibility for specific tasks is not as important in today's definition of family. It is more important to adhere to a meaningful definition of 'family', similar to what was proposed in the beginning of this chapter. Thus it may be stated that, now and in the past, every culture prescribes basic tasks that are essential for every family to perform. When these tasks are not adequately performed, societies intervene. Duvall and Miller (1985) have outlined eight tasks expected by the American family. These tasks may be adapted to changing family norms and groups. Noteworthy among them are these four: the provision of food, clothing, and shelter; the determination of who provides the care, support, and management of the home; the establishment of ways to communicate, interact, and express affection, aggression, and sexuality; and the maintenance of morale and motivation, reward and achievement, meeting personal and family crises, setting and attaining goals, and developing family loyalties and values. The absence of any one of these or the other four tasks could constitute a loss in itself; and certainly when individuals present issues of loss in counselling, these basic tasks of a family (or tasks unique to a particular culture) must be taken into consideration in assessment. An example of this was an ethnic family of three generations who came for counselling following the murder of an adolescent girl by a boyfriend from another race and culture. Besides her death, there were other losses past and present in this family's history. Included as a loss was the belief held by the grandparents that the family had been shamed, and there was a loss of family loyalties and values. They firmly believed that one should not develop intimate relationships outside their own race. In their eyes their granddaughter had already been lost; and moreover, she had been disloyal by having disregarded deep-seated family values. The parents of the deceased girl felt that they had failed as parents in their basic roles of providing care and establishing effective communication with their daughter. Their expectations of parental roles and the demands of their particular culture had to be understood and addressed, along with the obvious issues of current grief.

Family Development Tasks

In addition to some basic family tasks, developmental tasks within a family or stages of the family life cycle (Table 4.1) must be also considered. Duvall and Miller (1985) refer to these tasks as being relative to a given stage of development in the life cycle of a family. When counselling a family it is important to assess

Table 4.1   Stage-sensitive family developmental tasks through the family life cycle

Stage of the family life cycle	Positions in the family	Stage-sensitive family developmental tasks
I. Married couple	Wife Husband	Establishing marital dyad
2. Childbearing	Wife-mother Husband-father Infant daughter or son or both	Rearing tasks
3. Pre-school age	Wife-mother Husband-father Daughter-sister Son-brother	Adapt to needs of pre-schoolers
4. School age	Wife-mother Husband-father Daughter-sister Son-brother	Adapting to the community of school-age families

5. Teenage	Wife-mother
	Husband-father
	Daughter-sister
	Son-brother
		(a) Balancing freedom
		  and responsibility
		(b) Establishing post-
		  parental interests

6. Launching centre	Wife-mother-grandmother
	Husband-father-grandfather
	Daughter-sister-aunt
	Son-brother-uncle
		(a) Rituals for young
		  adults leaving
		(b) Maintaining a
		  supportive base

7. Middle-aged parents	Wife-mother-grandmother
	Husband-father-grandfather
		(a) Refocus on marital
		  dyad
		(b) Ties with older and
		  younger generations

8. Ageing family members	Widow or widower Wife-mother-grandmother Husband-father-grandfather	Coping with endings and transitions

Source: adapted from Duvall and Miller, 1985: 62

where each member is in his or her individual stage of development and where the family (in which they currently hold membership) is. Even if the family is not seen in counselling as a group (i.e., the client comes for individual counselling), this does not negate the importance of assessing the individual's family's stage of development. These tasks have been defined as growth responses that arise at certain stages in the life of the family, 'the successful achievement of which leads to present satisfaction, approval, and success with later tasks; whereas failure leads to unhappiness in the family, disapproval by society, and difficulty with later family tasks' (Duvall and Miller, 1985: 47). From this it becomes understandable that every individual has the potential to be working on more than one issue simultaneously. An individual who requests counselling for a specific loss event that he or she believes is unrelated to any other facet of his or her life may not be aware of unresolved family developmental tasks (past or present) that are contributing to the present loss event. The eight stages outlined in Table 4.1 range from the newly married couple, through the age-related tasks of caring for children, through middle age, ending with tasks that face aging family members and their families. Based on the prior discussion in this chapter, this model will need revision to accommodate new and changing definitions of the family; however, every model will include a beginning stage of basic family organization and move towards middle age and aging-related tasks. Whether or not all future families will include children will not preclude the concepts of a life cycle or tasks. When a major loss such as death, divorce, or chronic illness occurs unexpectedly during a critical period of a family developmental task, it is often doubtful that effective coping, attention to the family developmental task and individuals' developmental tasks, and healthy resolution of each member's issues of bereavement can be accomplished satisfactorily without support, education, and specific therapeutic interventions.

Researchers Jordan (1992) and Walsh and McGoldrick (1988) have outlined family tasks in adapting to a loss. They have also noted that the interaction of a number of other factors with the loss creates more difficult outcomes for the family. Some of these factors include the

- timing of the loss in the family life cycle;
- the effect of concurrent stressors;
- the family socio-cultural context; and
- the impact of previous unresolved losses in the family history.

Considering the above factors, it is important to determine where the family is in the family life cycle, and the possible application of the above factors. Moreover, it is also important to keep in mind the definition and purpose of a family in terms of the health, growth, and well-being of its members. A family in grief may not be capable of addressing family tasks, and this might have long-term effects on the ability for individual members to create their own healthy and functional families in the future. Counsellors may decide that it is best to address first the individual and family developmental tasks before issues of grief.

Family Concepts within the Family Therapy Approach

Not every family, or individual within a family, will need counselling; however, an understanding of the major theoretical concepts of family will prove valuable in the counsellor's general understanding of the relationship of an individual within a family or families to concepts of bereavement. Family therapy has incorporated theory from various disciplines, including concepts from systems theories, structural approaches, symbolic interaction, and attachment theory and styles, and constructivism. All of these offer insights and tools for assessments and interventions, and can be adapted to counselling for those experiencing loss and grief.

Communications, Systems, and Structural Theories
Communication theory includes concepts from cybernetics and general systems theory. This theory encourages exploration of patterns of communication within a

family setting in order to assess present behaviours and issues. Messages sent among family members are said to have report (content) and command (defining relationships) functions. Jackson (1965) observed that one can discern what the family rules are by listening to the report and command functions and the regularity of these types of family messages. These rules have the primary purpose of maintaining family homeostasis or balance. Homeostasis can be further understood by using concepts from general systems theory which has promoted the idea that a system is more than the aggregate of its parts. In terms of family therapy, this concept has been adapted to propose that a family system should be viewed as more than a collection of people, and that therapists should investigate what is helping to maintain the system. Symptoms are often considered to be mechanisms that maintain a dysfunctional system. Homeostasis (as a self-regulatory mechanism), involving positive and negative feedback loops, is a central principle in this theory, as it was in the theory of cybernetics. Nichols and Schwartz (1991) discussed the relationship of positive and negative feedback loops, family rules, and homeostasis to family therapy. The rules, both spoken and unspoken, that govern family behaviours are regulated by the need for a family to keep things in balance and control. This balance can be good for family functioning and survival; however, taken to an extreme it can become rigid. Negative feedback helps enforce the rules and minimize change in behaviour, whereas positive feedback allows or promotes change. Both of these feedback loops have a place in the overall functioning of a family, and both need to be evaluated at any given time for their potential deleterious effects on normal functioning. This model does not attempt to discover what the real problem is; rather, the main focus is on the system as the problem and how it is being maintained.

A leader in family systems therapy was Murray Bowen (1974), who based his theoretical-clinical model on psychoanalytical theory and practice. He stated that there were two central forces that needed to be kept in balance: differentiation from family and fusion (togetherness) with one's family. Differentiation was defined as being intra- and interpersonal. 'Intrapersonal' meant that one could differentiate between thoughts and feelings; that is, it was possible to have strong emotions, and to remain rational and in control of personal cognitions. 'Interpersonal' meant that one was able not to overly react to others. The second force, fusion, taken at its extreme, meant that one was enmeshed in a dysfunctional family structure. Bowen saw families as falling on a continuum between these two forces, with the healthier ones being closer to differentiation, where it was possible to think rationally yet continue to be emotionally connected to others. He also believed that present issues were rooted in past family experiences and that there was a transmission of emotional processes through several generations. Unresolved past losses can be passed down through the generations and hinder present coping and eventual resolution. As a result he encouraged therapists to take an extended family history that covered at least two generations, asking questions that focused on the emotional integration of the family (over the generations), how families facilitated or hindered emotional expression, types of family communication patterns, and the roles provided by the deceased members.

Nadeau's (1998) research and subsequent strategies for assessment and intervention advocated a family construction of meaning. In addition to theories of symbolic interaction, she utilized concepts from family systems theory. This theory provided a number of systems concepts (as discussed in the preceding paragraphs) that were useful in identifying and describing family meaning making processes and the structural changes that occur in a family following a death. Family restructuring based on systems theory requires change from and adaptation to new roles, rules, and boundaries. The meanings that families ascribe to their loved one's death and the deceased often influence and are influenced by structural changes in the family system. Meaning making occurs at all levels of the family system, from the individuals to the entire family group. And, in keeping with systems theories, factors that inhibit meaning making include family secrets, insecure attachments, and family rules prohibiting expression of emotions.

Although there is overlap between systems and structural concepts, some researchers and therapists have favored a structural approach to understanding and working with clients. A leading theorist in this area of structural family therapy was Salvador Minuchin. Minuchin (1974) focused on three constructs: structure, subsystems, and boundaries. Structure was defined as a pattern of organization in which family members interact in predictable sequences. These sequences are repeated and form enduring patterns of family behaviour. The patterns involve sets of covert rules that govern family transactions. Subsystems within a family are determined by generation, gender, or common interests. Minuchin theorized that families were differentiated into various subsystems to perform certain functions. He viewed every individual as a subsystem, with dyads and larger groups making up other subsystems. Family members play different roles in the various subsystems, and individual family members usually belong to more than one subsystem within a family structure. Lastly, he proposed the concept of boundaries and stated that 'individuals, subsystems, and whole families are demarcated by *interpersonal boundaries,* invisible barriers that surround individuals and subsystems, regulating the amount of contact with others' (Nichols and Schwartz, 1991: 451). Boundaries are on a continuum between rigid (nothing is allowed to permeate) and diffuse (enmeshment, i.e., no sense of personal boundaries).

Included within family systems and structural theories are concepts of family patterns of relating and communicating, and dimensions of family functioning. Kissane and Bloch (1994) clinically observed and conducted systemic research on family grief. Thirteen families were covered in their report that indicated an association between avoidance of grief and family dysfunction. The family patterns that were most evident from their studies were an adaptive family response and three maladaptive responses.

Adaptive responses, initially described by Raphael (1984), include an open and honest disclosure of feelings. There is an ability and willingness to be intimate with each other, share their distress, and provide support and mutual consolation. These families operate flexibly and allow for individual differences in their members' grief experience. Moreover, they are capable of taking on needed roles and tasks to restructure the family's meaning.

> Sid had been a respected member of the community. He was an educator who had risen from being a popular classroom teacher to a high-level administrator over his 25-year career. He was a role model both in his personal and professional life. He and his wife had two children. Cancer was diagnosed unexpectedly after a

lingering virus. At the time of diagnosis it was at Stage 4, with little hope for remission. His attitude was exemplary and he continued to work and live a full and meaningful life for well over a year. His wife sought counselling before and after his death, both for her own needs but more so for the children. Their grief was not easy, despite the anticipation and preparation. The children were 17 and 18, with developmental issues facing them as well as the untimely death of their father. Based on the above description of an adaptive family, this family were intimate with their feelings, yet allowed individual differences. All willingly shared the tasks and roles that had been their father's/husband's. His wife was insightful in terms of her children's developmental tasks and where the family was in their life cycle. She encouraged differentiation as they prepared to leave home for college, yet they pulled together for the three years following his death to restructure the family. The stories are still shared and dad continues to be remembered in the community through established educational scholarships. The legacy of this man continues to live on and the family he co-created continues with new chapters of the family narrative.

In contrast, maladaptive patterns of family response to grief promote dysfunction of its members. The key mechanisms underlying these responses are avoidance, distortion, amplification, and prolongation (Lieberman and Black, 1982; Bowlby-West, 1983; Raphael, 1984).

Avoidant families cannot share genuine feelings of intimacy and support for one another. They intellectualize and keep family secrets. The more dominant members control this pattern and prohibit any expression of members who desire to share. In a similar manner, distorted family patterns include idealizing, blaming, and angry responses. Amplification is a response that sees the distress reverberating to others. It disrupts cohesive bonds and fractures families. Relationships disintegrate within the family, often resulting in separation, divorce, rejection and neglect. Lastly, prolongation refers to the results of the family dysfunction on its members as evidenced by chronic long-term problems (e.g., chronic depression) and the never-ending process of grieving.

Marnie was a 16-year-old girl who was referred by her guidance counsellor after a friend reported that Marnie's father had thrown a remote control at her head. The school counsellor was concerned because she knew that Marnie's family had never been able to support each other and were continuing to avoid issues related to a drowning accident of their oldest son, Mark, three years ago. Marnie had been driving the boat when Mark fell off and drowned. Marnie would not share the details of the accident and mother would only say that she continued to hear her son's screams for help. During the initial assessment Marnie stated that she didn't want to be here because she belonged to a 'grief group' at school for the last three years and the group was all that she needed. She stated that her main problem was her father because he still blamed her for her brother's death and he frequently told her that when he was angry. Mother agreed that her husband felt this way towards their daughter, but she assured me that she believed that it was an accident and no one's fault. It was clear that dad was the dominant family member and that this family could not talk about the death nor share feelings. Although Marnie had a good relationship with her mother, she refused to share her emotions with her. Marnie had been getting her emotional needs met through the school support group; yet in three years she had never told the group the details of the drowning.

Individual sessions that followed were non-productive. Her resistance remained high. Other than feeling secure in the school group, there was evidence that this group was also enabling her silence. After a few sessions it was clear that individual and group counselling was not effective, the family was dysfunctional, and the maladaptive patterns of communication and relating to one another had been established years before the death. For any progress to be made, interventions needed to be directed towards the family system. Although the father/husband refused to come, future sessions were attended by mother and daughter together. Both were open to understanding the concepts of family systems and how they were relevant in their family dysfunction (past and present). Sessions focused on revising patterns of communication between the two of them. Anxiety was high, as neither of them had ever shared emotions together. Sharing stories of Mark was encouraged in order to facilitate the grieving process and to help them become comfortable with their anxiety. Mother was able to tell Marnie why she had never been able to touch anything in his bedroom for three years, and Marnie was able to share her feelings of guilt and her belief that her parents wished that she had been the one who had died.

Although full resolution had not been achieved, both understood the work that still had to be done. Mother was no longer going to tolerate the dysfunction, knowing full well that her husband had always been a negative and angry person since the beginning of the marriage. By the last session she had stood up to her husband and had made a decision regarding the future of her marriage. She stated that she had lost her son through death, and that she wasn't going to lose her daughter in a different way by enabling these unhealthy patterns. Their farewell to me was sharing their matching tattoos with Mark's name inscribed in loving memory.

Symbolic interaction

Symbolic interaction was the first theoretical construct utilized by Nadeau in her research that investigated the process by which grieving families constructed meanings and the nature of those meanings. In her 1998 research she studied patterns of ten non-clinical, multigenerational families. Her thoughts guiding the research were that we know very little about the manner in which families construct meanings. Most of what we know comes from an individual's perspective. Yet individuals don't grieve in isolation. Grief is a family affair.

Symbolic interaction theory provides a way of thinking about how meaning is jointly created. It has proven useful in understanding a variety of family phenomena because it emphasizes the relationship between mental and social processes. This theory includes the assumption that humans live in a symbolic environment as well as a physical environment and that humans acquire a complex set of mental symbols (Rose, 1962). Symbolic interaction also reflects Thomas's (1923) belief that if people define situations as real, they are real in their consequences. If this is correct, one could expect to find a connection between how a family construes a particular event of loss and how they respond to it. From this perspective it is not as important to know whether an event actually occurred than whether or not people believed it had, because all interaction emerges from the meanings with which people imbue events (Rosenblatt and Fischer, 1993: 168).

Attachment theory and styles of attachment

Chapter one discussed the relationship of Bowlby's (1969) attachment theory to concepts of loss and grief. Building on this conceptual framework, Kissane and Bloch (2002) proposed that this theory can be applied to an understanding of a family and their reactions to loss. They included concepts of attachment style, originally proposed by Ainsworth (Ainsworth et al., 1978) in her description of attachments in early childhood. *Secure attachments* imply the ability of children who are comfortable to independently explore their environments as they know that their parents will return and welcome them. *Insecure attachments* suggest the opposite behaviours and expectations. *Avoidant, ambivalent,* and *disorganized* are the three patterns that can be observed. The authors first utilized these concepts as they explored family response under the threat of cancer. The notion is that a life-threatening illness activates a threat of separation and loss. Illness and death of a family member reproduce a learned pattern of relating and caring for each other. *Insecure attachments* that are a core characteristic of a grieving family are dysfunctional and do not promote effective grieving or resolution. Assessment of a family's attachment patterns provides an opportunity for counsellors to reinforce existing patterns of *secure attachments* or to educate family members regarding dysfunctional patterns of attachment and design strategies to revise them. The case example of Marnie and her mother previously discussed provides an example of insecure patterns of attachment that had existed prior to Mark's death. Their insecure ways of relating negated the ability for the individuals and the family as a unit to tolerate the anxiety related to the death long enough to experience it and process the accompanying grief. Encouraging stories of Mark promoted a safe way to commemorate his life and tolerate the emotional pain connected to the memories. Gradually these stories led to the family narrative and subsequent revision of the insecure attachments and overall dysfunction.

Constructivism

Lastly, principles from constructivism add insight and offer practical applications to family therapy. This theory has had a variety of interpretations, many of which have been controversial. One of the basic premises of this theory is that reality does not exist as a singular entity, but that there is more than one reality. This concept is a core principle of postmodern thinking. Within family therapy this philosophy has been used to facilitate a different way of assessing and conceptualizing family issues. Counsellors have become more aware of the fact that they were viewing right and wrong and good and bad based on their own values. Previously, professionals in the helping professions imposed their meanings of reality upon a client, especially upon a family. Constructivism asks these professionals 'not to consider what they are seeing in families as existing in the family but, instead, understand what they are seeing is the product of their particular set of assumptions about people, families, and problems, and their interactions with the family' (Nichols and Schwartz, 1991: 142). This theory has particular relevance for bereavement counselling. It has been our experience that the advice offered to those in grief, in large part, is based on personal experiences and belief systems. Such a frame of reference more often impedes than promotes healthy resolution. As proposed in the underlying tenets of this approach, counsellors should be collaborators in a process, and not the experts. Only the individual client or family knows the depth and meaning of their grief experience. We cannot and must not put all grievers into presupposed categories, treating them all the same, based on a presumed category of their loss. A bereaved mother will not have the same issues or experience as another bereaved mother, even if they have lost a child the same age to the same circumstances.

The theories presented provide a conceptual framework that counsellors need to take into consideration during their initial assessment. Common to all the theories is an underlying notion that loss affects individual members of a family in various ways. As asserted by Raphael (1983):

> Bereavement will affect the family system in many ways. The death of a member means the system is irrevocably changed. Interlocking roles, relationships, interactions, communications, and psychopathology and needs can no longer be fulfilled in the same way as before the death. The family unit as it was before dies, and a new family system must be constituted. The death will be a crisis for the family unit as well as for each individual member and each component subsystem. The family view of itself, the family myth, may be impossible to maintain, and all that it avoided may have to be confronted. The threat to the integrity of the family unit may come not only through the change that loss of a family member brings, but also because that member may have occupied a key role in maintaining the system, or perhaps in regulating it in crisis. (1983: 54).

Another factor to be mindful of is the fact that a family is usually not in the same stage of their grief experience at the same time, even though their grief is emerging from the same event, thus making it difficult to muster emotional resources for each other on a consistent basis. And lastly, each person in a family has had a unique relationship with the deceased, thus necessitating different issues to grieve and resolve. Family discord can arise and cause additional grief if family members fail to see each other as individuals, with idiosyncratic ways of grieving, coping, and resolving their pain.

Strategies for assessment and intervention

Based on the constructs discussed, an initial consideration for assessment is to determine present and past individual and family functioning. Effective strategies are based on a clear understanding of pre-morbid functioning. One of the first areas to evaluate is an individual's prior independence and differentiation from their family of origin in which the loss has occurred. As stated, families in grief are more vulnerable and have the tendency to become less differentiated as individuals. In order to communicate and share expressions of grief, this can be viewed as a positive move. Healthy families will revert in time back to being differentiated; however, dysfunctional families will remain in fusion.

Grief produces anxiety. Life has changed. How one functions in his or her predictable world is no longer the same. It is understandable that anxiety and a severe sense of loss of control will initially dominate the grief experience. Thus family members have the tendency to reunite and create a sense of fusion, supporting each other for the common good. In order to facilitate an eventual return to differentiation, counsellors must continue to be aware of the anxiety of each individual and the family as a unit. An ongoing therapeutic goal is to decrease anxiety and increase differentiation among the members. This is achieved by encouraging the family to talk. Simply stated, for a family in crisis, encourage them to continue to talk until their anxiety calms down. It is at this early time of loss that families who cannot talk together become avoidant and emotionally unavailable for supporting the needs of its members. It is often at this point that individuals become lonely in their grief, setting the stage for future complications.

Past the initial crisis of a loss, encouraging communication continues to be a preferred strategy. Change and resolution require talk and the willingness to listen to one another. Nadeau (1998), who proposed family meaning making strategies, suggested specific ways of communicating: *story-telling*, *dreaming*, *comparison*, *coindancing*, *characterization*, and *family speak*.

Story-telling

According to Nadeau (1998), was the most common strategy used by the research participants. Most families can easily provide a favorite story about their loved one, and these stories are usually embedded in rich meanings. Stories often have themes that involve characteristics of their loved one, the type of life they lived, and often the care and type of death that the family provided for their loved one. There is comfort in these narratives and the memories promote healing.

> Joe's dad was on a respirator in intensive care. The night following surgery he suffered a heart attack, but remained alive because of the machine. He could not talk, his eyes remained closed, but he would hold and squeeze family members' hands in his attempts to communicate. The family was told that it would only be a matter of time until he died. However, until his blood gases improved he could not be removed from the respirator. The family did not know what to do, but did not want him to be left alone. At this point they made a commitment that someone would always be there to hold his hand and to talk to him. Ten days went by before he could be removed from the respirator, and he was never alone. Members shared their favorite stories, and often he would squeeze a hand responding to a joke or a treasured memory. The stories represented how he lived and who he was. Stories after his death focused on the 'good' death that they had provided for him. Healing was enhanced knowing that he wasn't alone and that somehow they eased his transition from life to death. Years later the stories continue to commemorate his character and the family maintains comfort in the meaning that they were able to provide during his final days.

Dreaming

Another strategy that can be utilized to make sense of a death are dreams, especially those which include meaningful interactions with loved ones. Moreover, dreams in which their loved ones appear healthy and no longer ill are especially comforting and provide a sense of hope for an eternal reunion. The counsellor's role in these situations is to encourage the full narrative of the dream experience and to provide appropriate feedback. It is not wise to offer an interpretation at this point. The goal is to understand the meaning that the bereaved derives from the dream and to facilitate an experience that promotes integration and healing.

Comparison

Is the third communication strategy suggested. Most individuals and families have a need to compare their loss with others' losses (death and non-death) inside and outside the family. They attempt to make sense of their loss in terms of its intensity and whether or not it can be resolved based on their perceptions of their prior losses, others' losses, and past abilities to cope. Karen, who had lost her only child (Chapter 2), continued to use this strategy for several sessions. She compared this death to the death of her parents when she was 19, to her son's 10-year incarceration, to a co-worker who had also lost a child many years ago. Her comparisons seemed to be an attempt to see where she fitted on the continuum of loss and if she could survive her own grief. Her conclusion was that she could survive, but that no loss in her past or the losses of others could compare to the death of her only child. In this example, *comparison* allowed her to conclude that she would survive his death; however, it was now important to promote a more productive strategy.

'Coincidancing'

Was a term given by Nadeau (1998) to describe the tendency that families have to connect coincidental events associated with their loved one's death in order to make sense of the death event. The *dancing* component refers to the fact that in families this strategy is interactive.

> Marge died in her sleep and was found the next day by her adult daughter, Sue. While waiting for the coroner to arrive, Sue began washing the dishes left in the kitchen sink. After turning the faucet on, black dirt gushed out, an indication that the well had run dry. Sue was certain that this event was symbolically linked to the death of her mother. For days later family members marveled at the significance of this and offered individual interpretations. Each individual's perception of the two coincidental events contributed to the total family's need to make meaning of Marge's unexpected death. Meaning making as a family also encouraged expression of a full range of emotions, paving the way for a healthy grief process.

Families often perceive deaths and births as meaningful coincidences.

> Pat's daughter, Linda, died on the cancer floor in a local hospital, following a lengthy cancer battle. At the same time, a close friend (three floors below) was giving birth to her first child. The baby was named Linda, and Pat was honored to be named the godmother. Pat perceived this as a divine coincidence and the event provided a meaning for her that cushioned her grief. Pat, her husband, and son felt that Linda's spirit would live on in this child.

Counsellors need to listen to the expression of these coincidences and ways in which families, individually and together, have made meanings that promote expression and healing. Families provide rich, meaningful material that encourages collaborative counselling experiences. It is important to keep in mind the importance of listening to each individual's story and not imposing professional opinions as the only criteria for interventions.

Characterization

As a strategy this overlaps with *story-telling*. Talking about the character of the deceased and the value of the life that had been lived gives a special meaningfulness to the importance of that life. Often families have to first make sense of a life that has had meaning and purpose before they can begin to make sense of the death. This strategy also encourages expression of the 'not so good' qualities of their loved one. The good and the negative must be expressed for healthy meaning and resolution.

Family speak

Basically describes the ordinary manner in which family members speak to one another in order to make sense of the death. It includes all forms of family communication: agreeing and disagreeing with each other, interpreting each others' thoughts, elaborating, and finishing each others' sentences. Encouraging all forms of family speak increases the family's tolerance of its members' expression of feelings. Counsellors must first observe family conversations in order to understand the essence of their meanings as members attempt to make sense of the loss. At times they must be prepared to join with the family to direct the talk so that meaning can be made that promotes healthy processing. Adaptive and securely attached families need little direction, whereas more dysfunctional families will require education regarding the strategy and direction to keep the discussion moving towards the goal of meaning making and healthy expressions of grief. The benefit of this strategy is that the family, by agreeing, disagreeing, elaborating, etc., arrives at meanings that could not be made by any one member.

Counsellors are encouraged to familiarize themselves with additional strategies utilized by family therapists that can be adapted to situations of loss and grief. It is beyond the scope of this book to discuss all of these additional strategies. However, the following suggests some interventions that are especially relevant to grief counselling. Bowen (1974), who proposed that multigenerational issues could impose a grief that extended beyond the immediate nuclear family, encouraged an extended family history assessment of at least two generations. In addition to specific questions to gain insight into past family losses and the emotional integration of the family, the use of the geneogram is a valuable tool for both the counsellor and the family. Bowen believed that the present problem needed to be placed in the context of the multigenerational system. A geneogram helps the counsellor trace the patterns of family issues. Using the geneogram, it is necessary to pay attention to process and structure. Process refers to the patterns of emotional reactivity and structure refers to patterns of interlocking triangles. Bowen's notions of differentiation, fusion, and the forces involved and Minuchin's concepts of structure, subsystems, and boundaries provide a framework to ask relevant questions and co-construct a geneogram.

The counsellor presents the individual and/or family with a basic geneogram (Figure 4.1) and creates symbolic and visual patterns that illustrate process and structure by asking questions about relationships with members in the nuclear and extended families. This visual diagram of the family over two or more generations combines the usual demographic information, key events, and important relationship structures and patterns both past and present. As the counsellor gathers information, he or she gains insight into the family's cultural development, traditions and beliefs and constructs a visual blueprint that provides a rationale

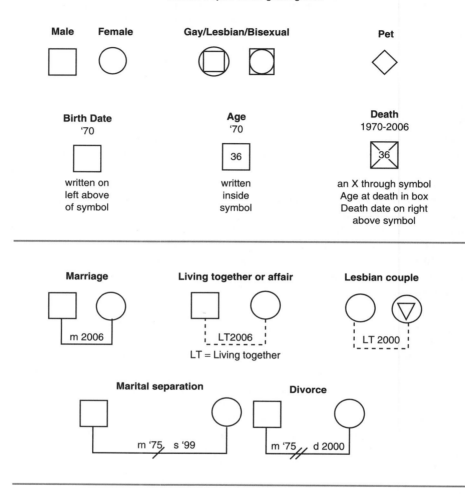

Standard symbols for geneograms

Male   **Female**

Gay/Lesbian/Bisexual

Pet

Birth Date
'70

written on
left above
of symbol

Age
'70

written
inside
symbol

Death
1970-2006

an X through symbol
Age at death in box
Death date on right
above symbol

Marriage

m 2006

Living together or affair

LT2006

LT = Living together

Lesbian couple

LT 2000

Marital separation

m '75   s '99

Divorce

m '75   d 2000

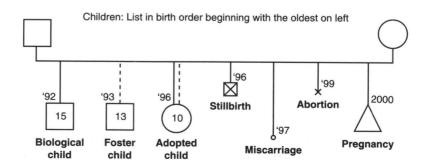

Children: List in birth order beginning with the oldest on left

'92
15
Biological child

'93
13
Foster child

'96
10
Adopted child

'96
Stillbirth

'97
Miscarriage

'99
Abortion

2000
Pregnancy

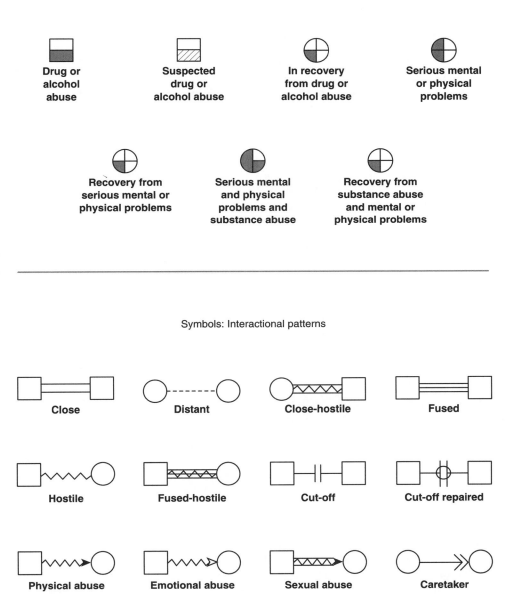

Symbols: Addiction and physical or mental illness

Drug or
alcohol
abuse

Suspected
drug or
alcohol abuse

In recovery
from drug or
alcohol abuse

Serious mental
or physical
problems

Recovery from
serious mental or
physical problems

Serious mental
and physical
problems and
substance abuse

Recovery from
substance abuse
and mental or
physical problems

Symbols: Interactional patterns

Close

Distant

Close-hostile

Fused

Hostile

Fused-hostile

Cut-off

Cut-off repaired

Physical abuse

Emotional abuse

Sexual abuse

Caretaker

Figure 4.1   Basic geneogram (adapted from Multicultural Family Institute, 2006)

for change in the family system. In addition to assessment and education, the geneogram is an effective strategy that encourages family members to lower tensions, neutralize destructive conflicts, and externalize issues that can be mutually resolved (Guerin and Pendagast, 1976).

Using geneograms with Sam and Gina

Sam was a 36-year-old male who had been diagnosed and treated for a malignant brain tumor 18 months prior to counselling. He had been married to Gina for 14 years and had two children, a son age 12 and a daughter age 9. He was the youngest of three children. His parents divorced when he was five and the children remained with their mother. His brother had left town five years ago and nobody had known his whereabouts until Sam's surgery, when he called to express his concern. Since then there were some attempts (telephone calls) to renew a relationship. His sister lived in another state and they visited each other once a year. His parents lived nearby, but offered little support during his surgeries and treatment. Sam did not appear to have any resentments towards his parents, despite their emotional distance. He viewed his relationship with them as normal and satisfactory. He was curious about his older brother's disappearance for five years, but had little emotions about the situation.

Sam had been a truck driver for a local company for 16 years. Despite the fact that he was now in remission, he had a terminal prognosis of three to five years. Prior to the cancer diagnosis he had experienced seizures, which immediately terminated his driving career. During the next ten months he had two surgeries and four months of radiation and chemotherapy. The physical and psychological effects of the cancer and the treatment resulted in a pervasive sense of loss of personal control that showed little improvement despite psychiatric medication. Counselling was recommended with the hope that issues of ongoing losses and his mortality could be addressed. Most of his sense of self-worth had been based on his ability to work and provide for the family. He had built an expensive new home six months before his illness, and now it was a financial concern. His wife, Gina, did not work and the need for her to get some form of education or training to prepare for an uncertain future was another major issue. Sam would be able to go on permanent medical disability in six months, but his wife and children would not be eligible.

Gina had several individual sessions before relationship counselling was initiated. She had a number of personal issues and a dysfunctional family of origin. She never had any self-worth. Her parents divorced when she was 12-years-old. Her older brother chose to live with their father, and Gina became the caregiver for her alcoholic mother. She lacked friends and activities as her mother's needs were all-consuming. She married right after high school to get away from her mother. After her marriage she developed a relationship with her father, whom she had not seen since her parents' divorce. This relationship ended five years later when her father died unexpectedly following a heart attack. She inherited her father's home and lived there with Sam and her two children until they moved two and a half years ago. This move was difficult for her as she did not want to move to a 'higher-class' neighborhood; moreover, her father's home was all she had left of him. Sam never understood this attachment and it was a major conflict well before his diagnosis.

During the past year her relationship with her brother had become estranged due to some unresolved conflicts, and the enmeshed relationship with her mother intensified as she was torn between Sam's needs and her mother's demands.

(Continued)

In addition to the parents' issues, the children were also showing evidence of the stress. Both children had an understanding of their father's illness; however, neither child knew about the prognosis. Their son, age 12, coped with the family's stress by internalizing his emotions and distancing himself from the family. He was always seeking activities outside the family setting and never asked any questions. The daughter, age 9, who had previously showed some learning problems, developed further problems in school, had nightmares, and slept on the floor in her parents' bedroom. Gina realized that she feared that her dad might die, but the topic was never addressed. Both children had always manipulated Gina and overwhelmed her. Sam was never an involved parent and ignored Gina's current demands for his help.

The issues presented by Sam and Gina needed to be addressed on individual and marital levels. Finally, the family as a system needed further evaluation and reorganization in order to meet the present challenges and prepare for future change and losses.

Individually, Sam needed to address his emotions regarding his illness. He was angry that he was so young, had taken care of himself, and yet was the victim. He also needed to address his debilitating symptoms of depression that impaired his relationships, daily functioning, and willingness to engage in any activity outside the home. Lastly, he had to address losses that had already occurred and anticipate future losses. Validating his multiple losses and emotions (especially anger) was the immediate goal. His lack of relationship skills and involvement in his nuclear family was consistently addressed throughout the sessions. Work, which had been his identity, was the third important focus, along with finding meaningful activities to alleviate his symptoms of depression.

Individual sessions addressed Gina's issues of low self-worth, her dysfunctional relationship with her mother, and concerns for personal and family changes in the future.

Relationship counselling began a month after the individual needs were identified. Education regarding multigenerational issues and present system and structural patterns provided the foundation for future interventions.

Structure, roles, and responsibilities had been mutually agreed upon after their son was born. Gina had worked part-time as a waitress and willingly gave it up to be a full-time mother and provide a family life for the children that neither one of them had had growing up.

The demands of child-rearing removed her from activities outside the home, which in hindsight was a negative influence on her pre-existing low self-worth. Currently, the thought of returning to work and being the primary provider challenged her insecurities and lack of confidence. Sam felt that he had always dealt with her insecurities; however, at this point he could barely deal with his own issues and threats of mortality. Gina's perspective was that Sam had never been able to communicate with her and had never been affectionate. She willingly had been his only caregiver for the last two years, and he never showed any appreciation. Instead, she felt that he continued to use her as an outlet for his frustrations. At this time she questioned if he had any love for her. She verbalized her needs for affection and communication. His only response was that it wasn't his style and that it made him feel awkward. She verbalized in session that if she was the patient with a terminal prognosis, she would be doing everything she could to give and receive love from her family. Despite her forthright communication, Sam remained emotionally distant. This was not unusual in their relationship; however, given the circumstances, she felt that she couldn't tolerate his aloofness along with everything else.

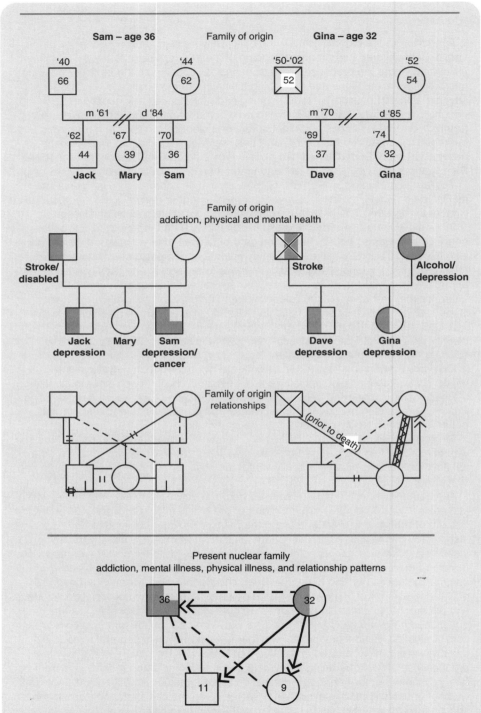

Figure 4.2   Geneogram : Sam and Gina

(Continued)

The present situation required Sam and Gina to understand their individual issues within their dysfunctional system and be willing to redefine their marriage and family life. Multigenerational patterns of roles, rules, and communication needed to be altered in order to find new meanings in their lives that would never be the same again.

Additional strategies

Additional interventions for families can be adapted from individual and group assessment and counselling strategies discussed in Chapters 2, 3, and 5. Noteworthy among them is the use of rituals. Rituals are behaviours designed by the bereaved that encourage expression of difficult emotions and promote opportunities of transition during the grieving process. Families need to grieve the death of the family system as it was formerly known as well as the loss of the individual before they can reconstruct a new family identity. Writing a family letter to their loved one, sharing memories, commemorating, and passing down treasured objects are all therapeutic and effective in promoting family healing and reconstruction.

The year after the suicide of their middle son, Arnie, the Harris family decided that their son's life needed to be commemorated on the first anniversary in a way that validated the essence of his character and the life that did have meaning and meanings. In order to validate other parts of his life and to encourage a healthy reconstruction of the family narrative, Jim and Alice (his parents) designed a ritual that encouraged the family to remember his entire life and not focus on the final year.

As the first anniversary approached, the adult siblings and extended family members were invited to share a meal and memories that validated the positive aspects of Arnie's life. Each person was asked to bring a favorite food of Arnie's and a favorite memory to share with the group. The ritual provided the opportunity for both individual and family expression of unexpressed difficult emotions. Moreover, it promoted the necessary transition towards eventual resolution and healing.

Lastly, counsellors are reminded that an important component of their services is education. Individuals and families often do not understand their grief as it relates to themselves or to their families as a whole. Knowledge is power. Information from a professional often validates their experience as *normal*, which then has the benefit of reducing their anxiety in order to tolerate their pain and travel together through the bereavement process.

Offering information based on family systems theory, additional family concepts discussed, and the process of grief provides a necessary foundation for the bereaved to make sense of their experience of loss, have a healthy expression of their pain, and the potential to regain a sense of control in their lives.

Grief Issues for Individual Family Members

Family members do not grieve the same, and often do not have the same issues. Each person in a family had his or her own unique relationship with a deceased member, thus necessitating an idiosyncratic grief experience. The following offers some guidelines for pertinent issues of various family members, following a death in the family.

Death of a spouse

The death of a spouse includes the loss of many roles. The spouse was not only a husband or a wife, in the broadest sense; he or she was friend, confidant, lover, provider, supporter, and sometimes 'the better half'. Often a spouse is the primary person who confirms one's sense of identity and self-worth. Adjusting an identity from a 'we' to an 'I' is one of the poignant issues to contend with. Very often, one's social world also ends with the death of a spouse. The loneliness that will be experienced will be physical, sexual, social, and emotional. This type of death affects the family in various ways, with different issues. One of the primary factors for consideration is the age of the children and all the related issues and concerns that are associated with this factor.

Death of a parent

As an adult, when one's parent dies, the experience is often a lonely and unrecognized loss. Many do not live where their parents live; thus, most of the friends who would attend the funeral or be available for support have little to offer because of their lack of association with the deceased parent. Moreover, this death is often not socially sanctioned because we are told that we should expect our parents to die before us. Parents have one of the most unique roles in our lives. They are the first relationship and are our ties back to our pasts and our childhoods. As long as parents are alive, it is possible to deny one's own mortality, as they are a buffer between oneself and death. When it is the death of a second parent, the individual experiences what it is like to be an orphan.

Various other issues emerge depending upon one's age at the time of a parent's death. An example is a 20-year-old male whose father died of a heart attack at age 56. The grief reactions and fears of one's own mortality may become more acute when that son approaches his 56th birthday (anniversary reaction). When a parent dies during one's childhood or adolescence, one should keep in mind for these age groups that the loss of a parent must be understood according to the developmental level of the child or adolescent, and that these normal developmental tasks must be addressed. Moreover, this age group relies upon denial, repression, and suppression. Grief may not be fully addressed or resolved until early adulthood. Children and adolescents must grieve fully; however, they must be allowed to do so on their timetables, and with ongoing, available support systems. With each stage of development, new questions and new issues will emerge that need to be re-examined and answered in light of more cognitive and emotional growth.

Death of a sibling

At any age, the death of a sibling has its own and unique issues. A sibling is an individual that shares similar, genetic characteristics with you. This is an individual (in addition to one's parents) in whom one can often see a reflection of oneself. This is a person with whom one has shared a unique co-history, often marked by ambivalence and more difficult issues to grieve.

When a sibling dies, the surviving sibling(s) experience a variety of thoughts and feelings. Often the survivor feels that the 'favorite' child has died, and that it is important to take on characteristics or behaviours of the deceased to lessen the grief of the parents. Role reversals (children assuming parental roles) occur also in attempts to alleviate parental pain. Guilt is a frequent emotion, as many siblings have harbored ill will towards each other over the years, and the reality of the death is difficult to adjust to. Many siblings have lost a close and trusted companion, and the grief will emerge during many milestones of their childhood and adult life. Davies (1990), in a seven-year longitudinal study of siblings who had died from cancer, found that siblings frequently thought of the deceased and grieved. Life had moved on; however, thoughts and feelings were close at hand.

For many adults whose siblings die, the current support systems may be unaware of the special bond that may have continued for years. In mobile societies people may not live where they were born; thus, present friends and potential support systems may not know what to say or do. This often increases a sense of aloneness in one's grief, as it is often difficult to feel connected to those around who were not part of this relationship.

Death of a child

No other loss has as many issues, and there is no other role that is governed by more rules or social sanctions. It is referred to as the one area in family life where society will step in and take over if the responsible adults do not perform according to certain dictates. Thus, when a child dies, the parents experience incredible guilt for a role in which they have not succeeded. There are differences in the ways males and females grieve, and when this is not understood, it may cause discord in the marital dyad. There may be problems parenting other children, and frequently one of the spouses closely resembles the deceased child, causing additional pain. This type of grief cannot be compared to any other type of loss, and counsellors should avoid trying to fit this grief into a current model for grief resolution.

A common question following the death of a child is the concern over potential, future divorce. Many believe that statistics are high for divorce following the death of a child, yet others do not see the correlations between death and divorce. Rando (1993b) believes that statistics have inaccurately represented the reasons for a divorce following the death of a child. Her view is that the divorces that do occur represent marriages that had been previously troubled, and following the death of a child, one of the partners will make the decision that he or she is not going to put up with any extra grief. That is, they express that they had endured a difficult marriage before the death, but now they only have the energy to deal with the death that is at hand. From a systems viewpoint, the triangular third party that allowed the marriage to continue is no longer available.

Death of a partner in a gay/lesbian relationship

The loss of a partner in a gay/lesbian relationship may be significantly different than a death in heterosexual relationships. Often the relationship has not been accepted by society or the extended families. As a result, rituals for funerals and ongoing bereavement services are not legitimized. Disenfranchised grief is often inherent in these deaths, making them lonely losses that are more difficult to resolve. Even before the death, especially if there has been a lengthy illness, there often is a lack of supportive resources available to these couples/families. Considering these and other possible issues, counsellors should initially evaluate current systems of support and be prepared to understand the variety of issues that these couples must contend with.

The following case presents Les, his partner, and his family of origin. It is an example of initial rejection, estrangement, and eventual reconciliation during his final stages of illness and death.

Les was a 39-year-old male who had lived with his partner, Jeff, in a committed relationship for over 10 years. It was an open relationship that had not been readily accepted by his family and siblings. As a result, their relationship with Les was estranged for many years. With Les and Jeff living 500 miles away, it was easy for the family to remove themselves from the realities of their son's/brother's life. No one in their town knew about his homosexuality, let alone the relationship that he had with Jeff. Because there had been little contact with Les, the family had been unaware of his diagnosis of AIDS. It was only when his condition worsened that Jeff encouraged Les to tell his family about his prognosis. Jeff felt that he and his family had important issues to discuss before it was too late. He was well aware of the anger that the family, especially his father, had with Les's lifestyle. Giving into Jeff's viewpoint, Les called and reinitiated contact with his family.

His family responded, and during the two remaining years they visited frequently. At first there was hesitancy to honestly discuss issues and emotions that had been repressed by all members of this family over time. Les felt that he had always been different, even as a child, and that his differences had never been acceptable in his own family. He felt shunned by his siblings, yet they believed that he was not interested in their lives. His parents' perception was that he felt superior to them and chose to remove himself from family gatherings. His father finally admitted his anger and shame upon learning that his son was in a relationship with a male former teacher. The family had never discussed their reactions to Les's relationship. His lifestyle became the dark family secret, repressed with unhealthy emotions of anger, disgust, and shame. His parents also bore the burden of guilt, believing that somehow they were responsible for their son's homosexuality. Les was surprised by their emotions, realizing that he had been so absorbed in his own feelings of anger and resentment that he never considered that his family might have their own difficult emotions. He was also surprised that his parents had never read or tried to understand his homosexuality. Even now his entire family was uninformed. Over the next several months, Les talked about himself and how he tried so hard to deny what he felt growing up. He hated being different, but by high school he knew he couldn't be like his siblings. He knew his family would never accept him, and he had grieved that a long time ago. However, his grief had turned into buried, festering resentments.

(Continued)

Over time, it was easier to disengage from them entirely. Now Les and his family were finally free to experience all of their feelings together.

During the two years that he had remaining they all tried to 'make up for lost time'. They came to know, respect, and care for Jeff. Les and his father were able to communicate on meaningful levels and their relationship grew. During the final stages Jeff remained committed, caring for Les until his death. At the funeral Jeff was invited to sit with the family and at the family's request delivered the eulogy.

Death of a grandparent (when grandparent has been primary parent/caregiver)

For various reasons and circumstances, grandparents have assumed parenting roles for their grandchildren. Often an adult child returns home after a relationship ends, works outside the home, and depends on a parent/grandparent to take on a caregiver role. Other times a biological parent might be declared emotionally or physically unable to care for their own children and the grandparents are given legal custody. Reconstructed families that put grandparents into parental roles have the potential to provide consistent nurturing environments and secure attachments that are crucial for a child's development. However, based on the age and well-being of the grandparents, these situations may present a threat of an additional loss. For youth who are still dependent on adults, losing a grandparent during this time creates additional developmental complications and risks. Thus, assessment and treatment strategies for these individuals must consider normal developmental tasks, family structure and patterns, and potential grief issues that may emerge throughout childhood and adolescence.

In the consideration of the issues inherent in the loss of a grandparent who has virtually been the parent, it is also important to understand the unique issues of an adult who experiences the death of a grandparent. It is not unusual to have adults seek counselling following this loss. Cognitively they are aware that this was their true parent figure. However, emotionally they do not understand the internalized experience of this relationship and what needs to be grieved. These bereaved have appreciated the roles assumed by their grandparents, but they may have never understood or processed the earlier childhood loss of the biological parent who did not raise them. The adult, who is now grieving the grandparent, may also need to grieve (for the first time) the death or non-death loss of the biological parent.

Family losses other than death

Death is not the only loss that most families have to cope with during their life cycle. Moreover, death is often not the most difficult or deleterious loss. Illness, desertion, divorce, adoption, foster homes, abuse, job loss, and disasters, such as fires and floods, are only a few to mention. Although general concepts and theories from loss may be used, along with tools such as the perspectives, the history of loss, and psychological needs assessment, these losses will have specific issues to address, cope with, and resolve. It is beyond the scope of this book to thoroughly discuss every type of loss; however, the fact remains that families continue to live with a variety of non-death losses that often present more challenges than death, and these losses often are catalysts for complications in resolution and issues of victimization.

The following case discusses a 13-year-old boy who had been removed from the home of his alcoholic mother at the age of 7, had lived in four foster homes over 6 years, and was currently being considered for adoption by his present foster family.

The Case of Pete

Pete was a 13-year-old boy who had been mandated for counselling by the county's children protective services and juvenile court. He had had four foster home placements over the last six years, failed three grades, had been diagnosed with ADHD, and had severe anger problems. The initial assessment (plus past records) indicated multiple issues of loss over his entire lifetime. He was the oldest of three children and had taken on the role of protector for his alcoholic mother and two sisters when he was 7. In addition to mom's alcohol abuse, she had had multiple abusive relationships. Pete prided himself on beating up one of mom's boyfriends with a wooden board when he was 11. The pattern over time showed that mom had multiple attempts to reclaim her children, but was not capable of any consistent stability. Pete's foster home placements were never successful. He always found a way to sabotage himself and develop a negative relationship with any adult or system that offered support. His present foster home was in a neighboring county. These foster parents seemed different to him. They had taken an active interest in his welfare, especially his education. Over time he dropped his defenses, allowed himself to like this family, and began to trust them. When the family discussed adoption, Pete realized that his future could have potential if he stayed with them. Adoption plans proceeded until Pete learned that his mother had to sign over her parental rights to this couple. Pete continued to love his mother despite her substance abuse, and this became a major issue for the next several months. Although Pete had sustained numerous losses over his life, this current situation was more than he could tolerate. He couldn't face his mother and had stopped his visits with her. He was torn between wanting to have a better future, yet not hurting her. Counselling addressed this conflict and the inherent issues of loss with either choice. Education in the sessions that followed focused on concepts of continuing bonds (Silverman and Klass, 1996) and the ability he had to continue to love his mother, maintain an inner reality of her, and yet make present choices that would better his future. His situation was a legal matter. He should not be put in the emotional predicament of choosing his adoptive mother over his biological one. The goal was to help Pete understand that he did not have to give up his love for his mother, nor did it mean that he would not have a future relationship with her as an adult.

Pete followed through with the adoption plans. As he told his story to the magistrate, he openly wept. Finally he grieved, and the years of buried hurt surfaced and found healthier outlets. Now was it possible to emotionally and behaviourally reconstruct his life with a sense of hope and purpose for his future.

Every individual in counselling represents, and has been influenced by, at least one family. Losses within a family unit (past or present family systems) mean that a family, as it had once existed and had been known, is now dead. Although counsellors mostly see individuals in counselling, it is important to consider the concepts and examples presented in this chapter for a more in-depth assessment and understanding of underlying issues as they pertain to individuals as members of some type of family.

5 Group Counselling

Group counselling offers an excellent choice for therapeutic intervention. It is not the intention to recommend groups over individual counselling; rather, the intention is to highlight some of the contributions of group counselling in general, to discuss specific features of grief groups, and to outline various components of the sessions of structured groups that can facilitate the process of grief counselling.

Therapeutic Factors in Groups

A group is a representation of the family and community to which individuals belong. Issues that emerge in a group often have origins in past and present family and community relationships. Often the dynamics of interpersonal relationships are not on a conscious level of awareness. For many, the group experience will offer the initial experience of personal insight into their relationships with others. Within the format of the group, a process occurs that is not possible in individual counselling. There are more people to relate to in a group and common issues of the human condition emerge that facilitate exploration of personal issues. Yalom proposed 11 primary factors that he viewed as being the basis of the therapeutic experience of group work: instillation of hope, universality, imparting of information, altruism, the corrective recapitulation of a family group, development of socializing techniques, imitative behaviour, interpersonal learning, group cohesiveness, catharsis, and existential factors (1995: 1).

Individuals attending a grief group have the opportunity to experience many of the above-mentioned influences. Instillation of hope occurs as members observe positive changes in each other and anticipate forward movement in their own process of bereavement. As they take risks to fully experience the pain of grief, they come to understand that the pain will not further destroy them; rather, the pain becomes a healing element. The universality of some of the common aspects of grief promotes a bonding and a sense that one is not alone in grief. However, although grief is the common denominator, initially individual differences will need attention. Members may not be experiencing the same type of death, nor the same issues. Even within a family, no two family members will have the same grief experience. The relationship each person has had with the deceased has been different, and the various perspectives discussed in Chapters 1, 2, and 3 will influence each person's grief process in a different manner. In the early, acute period of grief an individual will not feel connected to others. They believe that their grief is more painful than anyone else's, and they do not want to be compared to another's grief experience. From a philosophical perspective, one must face this aloneness, meaninglessness, and despair in isolation before one can connect with others in the universal aspects of grief. There seems to be a sense of readiness to connect with others and be part of a group six to eight weeks following a death. Before this time there are pervasive feelings of unreality, numbness, and a general desire to turn inward in one's grief. To experience a universality that promotes cohesion and a sense of belonging takes time and willingness on the part of members to risk joining with others. Many express reluctance at self-disclosure because they have believed that others would not view their issues as valid or important. Many individuals remain lonely in their grief because they believe their needs to be petty or selfish.

Early on members need to know if their individual needs will be met in a group where they view themselves as being different from others, even though they are there for similar reasons. From the first session the group is structured to foster an atmosphere and environment that assures members that their needs will be met. The promotion of universality and cohesiveness in the sessions builds hope. Those in grief together begin to rely on each other; they can begin to hope for diminished pain and new futures. They begin to learn from each other and realize that mourning will not be forever.

Members know from the first session who will be in the group. This facilitates the process of building trust and cohesiveness. As this process occurs, members begin to support each other and experience further healing from their efforts of altruism. They begin to understand that their grief is lessened by helping others in similar circumstances.

As mentioned above, members want to know if their needs will be met in this group. All have come from some type of family group, with positive and negative experiences. Many have been told by family members that they should 'get on' with their lives, or that their grief is a sign of weakness. The support group has the potential to be a corrective recapitulation of a family. Members will find someone in the group who reminds them of a family member. Thus an event that occurred many years ago within someone's family can still be experienced, cognitively and emotionally, in present time. Through the power of the experience of the group, members can address past experiences, rethink and cognitively correct them, and understand their influence on the present experiences. Connections will be made, and members may see that they are reacting to a present situation that has components which represent something in the past. Opportunities are present to practice new behaviours that can be used in real-life settings. Generally speaking, a group has the potential to become a therapeutic community, offering opportunities for support, self-exploration, insight, behaviour change, and the development of new socializing techniques. Bereaved members often express the fact that they no longer hear from old friends, or that they feel that people are avoiding them because of their grief. Within a group setting, members accept and support each other in their grief, and move together to develop new skills for socialization. One support group had four widowers, who had been totally dependent upon their wives to provide their social life. After the third session, one of the men suggested that they all meet for dinner each week before the group. He said that he had never done anything like this before, but if women could have their hen parties, men could have their rooster parties.

Groups set the stage for imitative behaviour. Members will observe how others try to cope with their grief and imitate each other's efforts. This is especially true when one comes in and reports that the pain of grief did not defeat him/her this week, and that a way had been found to cope with it. In the course of a several-session group, most members will adopt aspects of each others' ways of behaving. This illustrates interpersonal learning; that is, the group learns from each other, not just from the counsellor. Those in pain are often the best teachers for each other, as they have acutely known the experience of grief. Basic information for surviving and coping is shared on a weekly basis. This type of interpersonal learning cannot take place in individual counselling.

Group cohesiveness is one of the most therapeutic factors in a bereavement support group. Members whose worlds have been made less rich after the death of a loved one need cohesion or a sense of belonging. They all enter a group feeling shattered and bereft. The trappings of pretense and the wearing of masks are usually not part of a group experiencing deep grief. The outer layers of human defenses are cut through quicker and a sense of cohesiveness and trust is more readily built. Activities, such as sharing pictures and stories about the deceased person, promote the goals of cohesiveness. Catharsis in a group that fosters a healthy expression of emotions is an integral factor, and one that needs little facilitation. Counsellors may have to state up front that sharing tears together is encouraged, and that it is a way to build inter- and intrapersonal strength.

Lastly, consideration is given to Yalom's existential factors brought to the surface by grief. As discussed in Chapter 1, existential anxieties are part of the philosophical perspective in the loss experience. Sharing common feelings of a deep sense of aloneness and questioning the meaning of life set the stage for feelings of cohesiveness, and direct the process towards integration of the experience of loss and eventual rebuilding and resolution.

To illustrate the emotional connection among group members, the following letter reveals the personal experience of one member:

My Dear Friends,

Tonight is our last session together as a group but I hope it's not our last time together as friends. When I first came here, and for about the first four weeks, I thought I couldn't possibly continue the grief sessions, but for some unknown reason to me, I continued to come back, and now I am very sorry to see it end.

You have all reached out to me and touched my life, and through our mutual grief, we have come to know one another, and to care for one another. You have tried to help me understand the whys and have tried to show me reasons why I must go on and somehow, someday, perhaps be able to build a new and meaningful life for myself.

I will never forget your kindness and your love, our coffee breaks after the meetings, and your allowing me to share my dear and precious son with all of you. I know that if I never see some of you again on this earth, there will come a time when we shall be together with our loved ones and with each other on the other side of the mountain.

(43-year-old bereaved mother)

Following is an illustration of a semi-structured adult support group which capitalizes on Yalom's (1995) therapeutic factors.

Adult 10-week Support Group*

The adult 10-week group is semi-structured. Each session has a theme related to grief, the process, and potential resolution; however, individual needs are addressed as they emerge, and the facilitator must be flexible enough and trust the group process to put the agenda aside as needed. The group has closed membership (8 to 12), with specific goals and objectives for each session. Although a grief group is mainly supportive, it also has the goal of education, or imparting information as described by Yalom. The educational portion of the group sessions is an essential component of intervention as there is often a lack of accurate information about the grief process. Information shared not only validates and normalizes the grief experience, it also educates regarding healthy ways of expression and resolution.

Selection and screening
This group is intended for those individuals who are experiencing grief following the death of a significant person in their lives. The group is not intended for those who have additional and perhaps more intense issues other than grief. Examples would be intense anger, guilt, or prior issues that may need individual counselling. Moreover, those who are involved in legal or business matters following the death of a loved one may be too preoccupied to focus on the work involved in the grief process in general and the group work in particular. Lastly, it is advisable to suggest waiting one to two months before joining a group. There is either an initial period of numbness or unreality or there is intense, acute grief requiring individual attention that lasts for this period after a death.

The selection and screening process necessitates a pre-group intake session. Following the guidelines in Chapter 2, this session assesses the needs and the functioning of the bereaved and discusses the goals, objectives, and methods used in the support group.

Goals
The goals for this group are to provide an environment that allows and promotes a healthy expression of grief, to increase an awareness and understanding of the broader issues of loss and grief, to educate regarding the process and resolution of grief, to identify effective coping strategies, to facilitate a sense of personal control and decision-making, and to introduce the concepts of memorialization and reinvestment in life.

Session 1: Getting Acquainted and Goal Setting

Open this first session with introductory statements of welcome and acknowledgment of the strength that it takes to become part of a group that takes the

---

*Although this group is for death-related loss, it can be redesigned to address any loss. For example, this format has also been used for divorce and work-related losses. The sessions can use the same themes, but address the specific issues of the loss involved.

risk to explore their grief and share it with others who are strangers. State that care will be given to understand and address each member's particular grief and their ability to cope with it at the present time. Point out that there is no one right way to grieve and that members should not compare themselves with each other or believe that someone else is doing better in their grief work. Encourage members with words that express hope for emotional improvement. Comments such as: 'Tonight everyone is quiet and somewhat fearful. In two to three weeks, there will be talking and laughter among you. As a matter of fact, it will become difficult for me to get your attention. I know that you might find this difficult to believe now, but this will happen.' The letter shared by a member in the beginning of this chapter can be read at this point for additional encouragement.

Objectives

1. To make preliminary introductions and to discuss group rules, expectations, and the content of each session.
2. To provide an opportunity for members to become acquainted and to learn about the loss (death) of each member.
3. To initiate feelings of universality in the experience of grief.

Interventions

1. Members are asked to introduce themselves and to tell the group something about themselves that is not related to their loss. For example, suggest they tell about their work, areas of interest, or other family members.
2. Group rules, procedures, and expectations (Table 5.1 below) are discussed. Members are encouraged to express concerns about the procedure, and to clarify their expectations of what will be accomplished within the ten weeks.
3. Members are matched in dyads based on information obtained during the pre-group intake. Attempts are made to match on perceived similarities of issues related to the loss, age, sex, or personalities. Each person interviews the other, discussing specifics of the loss, feelings then and now, and other areas of difficulty. About 20 to 30 minutes are allowed for this exchange. In the large group, members introduce their partners and the loss that they have experienced. This activity sets the tone for a non-threatening environment, recognizing the pain of grief and the possible difficulty involved in telling a group of strangers about the death. Moreover, it provides an initial opportunity to meet someone who is similar and begins the process of universality and cohesiveness.

Homework

Tell members that each week an assignment will be given. They are not forced to do this homework; however, advise them that the more effort they put into these ten weeks and their willingness to take risks, the more they will get from the experience. Explain that the homework is designed to promote thought and reflection on the session just experienced, and also to prepare them for the topic of the next week's session. Explain that grief work is painful and difficult. It is normal upon leaving a session to experience a surge of pain. This will diminish over time, and

Table 5.1   Group procedures and expectations (example of handout given to group members) from Adult 10-week support group

Confidentiality is expected.

Members are encouraged to participate but are not pressured to do so; they may pass.

Co-facilitators are available between meetings.

Homework assignments are given weekly, but are not required to be shared.

The group is supportive in nature, not confrontational.

Others' grief should be left at the meeting, not taken home; each person has enough of his/her own.

The first few meetings may increase the pain and distress of the members; this is normal.

Please attend at least three meetings before you decide to stay or withdraw. If you decide to withdraw, please discuss this with the group leader before withdrawing.

If you cannot attend a session, please call. You are encouraged to attend every session. You are important and the group is not the same when members are absent. Your presence means a lot to everyone and adds support that you may not realize. Everyone is valuable to the group.

We encourage you to share, but we may have to 'move on' sometimes so everyone in the group has an opportunity to talk. Please do not be offended if we have to interrupt.

the early sessions are the most difficult. Invite and encourage members to call you in between the sessions if extra support is needed. Caution them that they should not be alone in their grief.

1. Ask members to identify three possible goals that they want to accomplish during the ten weeks. Give guidelines for setting effective goals: simple, not complicated; concrete, not abstract; something to do, not stop doing; self-initiated (i.e., not dependent upon others' help); and immediate (now and not in the future). Examples should be given to illustrate realistic goals that can be set along these guidelines. For example, a goal that states 'I want to feel better in ten weeks' is too abstract and could be self-defeating. A more specific, concrete, and attainable goal would be one that proposed eating breakfast every day in order to feel better physically. Other possible goals would be to watch the amount of caffeine intake in order to sleep better, to begin daily walking, to get up before noon, or to make one small decision each day in order to regain a sense of personal control.
2. Discuss the therapeutic value of journal writing and encourage members to begin this type of writing for identification and expression of feelings, and potential growth of self-insight.

Special considerations

The facilitator is relatively directive during this session. Guidelines are set and expectations checked. Members want to know if they will get their needs met in this group. Many start to compare their grief with other members. Occasionally, negative judgment will be expressed: 'What is she doing here? I lost my child and she only lost her 95-year-old mother who lived a full life.' If this occurs during the group session, you as the counsellor can choose to ignore it with the understanding that this is normal and that it will change in the next few weeks; or you can address it as it happens within the here-and-now context of the group. You can acknowledge what you have heard and state that this is a normal reaction until members get to know each other better; but validate the feeling and concern that are being expressed. Often reactions such as these are expressed to the counsellor outside the group. In these situations acceptance of their feelings is appropriate, with the acknowledgment that others from past groups have had similar reactions, which change as members become better acquainted. Others become overwhelmed by the grief of another: 'I don't know if I can come back. I hurt so much because of my own grief; I feel that I can't bear hearing about theirs.' For many it is the first time they have verbalized their loss outside the family, and it creates additional discomfort to hear others' loss at the same time. Assure members that these are typical reactions, but that everyone present has the ability to cope with their pain and it is not necessary to take on the additional grief of other members. Tell members that over the next several weeks they will see improvement in each other, and that laughter shared together will replace the initial pain and trepidation.

During this first session assess those who may have the tendency to monopolize with their grief or present their grief as more severe and more worthy of attention than others'. The counsellor can encourage members to talk; however, in order to give everyone the same opportunity, you may need to gently interrupt and ask others to contribute.

Another concern during this first session is that members may tend to rationalize their grief as not being as bad as others'. It is not necessary to intervene at this point; however, if this becomes a pattern over the sessions, it may be necessary to remind members that each person's grief is the most difficult for them and that their grief should not be underestimated. Dependence on rationalization as a defense mechanism allows members to intellectualize the process and avoid experiencing the pain that promotes healing. On other occasions the grief of others may be horrendous. Murders, suicides, and other types of death can be overwhelming to those already burdened with their own grief. Care must be taken to observe and process the initial experience of members as they listen to each others' experiences. Validate the intensity of this first session and assure members that in the course of the ten weeks, this level of intensity will not persist. Assure members that after the third session there will be a shift in focus and effect within the group, and that those who address their grief will experience positive movement in the bereavement process.

Session 2: Understanding the Multiple Perspectives of Grief

Introduce this session with comments that promote an understanding of the perspectives involved with loss and the tremendous power of grief. Comments should reflect the fact that every aspect of an individual is affected by a loss event, and that in the process, one must continue to assess which perspective is emerging at the present time and affecting the bereavement experience. The philosophical, spiritual, psychological, sociological, and physical perspectives can emerge at any time and on multiple occasions during the process. However, each time they emerge there will be different issues to address. For example, the spiritual perspective initially may be influenced by the bereaved's belief that God could have prevented this loss; thus the anger is directed at God. Later on in the process, this particular perspective may emerge again, with issues of rebuilding a relationship with God.

Objectives

1. To introduce the theme of multiple perspectives of loss.
2. To educate members about the nature and process of grief.
3. To validate and normalize grief behaviours.

Interventions

1. Ask members to share the experience of the first session and process the homework assignment (namely, goals and journal writing). It is important that the group give input to each other regarding goals and possible strategies. At this time it may be necessary to subdivide into groups that represent the same types of loss (e.g., spouse, child). Journal writing is shared for both the content and the affective components. Members begin to interpersonalize through this process, as they begin to realize that others share similar feelings and often have the same difficulties coping with everyday living.
2. Refer to your opening comments on the perspectives of loss: significant loss affects one philosophically, spiritually, psychologically, sociologically, and physically (see Chapter 1 for discussion on perspectives). Bereaved individuals do not understand the tremendous power of grief. They feel out of control, and many fear that they are going crazy. A 10-minute presentation to the group regarding these perspectives of grief is important and therapeutic. This information often provides the first ray of hope and reassurance of future resolution. Included in this presentation should be some reference to a model of grief. Models discussed in Chapter 1, especially the ones utilizing concepts of continuing bonds, narrative reconstruction, and dual processes, may be used.
3. Encourage members to share where they are in the grief experience, what has been helpful, and what are they doing to facilitate or hinder the process.

Homework

The next session will focus on the therapeutic value of remembering and developing healthy memories and inner realities of the deceased in order to create new sources of gratification and a sense of one's identity in the future. Sharing memories promotes the narrative process, the basis of meaning reconstruction. The narrative of shared past lives provides a connection to the future in order to reorganize and rewrite a meaningful life story.

Ask members to bring in pictures, items, and memories to share with the group that allow the group to experience the essence of the lives of the deceased loved ones. Give out copies of Table 3.6 (page 47) to encourage meaningful reminiscing. Encourage members to spend time reading this handout and thinking about the many dimensions of the relationship that has been lost through death. Also advise them that it is normal and healthy to have positive as well as negative memories, and that it is helpful in grief resolution to share both. Many need to share the fact that their loved ones had been demanding or self-centered, or that they had annoying habits.

Special considerations

Many will have unrealistic goals. The experience of grief is not thoroughly understood at this time, and many are still hoping for quick solutions and cures from a support group. Pain is still intense during this session, norms are being set, and members are not yet aware of the universality of their grief experience. Structure, direction, and support from the facilitators are important. Many times concrete suggestions will have to be given again to facilitate the goal-setting process.

Session 3: Remembering

Introduce the theme of remembering. Use the following as a guideline to introduce the theme.

Part of grief resolution entails the development of a realistic memory of the narrative of lives that have been shared. Many only remember the best features of an individual or relationship. Others become stuck in the memory of the illness or the death event that might have been traumatic. And for some, they cannot think of any positive aspects of the deceased's life. In order to emotionally establish an inner reality and to build a new relationship with the deceased, all the aspects of that individual must be remembered. Remembering, as an active part of the grief work, addresses the need to tell the story of a loved one's life. In this session the group members are encouraged to share pictures, items, or stories (positive and negative) about their loved ones. They describe memories that reflect the fact that we are all human, with human strengths and with frailties that often cause frustration. Through sharing, members allow others into their world. This session is often the pivotal session in which members no longer focus on why their loss is greater or why they are different from one another. Group cohesion and universality should be apparent after this session. If this is not the case, the lack of universality needs to be assessed by the facilitator and addressed with the group.

Others who have had conflicted relationships with the deceased find it difficult to remember anything positive. This can cause a problem in resolution. Unresolved, conflicted relationships foster an excessive focus on negative memories and unfinished business, leading to complications in the grief process. The following illustrates the potential for problems in the bereavement process:

> My mother died seven years ago. I didn't grieve much because I always felt we had a negative relationship. I adored my father, and my mother resented our relationship. I was cleaning things out of their home last year after my father died and I found her diary from when she was a teenager. I realize now I never knew my mother as a person. I also found that she had boxes of everything I ever made, with notes of pride about me on every item. Now I realize that I have to take this journey and go back and learn who my mother was – so I can put the memory of her within me – memories that will bring good feelings – instead of the hatred and anger that I have carried with me. (35-year-old female)

When memories such as the above are shared, acknowledge the pain being expressed, then focus on the positive that has come out of the process of sharing. Generate support and ideas from the group that will facilitate the process of finding new aspects about her mother. Contacting people who knew her mother might be one way she could learn more about the parent that she did not fully know.

Objectives

1. To develop an appropriate and realistic memory of the deceased.
2. To initiate creation of an inner reality.
3. To foster cohesion among members.

Interventions

1. This session draws entirely upon the reminiscences shared by the group. The only educational portion is a few minutes of introduction to the theme of the value of sharing memories, both positive and negative. It is important to recognize that our loved ones were human, with human qualities and frailties. All the memories have to be sorted out and processed. Some who only remember the good memories have a more difficult time of emotionally and cognitively integrating the loss. State that remembering is a valuable component of grief work and facilitates the process of eventually incorporating their loved ones within them in healthy memory. No one can take away the love that was once experienced, and no one can take away their memories.
2. Invite each member in turn to share pictures, items, and memories. For those who have little to share, encourage them to consider some of the questions posed in Table 3.6 on reminiscing, given to them last week to facilitate remembering.

Homework

Building on the emotions and potential issues identified during this session, the homework capitalizes on the need to gain insight into specific feelings and issues that need to be addressed. The assignment is to write a letter to the person who died. The letter can be stream of consciousness or structured to answer questions such as how I felt when you died, how I feel now, what I miss the most, what I do not miss, what I wish I had said or done, and what I wish I had not said or done. The structure allows for exploration and externalization of emotions that create conflict in grief resolution. Members are encouraged but not forced to write this letter. They will also be asked if they would like to share the letter or the thoughts and emotions experienced from writing it with the group. With difficult assignments it is helpful to give an example of those in other groups who benefited from this homework and how. Many have read the entire letter and have felt relief to share the burden of ambivalent emotions that they have harbored towards the deceased. Others have shared the fact that they have gained insight about repressed feelings, and now feel relieved or have a better understanding of themselves.

Special considerations

The intervention during this session relies greatly upon members' willingness to share meaningful memories with the group. The facilitators, however, must be prepared to generate discussion and move the sharing beyond mere factual reporting if necessary. This is accomplished by attempts to bring individuals into the here and now. This means that the facilitator asks individuals how sharing these memories have made them feel at this time, and how this sharing may have raised awareness of deeper issues. Linking, that is, asking other members if they have similar memories or feelings about their loved ones, often promotes cohesiveness and facilitates important connections between members. Another method is to ask members how it felt to share the memories with the group, and to ask other members if they have had similar feelings during this session. Those who monopolize should be gently reminded that others need time to share. A possible approach is to say: 'You have some great memories, Ann. Because we still have to hear from others, could you choose your favorite memory to share?' And lastly, if a member has only positive or only negative memories of the deceased, it is necessary to redirect their focus from highly selective memories to an exploration of that person's total life and their relationship with them.

Session 4: Identifying and Expressing Feelings

To introduce the theme for this session, focus on the need to identify and express all feelings. Explain that avoidance of difficult and painful feelings is one of the common problems associated with the healing process. In acute phases of grief one feels out of control, and there is a fear of losing more control if feelings are allowed to emerge. Moreover, many do not even know what they are feeling. To facilitate awareness of issues/feelings of commonality, participants are encouraged to share the experience of writing the letter or the reasons for not being able to accomplish the assignment. Once a person can identify specific feelings and acknowledge them and then be provided with an environment for healthy expression, one of the most difficult aspects of grief work has begun. It is a paradox that one can 'lean into the pain' and feel relief and renewed energy. Avoidance depletes energy. Grief work is hard work, and one needs purposeful breaks. Not to grieve or experience the pain is to deny the healing process and perhaps to complicate it. However, keeping in mind the dual process model (Chapter 1), it is important to remind members that the bereavement process requires an oscillation (regulatory process) between emotional grief work and restoration tasks that attend to life changes.

The following highlights the benefits experienced by one group member after writing a letter to his deceased father:

A male participant (age 37) had been referred to the group by his company's psychologist, who believed that current outbursts of anger were somehow related to unresolved issues of his father's death four years ago. In group, he was discussing his experience of writing a letter to his deceased father: 'Last night I was writing this letter on my word processor. I looked up at the screen and couldn't believe it. I was furious with my father. For two months I was the only one who knew he was dying. He wouldn't let me tell anyone, and he wouldn't let me talk to him about his dying. I was the one responsible for his care. He died and I never even got a chance to say the things that I needed to say.'

This member did not read his letter to the group; he was more intent on sharing the experience of writing it and the insight that he had gained regarding his anger and unresolved grief. It was therapeutic for him to share this experience; the group validated and supported the work he had accomplished through his letter writing. It was also therapeutic for the group as a whole, because those who had avoided writing a letter were able to realize the potential worth of such an exercise.

Objectives
To identify, validate and express painful emotions of grief.

Interventions

1. Ask members to share the experience of writing the letter within the group setting. As indicated from the above example, it can have several benefits, both for individual members and for the group as a whole. It builds trust and cohesion, and offers members the opportunity to imitate behaviours that have worked for others. Some choose to read their letters. Often, painful and not previously known feelings are elicited by this assignment, leaving an individual feeling even more overwhelmed. The group offers support by listening and generating suggestions. Most who have shared have expressed a sense of relief or a physical feeling of having a weight removed. There is a saying in bereavement counselling that 'a grief shared, is a grief cut in half'.
2. Discuss the nature of feelings for about 15 minutes. The handout called 'Feelings spiral' (Figure 5.1, see below) that shows a variety of emotions can initiate a general discussion. The handout shows the extremes of going from being very 'up' to being very 'down'. Grief has the power to create these swings, and the goal in this process is to come more towards the middle. Members are asked to identify emotions, both positive and negative, and the extremes of them. Discuss the fact that feelings are neither intrinsically good or bad; it is what one does with them that determines whether they are positive or negative. Feelings should not be avoided, but rather embraced and worked through.
3. Help members identify the negative and the positive emotions on the handout. Many are only aware of the more unpleasant feelings and are unaware of any positive ones. Investigate what is occurring when the more pleasant emotions are being experienced. Validate the need to have pleasant feelings in the midst of their grief. Emphasize the importance of living life again and restoring a sense of choice in an ability to complete tasks of daily living. This moves individuals towards empowerment. Many believe that things just happen for no reason at all. Many believe that if they experience a good hour or day, something 'out there' caused it to happen. Once we can facilitate awareness that they are doing something to cause this difference, they can begin to activate behaviours to feel better.
4. Discuss the history of loss (Chapter 2) and ways that repressed emotion from past losses can be contributing to the present loss and painful emotions. Connect this to the idea that feelings should not be avoided. It is important at this time to help

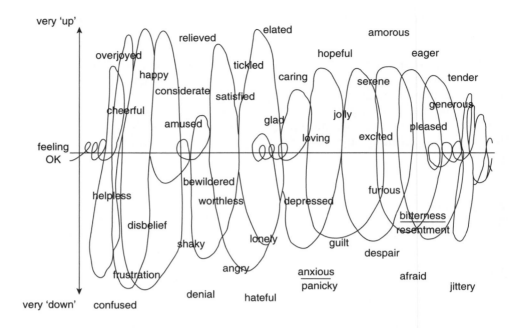

Figure 5.1   Feelings spiral (Source: Reprinted with permission of Grief Center, Inc., North Canton, Ohio)

members become aware of and assess past losses; many are often not aware that past events have been significant losses in their lives.

Homework

1. Advise members that next week's focus will be on changes made in their lives since the death of their loved one. Discuss the fact that relationships are built over many years, with numerous roles involved. Many do not understand the breadth and depth of grief work, especially as it applies to the many changes and lost roles. Ask members to focus on changes in their lives since the death of their loved ones, and what new roles they have had to assume.
2. Ask members to complete the history of loss chart (Table 2.5, page 33) and bring it to the next session. This activity provides additional insight into behavioural and emotional reactions to loss, and allows them to have a clearer understanding of role changes after different losses over their lifetimes. This is an important assignment as it raises an awareness of the impact of past losses and the effect they have had.

Special considerations

When doing the letter assignment for this session, some limit themselves to one or two areas. Others write lengthy letters and desire to read the entire letter to the group to complete the process. Others focus on what was difficult with this assignment, or what they learned about themselves from writing this letter. The assignment is structured, but flexible enough so that individuals use it for their needs and on their timetable. If members have avoided the assignment, encourage them to return to the task when they have more strength.

Session 5: Role Changes and Meaning Reconstruction

Introduce the topic of role changes and meaning reconstruction for about ten minutes. The following information and case example can be used.

Bereaved individuals are acutely aware of the physical loss of a person. An important aspect of group work is to address the number of roles or functions that are also lost (i.e., intangible losses) after the death of a significant person. A person is not merely a friend, a child, a parent, or sibling. Relationships provide meaningful roles and are the basis of one's identity. A goal of the session is to help members explore the roles that have been lost or redefined. This is not intended to add more grief or to promote self-pity. When taking into consideration one's sense of identity and narrative coherence, the bereaved must understand all that has been lost in order to reorganize their lives with some sense of meaningfulness and continuity to the past (refer to Chapter 1 for narrative constructs).

As members begin to understand the changes in functions and roles as a result of their loss, they are cautioned not to perform all the roles alone. However, they are also cautioned not to realign too quickly. Identities are established over time through the feedback that significant others give regarding roles, strengths, and weaknesses. To reinvest or realign too quickly often negates the opportunity for new aspects of an identity to emerge. Quick replacement is an attractive possibility because it can provide the opportunity to keep busy and avoid the necessary grief work. The ability to learn new skills and to take on new roles allows the bereaved to build self-confidence and regain a sense of personal control:

> My wife and I were high-school sweethearts. I never lived on my own. We had three sons and she stayed home and I worked two jobs to support the family. I never knew where anything was at home, let alone know how she did everything. Even though she wasn't well these last few years, she still ran the house. Last night I decided that I better figure things out if I am going to make it. I started by going through the kitchen. When I came across my favorite recipes that she made for me I couldn't stop crying [tears up]. Somehow I finally stopped, got up, found what I needed, and made it. It wasn't too bad, if I can say so. (67-year-old widower)

An example such as the above is indicative of responses given by members as they begin to understand the meaning of role change in their lives. Others may need more help to develop insight into these changes and support to initiate new behaviours. The group can be an excellent resource for generating ideas and offering opportunities for needed behaviour changes.

And finally, an important goal for this session is to foster a sense of survival and empowerment. Introducing concepts of resiliency, discussed in Chapters 1 and 2, is appropriate for use during this session. A focus on aspects of *I AM, I CAN, I HAVE* (Table 3.4, page 46) is especially relevant at this point, and can provide meaningful discussion and interaction amongst the members.

Objectives

1. To discuss and process the history of loss in order to gain insight into the effects of past loss and change on the present loss.
2. To understand the multifaceted nature of loss as it affects roles and identity.
3. To explore healthy role realignments.
4. To understand concepts of resiliency and foster meaning reconstruction and personal empowerment.

Interventions

1. Ask members to share their history of loss. They can share specific losses, general reactions or styles of coping, multiple changes endured throughout the years because of these losses, or how the past is affecting the present experience. In addition to the awareness and insight that this activity generates, it also provides a framework for designing interventions. For example, an individual may learn that he or she have had multiple losses and the way of coping had always been to avoid pain and to quickly replace what had been lost. As this individual now faces role changes after the death of a significant person, the tendency might be to try to replace this person quickly and have others take over the roles that had been provided by the deceased. This awareness leads to designing interventions that help this individual stop inappropriate past patterns of response to loss, and develop new ways of coping.
2. Initiate an activity that will visually demonstrate role losses and changes. The paper plate exercise (Figure 5.2) can be used. Members are given paper plates, markers, and scissors. They are instructed to think back six months to a year before their loved ones died, what roles they were involved in with them, and what percentage of their time was involved in each role. Many put down roles of caretaker, spouse, parent, church member, and so on. They are then instructed to cut out the roles that are no longer there or have changed. Many cut out the role of spouse and caretaker, and are left with a wedge that represents 20 percent of remaining roles in their lives. Others also cut out pieces from church and parental roles, if this had been a shared role. This heightens awareness of the voids in their lives, and gives expression to feelings of aloneness and emptiness, not thoroughly understood before this exercise.
3. Encourage members to share insights regarding changes, especially in terms of roles and identity.
4. Get input within the group regarding new roles that they have assumed since the death.
5. Discuss the need to have meaningful roles in life and the necessity to begin to think of new roles (not replacements). Roles are purposively chosen to give one a sense of identity. Replacements are not thought through; rather, a person or an activity is quickly chosen to fill the void that one feels after the death of a loved one.
6. Discuss resiliency as reconstruction and empowerment. Facilitate discussion among members in order to promote insight. Focus discussion on *I AM* (inner personal strengths), *I CAN* (interpersonal skills), and *I HAVE* (external support systems).

Homework

As members explore past and present losses, significant role changes, and the emotional impact on their lives as a result, they become more acutely aware of the stress that they are experiencing. This session has begun the process of a more in-depth investigation into change, and the stress created by change. The next session will help members understand the connection between grief, change, and

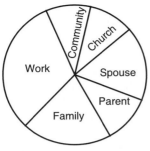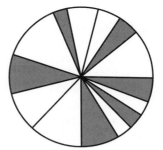

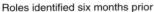

Roles identified six months prior

Roles – Present
Pieces of every role had to be
eliminated, leaving fragments

The shaded areas represent segments he had to eliminate. Although he still had a
portion of these roles, he became acutely aware of the involvment he and his daughter
had in each other's lives. He was a leader in her church your group, employed her during
the summer, attended her sport functions, and participated with her in a number of
community activities.

Figure 5.2   Paper plate exercise

additional stress. It is the intent of these sessions to help members break behaviours, thoughts, and emotions down into smaller components, thus making them
more workable. For this week's assignment, members are to write down what
upsets them during this week and how they resolve it. This assignment provides
the basis to concretize stressors. Many are only aware that they are experiencing
stress. Giving a stressor a name promotes concrete solutions.

Special considerations

The paper plate activity facilitates group cohesion and universality. Members
visually understand that they are sharing a common experience. Many of these
role changes have not been prepared for, such as the widower who has to cook
and do the laundry, or the widow who has to make decisions about the house.
Another important feature of this session is the insight gained regarding the
multi-faceted nature of roles. Many do not understand the diversity of roles and
the relationships involved, and try to replace the missing 'role' with a new 'wife',
'child', 'friend', and so forth. And, the introduction of resiliency concepts provides
the foundation for empowerment and reconstruction. Bereaved individuals are
acutely aware of what has been lost. They have little insight into inner strengths
or valuable support systems.

Session 6: Stress

Introduce the topic of stress for about five minutes. The following may be used as
a very brief introduction, and counsellors are encouraged to use the information
discussed in Chapters 1 and 2. Counsellors might also supplement the topic with
any additional information that they believe to be pertinent to the particular
group. For example, if the group has widows who are mothers, acknowledgment

of their particular type of stress (raising children/adolescents as single parents) may be appropriate. A brief introduction to the topic of stress follows.

Stress is a normal part of everyday life. Loss and grief bring additional stress. Often it is difficult to sort out and identify specific stressors. Some may only have a vague idea that they are 'stressed out'. Within the group it is helpful to identify specific stressors, when they occur, how often, how they have been dealt with, and specific ways for healthier ways of coping. The goal of managing stress is to change the problem that caused the stress and to regulate the distressful emotions caused by the problem (Lazarus and Folkman, 1984). It is not possible to change the problem that caused the stress (death of a loved one); however, it is possible to change some of the concurrent stress that is contributing to the grief experience.

In order to understand personal stress, members should be encouraged to examine it on three different levels: affective, cognitive, and behavioural. Often there is an affective awareness, as it is most intense on this level. However, stress is seldom present on only one level. Understanding the pervasive nature of stress is the main focus of this session. Additional attention this session will be on factors of resiliency, a concept introduced during Session 5. Factors of resiliency underlie personal empowerment and the ability to manage and survive all stress.

Objectives
To discuss the fact that there was stress before the death and that specific issues and feelings of grief increase stress. Many aspects of grief must go through a process that cannot be rushed; however, resolution in areas of stress can be beneficial. Often this is one of the few areas that the bereaved can gain some control and set realistic goals. Relief of stress is an empowering factor that initiates feelings of personal control.

Interventions

1. Ask members to share the homework regarding what was stressful last week and how it was handled. Generate discussion based on what was learned from the situation, what did they do that was helpful, and what needs to be altered.
2. Discuss (about ten minutes) stress in more detail, incorporating ideas from the introduction to this session and Chapters 1 and 2. Use any current information regarding the nature and effect of stress on the human body.
3. Give members the handouts that allow them to identify and assess areas and levels of stress, and to sort out those which are important/not important and controllable/not controllable (Tables 5.2 and 5.3). Promote discussion from members, based on the information presented and the handouts. Put responses on a chalkboard or a paper chart. Work towards helping members let go of stressors that are not important and to find solutions, even partial solutions.
4. Give members the handout that categorizes resiliency factors (Table 3.4, page 46). Refer to the introduction of the resiliency concepts discussed last session. At this time give examples for a better understanding of the concepts as they relate to issues of stress and coping. Encourage members to identify their current individual resiliency factors and ones that they wish to develop. Finally, promote discussion among the group to support the development of additional factors amongst its members. Members who can identify personal resiliency factors and give examples may serve as role models and encourage others.

Table 5.2 Levels of stress

I.	Emotional level:	Feelings of anxiety, nervous, panic, can't concentrate, go blank.
	Coping behaviours:	Relaxation techniques
		Breathing exercises
		Meditation
		Prayer
		Imagery
		Music
		Physical exercise
		Healthy expression of feelings
II.	Thinking level:	Beliefs reflect 'shoulds', 'musts', 'oughts'. Inaccurate appraisal of situations. Lack of confidence in coping abilities.
	Coping behaviours:	Rethink and change perceptions, beliefs, and self-statements. Get accurate information about events and examine possible and plausible interpretations of an event. Develop communication skills. Get assertiveness training.
III.	Behavioural level:	Stress can be caused by what you are doing or not doing (e.g. putting things off, acting before thinking).
	Coping behaviours:	Evaluate what you are doing. Change what you are doing. Make other choices. Re-evaluate, prioritize, make new plans. Learn new skills.

Table 5.3 Stressors

Stressors that are important		Stressors that aren't important	
controllable	uncontrollable	controllable	uncontrollable
1. Lack of things to do.	Family is not supportive.	Allow phone calls to go unanswered.	Rain/snow.
2.			
3.			
4.			
5.			

Stressors that are important and that we can control need to be worked on. Those that are unimportant and under our control can be either dealt with or ignored. Stressors that are either important or unimportant and out of our control should be let go of, as there is nothing that can be done about the uncontrollable stressors in your life. *Concentrate on the ones that are under your control.*

Homework

The next session will build on this one. Coping styles will be examined in more depth, and new possibilities for coping will be presented. Ask members to fill out a coping inventory (Table 5.4 below)*. Coping inventories offer a wide variety of coping styles. They help individuals see negative ways they might be coping and open up potential ways of coping. Present the idea that inability to cope at this time is not a sign of weakness. Past, effective coping strategies may not work with new situations. This exercise provides the opportunity to personally evaluate what still works, what is not effective, and what new strategies can be added.

---

*Table 3.3 (page 42) provides an alternative exercise. It focuses on the two major coping strategies and is suitable for individual assessment and group discussion.

Table 5.4 Coping behaviours

The following identifies a number of ways different individuals cope with stress in their lives. They represent positive and negative ways of addressing life's challenges. Often we depend on one or just a few ways of dealing with stress. Some situations demand additional coping skills or new approaches. Read the following and rate how likely you are to use the different behaviours. Then reflect on whether or not it is effective in every situation, whether it is helping you or creating additional stress, and what new ones from this list might be effective.

1 = Never
2 = Seldom
3 = Sometimes
4 = Usually
5 = Always

1.	Use drugs (nonprescription) or alcohol	1	2	3	4	5
2.	Talk with others	1	2	3	4	5
3.	Learn as much as possible about the situation	1	2	3	4	5
4.	Keep so busy that you don't have time to think	1	2	3	4	5
5.	Overeat	1	2	3	4	5
6.	Miss meals/eat sporadically	1	2	3	4	5
7.	Exercise	1	2	3	4	5
8.	Use humour as a release	1	2	3	4	5
9.	Ventilate through tears	1	2	3	4	5
10.	Try to forget	1	2	3	4	5
11.	Turn it over to God	1	2	3	4	5
12.	Find solace in nature	1	2	3	4	5
13.	Listen to music	1	2	3	4	5
14.	Make new choices	1	2	3	4	5
15.	Take on new roles	1	2	3	4	5
16.	Get medical help	1	2	3	4	5
17.	Take more rests	1	2	3	4	5
18.	Get a massage	1	2	3	4	5
19.	Learn relaxation techniques	1	2	3	4	5
20.	Meditate	1	2	3	4	5
21.	Find good in the issue/problem	1	2	3	4	5
22.	Rename the problem to make it solvable	1	2	3	4	5
23.	Hope for relief	1	2	3	4	5
24.	Get others' input for solutions	1	2	3	4	5
25.	Take a trip	1	2	3	4	5
26.	Keep a journal/write letters, etc.	1	2	3	4	5
27.	Take care of unfinished business	1	2	3	4	5
28.	Repress emotions	1	2	3	4	5
29.	Treat yourself as you would a friend	1	2	3	4	5
30.	Drive fast to let tensions out	1	2	3	4	5
31.	Immerse yourself in work/hobby	1	2	3	4	5
32.	Seek solace within church activities	1	2	3	4	5
33.	Shout, scream, bang doors, curse	1	2	3	4	5
34.	Make a plan to do something (take action)	1	2	3	4	5
35.	Accept it as unfair and let it go	1	2	3	4	5
36.	Reflect on ways past problems were coped with	1	2	3	4	5
37.	Wait for a miracle	1	2	3	4	5
38.	Act quickly (without thinking)	1	2	3	4	5
39.	Take others' advice	1	2	3	4	5
40.	Move - start over	1	2	3	4	5

Special considerations

This session is practical and is pivotal in facilitating awareness of specific stressors and potential solutions. In terms of the tasks of grief, it provides the opportunity to adjust to an environment that is different because of the loss. The ability to make new choices and to take some action provides a basis for rebuilding a future existence.

Session 7: Coping (including coping with holidays, birthdays, special events)*

Introduce the theme of coping as an active response to loss. As discussed in the previous session, the goal of coping is to activate purposeful change in order to regulate the distressful emotions caused by the event of loss and concurrent contributing events. Coping includes the ideas of accommodation and assimilation. As individuals relearn their worlds after loss, new information about themselves and their environments must be assimilated. The bereaved strive to somehow maintain the essence of their identities, yet adapt to new lives and environments. Coping involves identifying specific stressors and understanding what needs to be altered. Changes often have to be made in present coping styles. Options for coping are discussed in the group, ideas shared, and specific strategies are explored for each level (affective, cognitive, and behavioural) of stress.

Specifically, holidays and special events are highlighted as intense periods of stress and potential emotional pain. They cannot be avoided, and they need to be carefully preplanned. Holidays and special events have the potential to arouse a multitude of past memories, many very painful. Preplanning with other family members can be instrumental in avoiding unnecessary grief:

> I knew Christmas was going to be hard. This will be our first one since my husband died. So I called together my two daughters and we decided how we were going to cope with the actual day. We decided that giving gifts would be okay. However, we will exchange gifts the night before and not wrap them. We all agreed that unwrapping them would be too difficult. (55-year-old widow)

The above represents a typical response after permission is given within the group to alter traditions for celebrating holidays and special events. Individuals have solutions within them; most have not been given permission to express them or to act upon them.

Objectives

1. To identify coping strategies that help facilitate the grief process.
2. To identify time periods that create stress, e.g., holidays and anniversaries, and specific coping strategies for them.

---

*Refer to Chapters 1 and 2 for additional information on stress and coping.

Interventions

1. Discuss the homework regarding coping strategies. Are present ones effective? Explore specific areas of coping: mental, spiritual, physical, behavioural, and emotional. What are specific ways members have of coping in each of these areas?
2. Discuss the potential of holidays, anniversaries, and other events to elicit pain.
3. When appropriate, ask members to share plans and concerns of anticipated events or seasons.

Homework

Next week's session focuses on additional strategies for active bereavement: memorializing, rituals, and continuing bonds (creating an inner representation and interactive relationship with deceased loved ones).

In grief, one feels that everything is out of control. Memorialization, especially through the creation of rituals, promotes awareness of some personal control again. Ask members to identify what has been done to commemorate or memorialize their loved ones. Encourage them to commemorate beyond the funeral ritual. Most do not understand the therapeutic value of remembering or memorializing after the funeral rite. Suggest that they consider what was of value or meaning to their loved ones, and how this could be memorialized in a meaningful way. Give some basic ideas such as contributing to a charity or developing a scholarship fund in the name of the deceased. Also mention that in addition to memorialization and creation of personal rituals, next week they will also be introduced to current concepts of continuing bonds – an approach that encourages an inner relationship with their loved ones, while at the same time promoting the ability *to move on*.

Special considerations

This session has the potential to be helpful from day-to-day coping to coping with major holidays and events. Many realize during this session that they are having difficulty because they continue to use strategies that may have been effective in the past, but currently are not useful. It is often a relief to learn that it is not personal deficits or weaknesses that are causing coping difficulties. Most members are willing to try new behaviours at this point, and can usually select new strategies from the coping inventory or from each other.

Session 8: Memorialization, Continuing Bonds (Inner Representations and Interactive Relationships), and Therapeutic Use of Rituals

For this introduction, connect the theme of memorialization back to the theme of remembering in the third session. Memorialization implies a more active process, as it requires some action on the part of the bereaved. Memorializion begins with the funeral rite and can continue for an indefinite period of time. The goal is to incorporate a loved one in healthy memory and to reinvest in meaningful life. Not to invest in life again would negate the meaning of the life of a loved one.

Continuing bonds presented in the first chapter offer new understandings of the bereavement process. Reconstruction of new identities and reinvestment in meaningful life involve the ability to hold the deceased in loving memory and maintain an inner representation of them (Silverman and Nickman, 1996b). Development of these representations (i.e., new relationships) is not a passive process. Love does not end with death; caring and some form of attachment continues. Bonds of human attachment change over time, but a connection will continue. The ongoing attachment will depend, to some degree, on the survivor's ability to maintain an internal dialogue with his or her loved one. The paradox is that 'the deceased are both present and not present at the same time. It is possible to be bereft and not bereft simultaneously, to have a sense of continuity and yet to know that nothing will ever be the same. The reality is that there is an inner system that continues to be centered on the person who is no longer physically present. This inner reality may encourage the mourner to carry on' (Silverman and Nickman, 1996: 351). Although there can never be the same gratification shared during life, the ability to incorporate loved ones within has the potential to provide new sources of gratification in the future.

Rituals (Rando, 1988) can be utilized to facilitate memorialization and an inner representation of a loved one. During this group session, members learn about the relationship between rituals, tasks of grief, and grief resolution. They are encouraged to begin to identify where they are in the process and tasks of grief, and to explore possibilities for personal rituals.

The behaviour (ritual) is designed to express internal feelings of grief in order that others may better understand the depth and nature of the grief. A ritual may be done once, as in the ritual of the funeral, or it may be repeated. A ritual is structured and has a time limit. Thus family and friends may be more willing to participate if they understand exactly what is expected of them, and that there is an end point. Often support persons abandon the bereaved because they tire of endless grief, and they do not know what to do to help. Rituals provide a framework and a channel for emotional energy. They should be considered for memorialization and as an adjunct to facilitate the process and resolution.

Reinvestment in life does not mean forgetting or ceasing to actively remember the deceased. Loved ones will always be a part of us. The highest form of memorializing is to live a meaningful life as a tribute to the deceased. Any behaviour done in memory and with the purpose of reinvesting is a ritual. The therapeutic aspect of a ritual is that it empowers you to act upon the world. To symbolize this power to rebuild and reinvest, many choose an item as a ritual that signifies new life. Garden plants are frequently chosen as symbolic reinvestments in life.

Rituals can also be designed to promote meaningful expression of the bereaved's attempts to develop new relationships with the deceased. New relationships will have continuity with former ones, and the bereaved will continue to play roles and exert some type of influence in the survivors' lives.

Research conducted by Marwit and Klass (1996) suggests that these new relationships are based on past meaningful roles. For example, encourage the bereaved to remember and share the positive aspects of their loved one's life, then discuss how they can serve as ongoing role models. Thus a ritual might be to help the survivor design a behaviour or plan to emulate what they most admired while this person was alive. Encouraging an inner dialogue with the deceased regarding their plan, then contemplating their loved one's response, begins the process (paradox) of creating an inner reality while moving on and reconstructing one's life. Other ideas include seeking their wisdom (internally) when faced with moral dilemmas and life-altering decisions. Thus the deceased remain alive within us, providing a connection to the past while, at the same time, being available for ongoing guidance and support.

Objectives

1. To consider memorialization as an ongoing part of the grief experience.
2. To understand the therapeutic properties of rituals.
3. To begin the process of active reinvestment, continuing bonds, and the creation of inner representations (new relationships).

Interventions

1. Introduce the concept of memorialization. Process the homework assignment. Encourage sharing ideas of what has been done and future intentions to commemorate their loved one.
2. Discuss the relationship of rituals to memorialization, continuing bonds, and creation of inner representations (new relationships) for about five to ten minutes. (Use information and examples from the opening comments for this session and previous chapters.)
3. Encourage the sharing of ideas of possible personal rituals and rituals already enacted to facilitate the grief process. (Many have experiences to share that may have not been recognized or integrated as therapeutic rituals.)

Homework

1. Discuss the need for ongoing support systems and the need to identify who are the people who are presently providing needed support. Relate this need to concepts regarding resiliency factors previously discussed, especially the category *I HAVE* (Table 3.4, page 46).
2. Discuss the idea that some healing can be attained by helping others (*I AM, I CAN*, Table 3.4). Ask members to reach out and support someone who is experiencing a difficult time this week (e.g., greeting card, phone call, visit), and to process the feelings experienced afterwards in their written journals.
3. Distribute the psychological needs assessment and planning sheet (Table 3.6, page 47). This tool was discussed in Chapters 2 and 3.
4. Advise members that there are two sessions left. Ask if there are there any unanswered questions or new issues.

Special considerations

The notion of rituals is usually well received by the group. Once explained, it is not a difficult concept to grasp. It provides the opportunity to take some action, instead of constantly feeling acted upon by external forces. Many have already enacted rituals without realizing it.

Session 9: Assessing Support Systems and Rebuilding and Reconstruction

Introduce this week's theme by connecting it to the homework assignment. Bereaved individuals need to give and receive support. Giving support to those who are also in pain or experiencing difficulties is a form of altruism, which facilitates healing and reconstruction. Receiving support is an important concept in resiliency (*I HAVE*) and an integral part of the bereavement processes. It is important to assess what is currently available, and determine if these systems are effective. Often supportive friends and family give uninformed and unhelpful advice, or only tell the bereaved what they think they (the bereaved) want to hear. Often the most useful support is to tell someone that what he or she is presently doing could be harmful to his or her future well-being. This type of support is difficult to give to bereaved individuals because no one wants to cause additional pain.

Support is needed in many different ways over the course of bereavement. Without good support systems the grieving process is even more difficult. As the bereaved move from the acute phases of grief, they are often in a position to help support others. It can be noted that helping others is itself healing – the helper becomes helped. This effort often complements the grief process and begins the next phase of rebuilding. In addition, this facilitates other aspects of resiliency (*I AM, I CAN*). Rebuilding and reconstructing new identities cannot come before the pain of grief is fully experienced, yet many try to rush through this as if it were another 'daily' task to be accomplished. This is an active process that implies accommodation and assimilation. The goal is for the bereaved to regain a sense of empowerment and control.

Assessing support systems and beginning the process of rebuilding necessitate an evaluation of what has changed and what one still has. Rebuilding is based on what remains (i.e., what has not been lost through this experience).

Objectives

1. To assess current resiliency factors based on present support systems (*I HAVE*) and to understand the value of altruism in the healing process (the ability to give support: *I AM, I CAN*).
2. To understand what has changed, yet comprehend what is still intact and meeting psychological needs.
3. To begin the process of making new choices and reconstructing a new identity.
4. To understand the therapeutic functions of hope.

Interventions

1. Enquire if any members have unanswered questions or new issues that have emerged. Allow time to answer questions. If new issues have emerged, assess whether or not they can be addressed within the context of the group, or if individual counselling would be more appropriate.

2. Process the assignment regarding support systems. Introduce the concept of healing through altruism and the potential each member has to be a support system for another bereaved individual. If members do not have support systems beyond this group, use group time to help identify potential support systems. Many members will offer support to each other when they become aware of the needs of others.
3. Process the assignment regarding psychological needs. Involve the group in the process of helping each other identify future choices in the different areas of 'need'. Brainstorming techniques generate valid ideas to consider.

Homework

1. Remind members that next week is the last week and that the focus will be on evaluation of the ten weeks and on positive achievements. Ask members to think about one personal change experienced during the ten weeks and be prepared to share it.
2. Instruct them to be prepared to tell each member one positive change that they have observed about each other during the last ten weeks.
3. Ask them to think about their own uniqueness and gifts. Remind them that in session 3, items, pictures, and stories were shared to show the beauty of their loved ones' lives. This next session will honor and celebrate their own lives. In our experience, some members have brought in items that they have created. One member brought in several quilts she had made. Another member brought in his band instrument from 1923 and several music instruction books that he had written during his professional career. One man talked about his ability to cook and invited everyone over for a special dinner. And a retired art teacher offered free art lessons to everyone in the group. As this request is made, it is wise to share examples such as these, as the assignment can be confusing.
4. Ask members if they would like to bring light refreshments next week as part of the closure and celebration of life. If so, make arrangements at the end of this session.

Special considerations

Through the processing of individuals' psychological needs assessments, this session provides insight into what has not been lost through death. Many are surprised by what still remains and the options available for new choices. In addition, this session addresses the need to give and receive support. There will always be members who have little support available and little left to rebuild upon. It has been our experience, however, that as members become aware of this, they readily offer support in various ways.

Session 10: Closure/Celebration of Life

Open this session with statements of appreciation for each member and the risks that they have taken to share their pain with each other. Validate the fact that you have observed growth and change in everyone over the past ten weeks. Acknowledge the fact that today is the formal end of this group and that this often brings up additional feelings of loss and grief. Share the fact that many in the past have chosen to continue to meet informally and have benefited from ongoing mutual support.

Table 5.5   Evaluation

Think about your experience in this group. Please respond in the most honest way possible to the items below. This will be kept confidential. Do not be concerned if you have some negative feelings; people sometimes do and are hesitant to say so.

The responses are **Definitely yes, Yes, Unsure, No, and Definitely not**. In addition to a response, please give some specifics regarding your experience and opinions.

1.   In general, did you make good progress?
2.   Do you feel that the group leader (counsellor) had a good understanding of you and your individual issues?
3.   Do you feel that you were clear about what you wanted to accomplish in this group within the number of sessions (goals)?
4.   Were there certain things that you were afraid to share with the group leader or the group? If so, do you wish to indicate anything at this time that was/is a concern for you?
5.   Are you handling things better now than before the group began?
6.   Do you feel that you learned things about yourself? If so, what?
7.   Do you feel that the group leader shared with you all the information that you needed in order to cope better with your issues?
8.   Please list things that worked best for you during the course of the ten weeks of the group sessions.
9.   Please indicate things that did not work for you.
10.   Did you feel that you were able to connect to and relate with others in the group?

Objectives

1. To identify change and growth and bring attention to members' resiliency factors.
2. To share a unique aspect of self and to promote the idea of celebrating life.
3. To acknowledge the need for continued support as the 'formal' group terminates. Enquire if any members have unanswered questions that have emerged. Allow time to answer questions. If new issues have emerged, assess whether or not they can be addressed within the context of the group, or if individual counselling would be more appropriate.
4. To evaluate the experience and bring closure.

Interventions

1. Ask each member to fill out an evaluation form regarding the group experience (Table 5.5). Address any unanswered questions and recommend individual counselling for those who have additional issues that cannot be satisfactorily handled during this last session.
2. Encourage members to verbalize their own change, growth, and awareness of their resiliencies. Then ask them to share insights regarding other members' change, growth, and resiliences.
3. Ask members to share stories, pictures, or items that they have brought that will allow the group to experience a special part of who they are.
4. If food has been brought, allow time for this celebration of life as a way to formally close the ten weeks.

Special considerations

The final session represents another loss in the lives of those already coping with loss through death. Attention must be given to this additional loss and processed in the here-and-now setting of this final session. Encourage members to share how they feel about the fact that this is the last session. Move this process towards a discussion of coping strategies and continued support of one another. Most groups will appoint someone to organize future sessions together. It is not always the entire group that remains together, but some portion of the group will likely continue.

Groups will always mirror some part of each member's private reality and offer an opportunity to practice change that needs to be accomplished outside of the therapeutic setting. It has been our experience that the 'power of the group experience' brings issues to awareness sooner than in individual counselling and provides an appropriate environment to practice behaviours, to gain needed support, and to more expediently facilitate the full experience of grief.

6 Children and Grief

Children are not merely small adults. Rather, they possess distinct cognitive, developmental, and emotional constructs that make them distinct from adults. This means that the accepted concepts of grief and bereavement may not apply to children and therefore a distinct approach and interaction are necessitated. Moreover, children vary by age, experience, and their environment. This further solidifies the notion that there is no blueprint from which to seek directions when interacting with the bereaved child. There are, however, patterns of development and grieving that can aid in the counselling of a bereaved child. This chapter seeks to highlight these patterns and provide tools of intervention for the practitioner wishing to aid a grieving child.

Theories of Death Conceptualization

One cannot assume that a bereaved child accurately conceptualizes death. Rather, most theorists agree that conceptualization of death occurs in a sequential fashion. It is theorized that there are three basic concepts to understanding death as an entity: universality, irreversibility, and the non-functionality of the deceased. Universality refers to the understanding that death happens to all living things, is inevitable, and is usually not predictable. Understanding irreversibility signals that one understands that death is a final state of being that can have no alteration. Finally, understanding the non-functionality means that one realizes that all living processes have ceased (Speece and Brent, 1984).

For children, understanding all of these concepts and therefore death requires acquisition of certain cognitive and developmental milestones. Nagy (1948) postulated stage-based acquisition. First, the finality of death is not understood. Next, finality is understood but the person believes he/she can escape or 'cheat' death. Finally, death is perceived as final and inevitable as the child gains the ability for abstract thinking.

Modern theorists such as Fox (1988), though, believe in a task-based path to death conceptualization. The sub-concepts of universality, irreversibility, and non-functionality are viewed as tasks that are revisited at every developmental milestone of a child's life and accommodated into current schemata. Thus, at each milestone a bereaved child must simultaneously re-evaluate the loss with a new level of understanding and emotionally experience grief appropriate for their present age. The following section is devoted to reviewing how children of various ages experience the loss, what healthy grieving constitutes, and how professionals can help a child grieve.

Age-based Conceptualization of Death and its Behavioural Manifestations

A task-based theory to death conceptualization implies individuality to each child's death awareness. Still, generalizations can be made based on observations, studies, and developmental theories. These generalizations are important, for they provide a framework with which to observe and interact with a grieving child. They are also milestones that grieving children must acquire to assure healthy development.

Infants who experience a death do not comprehend it, yet still react. Bereaved infants between 0–6 months of age lack the consistency they need and seek. With inconsistency, they may become more irritable and exhibit changes in feeding patterns. As object permanency emerges between 6–12 months of age, the bereaved infant may demonstrate separation anxiety such as anger or withdrawal as the safe object has been taken away (Duffy, 1991; Bending, 1993).

Similarly, toddlers do not understand the concept of death. They do, however, struggle with the impact of death's irreversibility as it clashes with their developmental task of separation. Normally, separation anxiety emerges as a toddler learns that he is an entity independent from his caregiver. He is challenged each time the caregiver leaves, but is then rewarded with a reunion that reconfirms that the caregiver is a stable figure. This teaches the toddler to have expectations in his life. With a death, the reunion never occurs, his sense of consistency is threatened, and regressive or destructive behaviour can ensue (Couldrick, 1991).

Preschoolers can recognize that a deceased person is in an altered state but cannot comprehend the irreversibility, universality, or non-functionality of death (Kenyon, 2001). Additionally, they misappropriate causality to the altered state they witness. Developmentally, preschoolers are ego-centric and are equipped with magical thinking. This leads some bereaved children to believe they caused the death through a bad thought (Corr, 1995). Guilt and confusion can then occur and manifest as anxiety.

School-age children understand death's finality; however, they struggle with its causality (Kenyon, 2001). School-age children are concrete thinkers and ask directed questions as they seek an explanation of causality. Despite their questions, however, they often externalize the causality of the death into a mythical creature like the 'boogey man'. Such externalization produces anxiety as there is no predicting from whom the 'boogey man' will next steal life. School-age children seek protection from the 'boogey man' by distinguishing themselves from the deceased. They avoid discussions about the deceased and actions that may merit comparison to the deceased so that the 'boogey man' does not liken them to the deceased and take their life away next. In some children, this avoidance can lead to guilt manifested as 'acting out' (Corr, 1995).

Pre-adolescents comprehend the causality and universality of death (Smith and Pennells, 1995). As they gain biological knowledge and witness the death of living things, they learn to accurately attribute causality. However, they are still concrete thinkers so they often intellectualize death. For example, a girl might state that it was acceptable that her mother died because there was no cure for her illness. She intellectually is able to do this without acknowledging her emotional reaction. Additionally, understanding the universality of death can cause pre-adolescents to become preoccupied with their own death. Psychosomaticization, guilt over fearing death, or a reaction formation can all form as they attempt to suppress their worries.

Adolescents have a sophisticated understanding of death, yet are at risk of complicated grief because of their developmental needs. Erik Erikson (1980) stated that adolescents must define their identify or risk role confusion. Adolescents define themselves by exploring their capabilities, social identity, and beliefs. They engage in risk-taking behaviours to identity their own limitations, and in doing so learn their capabilities. Adolescents also seek friends and social situations to refine their personality. They look to their peers for acceptance and feedback. Finally, healthy adolescents often voice strong opinions on topics such as religion as they refine their belief system. They are becoming abstract thinkers and therefore re-think all the rules and morals they have been taught (Noppe and Noppe, 2004). Through all of this, healthy adolescents develop and take ownership of their identity.

Bereavement interferes with these necessary developmental tasks. Adolescents who experience the loss of a loved one may not be willing to engage in risk-taking behaviours. As adolescents, moving from concrete to operational cognitive abilities, they realize the finality, universality, and non-functionality of death and therefore the limitations of life. As a result, bereaved adolescents may never engage in risk-taking behaviours, and therefore never fully learn their capabilities (Fox, 1991).

Bereaved adolescents also struggle with the fact that they are different from their peers. Adolescents seek the approval of his peers and resist actions that will make them unique; thus they often repress their grief. Bereavement makes their position in the group distinct, thereby increasing the risk of rejection. Moreover, their friends lose a sense of conversational commonality and may withdraw out of fear of 'saying the wrong thing'.

Finally, death challenges adolescents' sense of justice and therefore their overall belief structure. There is no justice when a young person dies or a good person has a difficult death. As stated above, adolescents are re-thinking what has been taught to them, including death. They are able to abstractly contemplate death and the morality surrounding it, but lack the judgment and experience that adults have (Noppe and Noppe, 2004). As a result, bereaved adolescents may develop an ill-defined belief structure or one rooted in fear.

All of these clashes between development and a grieving adolescent can take dramatic manifestations. Some grieving adolescents become angry from the injustice or their lack of control. Alternatively, the grieving adolescent may withdraw as his or her sense of being different overwhelms their need for support. Such actions can isolate the adolescent, which can lead to grief with complications as discussed below.

The Grieving Process

Grief with healthy responses

Just as children perceive death differently to adults, children's grief is also distinct. As reviewed above, they have an incomplete understanding of death that impacts their grieving. Additionally, they possess insufficient coping skills, so they have an increased need to rely on others. Finally, children, unlike adults, need to continue their psychosocial development and must learn how to do this alongside their grieving. All of these factors cause children to grieve differently to adults; yet this does not mean that they will have complicated grief. Rather, most children experience healthy, productive grief (Fox, 1991).

Children who have healthy responses to grief have adults that allow the grieving process to occur. They are permitted to ask questions and are given concise, developmentally appropriate answers. Children with healthy grief have adults that ask questions to determine the child's level of understanding and to correct misinformation. They are also permitted to continue having these conversations as they grow older and their needs and comprehension change (Cullinan, 1989).

In tandem with this, Silverman and Nickman (1996a), utilizing data analysis from the Child Bereavement Study*, posit that children with healthy grief are allowed to have a continuing bond with the loved one. They are permitted to speak about the loved one, to reflect upon the loved one's life, and to symbolically carry on a relationship with the deceased. This allows bereaved children to incorporate the death throughout their development in safe and healthy ways.

In order to accommodate the death, bereaved children must also have the appropriate coping skills. However, they will not fully possess these skills until their early twenties (Fox, 1991). A child with healthy grieving has access to an adult with healthy coping skills and is encouraged to utilize and model these skills. They are able to lean on an adult and the adult has enough emotional strength to support both themselves and the child. Furthermore, children with healthy grief witness that it is acceptable to talk about the death and the associated emotions and model that behaviour. Through this they learn healthy coping skills they can utilize throughout their development (Cullinan, 1989).

Unlike adults, bereaved children and adolescents need to continue their psycho-social and cognitive development alongside their grieving. Children that have healthy responses to grief learn to juggle these tasks with short bursts of grief work. Stroebe and Schut's dual process model (1999, 2001) posits that healthy grieving requires oscillation between emotional work and restorative tasks. That is, grieving children must vacillate between dealing with the emotions surrounding the loss and the rebuilding of their life without the loved one. Too much time spent on emotional grief work will cause a suspension of the child's social development. Conversely, constant focus on 'being happy' without addressing the difficult emotions of grief may result in maladaptive expressions of these emotions. Children with healthy grief are playful, confident children who experience intermittent bursts of grief.

In healthy grieving, these short bursts of grief work will continue to occur over time. Worden (1996) posits that at every developmental stage a bereaved child must accept the reality of the loss, experience the emotions associated with the

*The Child Bereavement Study was a study sponsored by Harvard Medical School's Department of Psychiatry at Massachusetts General Hospital. It was co-directed by Phyllis R. Silverman and J. William Worden and funded by the National Institute of Mental Health, the National Funeral Directors Association, and the Hillenbrand Foundation.

Table 6.1   Risk factors for grief with complications

- Sudden or violent death.
- Child is less than 10-years-old at time of bereavement.
- Pre-morbid mental health issues in child.
- Unstable or cold family environment before or after death.
- Frail or dysfunctional adult.

loss, adjust to an environment devoid of the loss, and to find ways to memorialize the deceased in their daily lives. Children that grieve with healthy responses repeatedly address the aforementioned needs of grief work while continuing their psychosocial and cognitive development.

Grief with complications

When any of the aforementioned aspects of healthy grieving do not occur, children may experience grief with complications. They do not explore the emotions or the implications of the loss, and therefore do not learn to accommodate the loss into their daily living. As a result, children with complicated grief may manifest maladaptive or regressive behaviours.

Dora Black (2002) has revealed pre-morbid characteristics and environments that are risk factors for future grief with complications. Though Table 6.1 appears geared towards children who have lost a parent, it can also be utilized when a child experiences the death of a friend or an adolescent who has experienced either.

The nature of the death can impact children's ability to grieve. If sudden, children have not had time to prepare emotionally (Dent, 2005). This can lead to magical thinking in younger children that the loved one or friend will return. In older children, a sudden death can inspire a refusal to accept the death. A violent death can also negatively affect bereaved children. It may cause children to spend so much emotional energy fearing for their own lives that they cannot put forth the energy to grieve and process their loss.

The age of a child is also a risk factor for complicated grief. Black (2002) states that children less than 10 years of age are at risk because of their inability to comprehend death and its impact. This misunderstanding will then affect each stage of their development. Worse, bereaved children are at risk of arresting at whatever developmental stage they were addressing when the death occurred. The younger the child, the earlier his or her development is stagnated, resulting in poorer comprehension of the death and the greater ineffectiveness of his coping skills (Fox, 1991).

Children with pre-morbid mental health issues such as anxiety are at increased risk for complicated grief. Like children experiencing the violent death of a loved one or friend, children with other emotional issues may lack the energy to explore properly the various emotions associated with the loss. Moreover, their coping skills are already negatively affected by their emotional issues and may make them insufficient to deal with the death. Finally, adults have an increased desire to protect emotionally fragile children and may try to shield the child from the death. This may impede the open dialogue needed for healthy grief, thereby placing these children at risk of grief with complications.

Table 6.2   Red flag behaviours (adapted from Worden, 1996)

1. Not able to talk or hear about the deceased.
2. Anger accompanied by destruction.
3. Persisting anxieties/phobic behaviours.
4. Develops accident proneness.
5. Exaggerated attachment to surviving parent (over the years).
6. Stealing or other illegal behaviours.
7. Becomes a compulsive caregiver or extremely self-reliant.
8. Continues to blame self for the loss.
9. Child who fears revenge around the dead person.
10. Promiscuity that wasn't present prior to the death.
11. Child who wants to join a deceased parent through suicide (preoccupation through death).
12. Child develops an eating disorder.
13. Dramatic academic reversal.
14. Shows serious social withdrawal (when used to be social).

When children experience grief with complications, they often lack the language or the self-awareness to realize that they are having difficulties. Similarly, the parents may not recognize that their child is struggling with the loss. As a result, neither the parent nor the child seeks help. However, research has revealed 'red flag' behaviours (Table 6.2) that can be recognized as a cry for help. Of note, these behaviours are 'red flags' when they are present and continue a year after a death occurs. If any of the flags are present, an intervention by a counsellor or other professional seeking to help the child must occur.

Intervention Models

Resiliency

Resiliency is a concept that emerged in the 1990s from research that investigated childhood risk factors that led to negative adult behaviours. These studies showed evidence that identified risk factors such as violence or poverty created a negative cycle for future generations. However, this research also revealed that some children become healthy adults despite experiencing these factors. After extensive study of the environments and temperament of these children, the concept that emerged became known as resiliency.

Resilience has been discussed by Lifton as the the human capacity of all individuals to transform and change, no matter what their risks; it is an innate self-righting mechanism. That is, resilient children possess a set of skills that allow them to face adversity and succeed. Such skills include social competence, problem-solving skills, autonomy, and a sense of purpose and future (Benard, 1991).

Resilient children have social competence. They have the ability to engage others and derive support as needed. They laugh at themselves, thereby placing others at ease and allowing closer relationships. Children with resiliency are also more socially adaptable and flexible. They are able to blend into a group with ease and are able to change as needed to be part of that group. These skills give resilient children supportive networks in times of need (Bernard, 1991).

Children with resiliency are good problem-solvers. Like their social skills, resilient children's cognitive skills are flexible and they too 'think outside the box' when analyzing a situation. They are receptive to new ideas and are willing to test them. Moreover, they are able to think abstractly, which heightens their ability to generate new ideas. Thus, resilient children can see beyond their current situation and devise effective, innovative plans (Benard, 1991).

Resilient children are also autonomous. They have a strong sense of self and believe they can control their reality. For example, when placed in a dysfunctional environment, they do not despair or feel helpless. Rather, they recognize opportunities for improvement and act upon them (Benard, 1991).

Finally, resilient children have a strong sense of purpose and future. In conjunction with their sense of autonomy, resilient children believe they are living a meaningful life with a promising future. They maintain a focus on their potential regardless of their current situation and utilize all of their aforementioned skills to make a better future (Benard, 1991).

Arenas for intervention: the Bronfenbrenner model

There is the adage that it takes a village to raise a child. Similarly, it can be stated that it takes a community to heal a bereaved child. This sentiment is embodied by school counsellors, ministers, and neighbors who rally around bereaved children in their time of need. Children who best maximize this support are those with the resiliency skills to maximize the support provided by the community. However, if the child lacks resiliency, then the community should create a bereavement environment that allows the acquisition of resiliency skills to occur concomitantly with the tasks of grieving in order to minimize the complications of grief.

When designing these environments, a helpful model to utilize is the Bronfenbrenner's ecological systems theory (1979). His model places the child in the center of a multitude of environments that interact not only with the child but also with each other. The theory also provides a language and a visual schema when describing these environments and how they relate to the child.

Specifically, the ecological systems theory is composed of five systems. The one closest to the individual is the microsystem. This system is the environment in which a child lives, such as the home or school. The child is not a passive actor in these environments; rather, he or she is an active player who directly impacts the nature of these environments (Bronfenbrenner, 1979).

The next system is the mesosystem, which is the relation between the various microsystems in a child's life. The child's actions in the microsystem impact each of his mesosystems. For example, how a child behaves in school impacts on how his/her home life interacts with the school environment (Bronfenbrenner, 1979).

After the mesosystems are the exosystems. In these systems, the child does not have an active role in these environments but is nonetheless impacted by their presence. An example is the parent's workplace. Here, decisions and events impact on a parent's stress level and his/her ability to be emotionally and physically present in their child's life (Bronfenbrenner, 1979).

The fourth level of systems is the macrosystem, which represents the attitudes and ideologies of the culture in which the child lives. For example, every child experiences a political macrosystem, and the laws of this macrosystem influence his/her definition of justice (Bronfenbrenner, 1979).

The final system in the Bronfenbrenner model is the chronosystem. This is the system that represents the lasting effect of significant events that occur in a child's microsystem, macrosystem, or exosystem over time. For example, 9/11 has had a lasting impact on childrens' sense of security and how they will view others as they mature. On a smaller scale, a death in the family has not only an immediate affect, but also a long-term impact on a child's microsystem, mesosystem, and exosystem (Bronfenbrenner, 1979).

There is a constant interplay between all of the systems. An event in one system affects every other system, and therefore one must think of all systems when interacting with a child. Specifically, a death in a child's life has an impact in each system at the time of the death and throughout his development. To maximally help a child grieve and be resilient, therefore, all systems must be addressed and then readdressed as time progresses.

Bonnie Benard (1991) stresses three touch points when designing environments that foster resiliency. These are to provide care and support for the child, set high expectations for him or her, and elicit his or her participation. Such tasks can be woven into the ecology systems model to create a workable system that fosters resiliency. When dealing with grieving children, this information plus the knowledge of their developmental capabilities can be combined to design effective interventions.

Family interventions

A caring and supportive family environment is a fundamental building block of resiliency. Erik Erikson's first stage of his psychosocial developmental theory is 'trust versus mistrust' (1980). To complete the first stage successfully, infants must learn to trust. Such trust comes from a loved one that provides constancy, and therefore predictability. Armed with trust, resilient children will have the ability to depend on others in times of need.

Families that raise resilient children impose high expectations. They have an authoritative parenting style that provides clear rules and consequences. Such structure gives predictability, which fosters children's belief in the future. High expectations also strengthen their sense of empowerment. Someone is focused on their actions, thereby teaching resilient children that their actions impact on those around them (Benard, 1991).

Similarly, families that foster resiliency encourage participation. Resilient children are expected to perform household chores. When they fail to do the tasks they are reprimanded and thereby taught that their input is necessary for their family environment to function properly. Families that foster resiliency also encourage participation by giving children a voice in family decision-making. Through this, families grant a sense of control and encourage problem-solving skills (Benard, 1991).

When a child loses a loved one, counsellors and others seeking to help must assess the strengths and needs of the family microsystem. From there, interventions can be devised. Table 6.3 outlines a needs assessment to be utilized when initially interviewing a family.

Table 6.3   A needs assessment of the family microsystem

1. What are the coping skills of the parent?
2. What is the parenting style of the parent?
3. Is the parent able to express and demonstrate emotions?
4. Does the parent accurately understand the child's comprehension of the death?
5. Is the parent willing to educate the child about death and its associated emotions?
6. Does the parent know how to find resources to help educate and/or support the bereaved child?
7. What are the states of the parent's other microsystems, mesosystems, exosystems and macrosystems? What support does the parent have, and where is extra support needed?
8. What is the state of the parent's chronosystem? What aspects of it will positively and negatively impact on the parent's grieving process and his or her ability to help their child grieve?
9. What resiliency skills does the child currently possess, and how can they be utilized?
10. What resiliency skills are lacking, and how can they be fostered in this child?
11. Does the child have risk factors for grief with complications?
12. What is the state of the child's other microsystems, mesosystems and macrosystems? What support does the child have, and where is extra support needed?
13. What is the state of the child's chronosystem? What aspects of it will positively and negatively impact on his or her grieving process?

After completing this assessment, an appropriate intervention can then be designed and implemented. First, however, it needs to be determined if an intervention is needed. If the parent has adequate coping skills, is willing to discuss the death and its emotions, has the knowledge to find help as needed, and the child is resilient, no intervention may be needed.

Conversely, if deficiencies in the parent or the environment exist or the child possesses risk factors as outlined by Table 6.1 or 'red flags' as listed in Table 6.2 are present, then an intervention may be necessary. Though each intervention must be tailored to the needs of an individual child and family, there are several general aspects that can be incorporated. One point is that the parent's primary role is to support and educate the child. Often, this requires an intervention to augment the parent's coping skills. Similarly, an intervention by a grief counsellor, teacher, or doctor often needs to involve teaching the parent the resources that exist to educate the child. For example, bibliotherapy is an excellent tool for parents to use with children in order to both assess the child's death comprehension and to teach the child at a developmentally appropriate level.

Another general aspect that should be included in an intervention is the assertion of the parent as an authoritative figure. The parent's need to protect the child from sadness cannot replace the parent's primary role as the disciplinarian. The parent needs to understand that placing boundaries on the child will serve as a stabilizing, predictable force that can counteract the sense of insecurity that surrounds a death. With this, children will have the positive behaviours needed for grief work and play.

A final overarching theme of intervention must include an evaluation of the other microsystems, mesosytems, macrosystems, exosystems and chronosystems that are affecting the parent and the child. Both the strengths and weaknesses need to be assessed in order to augment the strengths and diminish the weaknesses present in each of these systems. An example is the potential of a school system to intervene when a parent cannot provide the necessary support because of his own grief work.

School interventions

School microsystems greatly impact on the social and emotional development of children. In an ideal setting, they complement a functional home microsystem. However, they can compensate for an inadequate family environment when necessary to create or aid resilient children by providing a caring and supportive environment, setting high expectations, and by encouraging participation (Benard, 1991).

Functional school microsystems provide caring and supportive figures. Resilient children will seek these figures and utilize them in times of need. However, a school can also identify at-risk youth and provide them with a stable, caring figure to encourage trust, and therefore resiliency (Benard, 1991).

School microsystems that foster resiliency have high expectations for its students. They set high academic standards and have clear rules. Moreover, schools that foster resiliency give the students the opportunities and skills to be successful. As a result, these schools have greater academic success and students with greater resiliency (Benard, 1991).

Finally, schools that foster resiliency encourage youth participation and involvement. They assign roles within the school to give every child a sense of purpose. Successful schools also give students a voice. The Perry Preschool Project revealed that 'inner city preschoolers given the opportunity to make decisions in their school environment had up to 50% less drug use, delinquency, teen pregnancy, and school failure at age nineteen' (Benard, 1991: 15). When given a voice, students are given autonomy, which fosters a sense of purpose and self-control to aid resiliency.

A school's commitment to building resilient children must be maintained in times of crisis. When a child experiences a death, the school should have an action plan that supports or enhances resiliency while encouraging healthy expressions of grief. To ensure this, Rowling (2003) states that a school needs to have a proactive approach to bereavement interventions. A school's health education curriculum should include discussions about death and bereavement so that the teachers and students develop an open dialogue prior to a child experiencing a loss. This then allows for a more natural conversation between staff and students following a death. Additionally, a school should develop a bereavement action plan prior to a death. Adults should be pre-selected and educated on grief and resiliency so that they are emotionally and cognitively prepared. They should learn how to discuss bereavement in developmentally appropriate terms and practice talking about death before one occurs, again to facilitate better interventions.

After the initial bereavement, a school can continue to impact a child's grief work. Schools can play a significant restorative role (Rowling, 2005). By continuing old rituals such as the morning announcements, a sense of familiarity can be provided to a bereaved child. Additionally, a school can create new and meaningful traditions that allow a child to have continuing bonds with the one he or she lost. For example, the school may choose to have a yearly tree-planting ceremony that commemorates the loved ones that have died. A school can also strengthen the mesosystem that resides between the child's school and family environment by increasing the number of parent–teacher conferences or by daily communications via email or paper notes. Finally, a school can continue to provide support by educating all adults who will have an interaction with the child throughout his school years about the death, in how to assess for risk factors or 'red flag behaviours', and how to encourage open communication that allows the developing child to re-assess the death as he or she matures.

Community interventions

The community is a macrosystem that defines the spirit of its microsystems. As with the various microsystems reviewed above, a community can impact on a child's resiliency by its level of support, its expectations for each citizen, and by providing opportunities. Through its governing body, a community chooses the level of financial and political support it will provide children's organizations, thereby impacting the quality role support structures that exist for its children. Through its cultural norms and laws, a community also defines expectations for its members. Finally, communities delegate opportunities for youth participation, thereby signaling how it values the voice and actions of its youth. Through all of this, communities determine their role in fostering resiliency within children.

When there is a grieving child, a community continues to have a crucial role. It can provide financial support and human resources for the microsystems that surround a grieving child. It can also create microsystems for grieving children to ensure that they experience healthy grief and that their skills of resiliency are optimized. Examples of such microsystems are Winston's Wish and Camp Lost and Found.

Winston's Wish

Winston's Wish is a 'community based child bereavement service' based in Gloucestershire, England that strives to support grieving children through prevention (Stokes, 2004: 15–16). They recognize that bereaved children are at risk if they lack the resiliency tools and the adequate social support to weather their grief throughout their development. Through its myriad of services, Winston's Wish seeks to support and educate bereaved children and their families who are at risk to prevent grief with complications.

As discussed in her book, *Then, Now, and Always* (Stokes, 2004), Winston's Wish offers open services to all the bereaved youth of Gloucestershire. Through a phone survey that everyone who contacts Winston's Wish undergoes, a needs assessment is generated. Often, advice is offered without further intervention by Winston's Wish because there are no 'red flags' during the interview. In these cases, Winston's Wish does not offer further services but assures future support as needed. For those children assessed to be at-risk, however, Winston's Wish then determines what level of service intervention is required. Among the various support services, there are assessments in the home, individual sessions, a residential weekend, yearly social events, email and web-based services, a newsletter, and a school-based program that empowers school nurses. In all of these venues, Winston's Wish has five clinical objectives (Stokes, 2004), shown in Table 6.4.

Table 6.4   Primary clinical objectives of Winston's Wish (Stokes, 2004: 33)

- Support, information, and education about death.
- Understanding and expressing grief.
- Remembering the person that has died.
- Communication within the family.
- Meeting others with similar experiences.

With these goals and interventions, Winston's Wish embodies the ideas discussed in grief with healthy responses, including the sense of continuing to
remember those who are gone, normalizing the experience, and continuing the
bond with the loved one. Similarly, Winston's Wish represents a functional model
of intervention to prevent grief with complications. It is a microsystem supported
by the child's macrosystem that utilizes resiliency and a working knowledge of
the child's developmental needs to create a brief intervention with a lasting
impact (Stokes, 2004).

Camp Lost and Found

In Canton, Ohio, The Grief Support and Education Center had similar goals when
it designed Camp Lost and Found. Camp Lost and Found was a day camp for
children and adolescents who had lost a loved one. Its mission was to create a
sense of normalcy for bereaved children while they learned to experience grief
safely and gain the necessary resiliency tools to continue their grief work throughout their development. The goals of the camp (Table 6.5) all reflected its mission
statement.

Table 6.5   Goals of Camp Lost and Found

- Children finding others like themselves.
- Demystifying death and grief.
- Teaching how to experience and control emotions associated with grief.
- Teaching that it is ok to still have fun.
- Teaching how to grieve and still have fun.
- Teaching and utilizing the skills of resiliency.
- Giving children a sense of empowerment and control so they can utilize their skills of resiliency
  while grieving and having fun.

Camp Lost and Found was comprised of two programs, one for school-age
children and one for adolescents. Each camp was five days in duration and
occurred at a local college where the participants had access to both the class-
rooms and the outdoors. The staff consisted of a grief director who oversaw the
camp's curriculum, licensed counsellors, art and music therapists who enacted the
curriculum, and a camp director who focused on providing fun activities to balance the hard work the children did with the counsellors and therapists. Finally,
there were guest speakers such as a priest and a pediatrician who came to the
camp and a funeral director whom the children visited on site.

The camp's curriculum was designed as a journey through grief. Each day had a theme and each subsequent day built on the realizations and skills acquired the previous day. There was a daily schedule comprising activities that reflected the day's theme. Various activities were offered so that every child found a venue to express and experience his grief. These tasks were then off-set by scheduled fun times to re-charge the children and to give the message that it is necessary to laugh and to grieve in tandem (Stroebe and Schut, 1999, 2001). The goal of the camp was for children to experience grief safely while learning the resiliency skills and coping mechanisms to grieve successfully throughout the remainder of their development.

Camp Lost and Found's 5-day program

Day 1: Understanding what happened and why
The first day focused on introductions and the creations of narratives. The children and adolescents were given activities that created a safe environment for sharing similarities of their stories.

Objectives

1. Introducing who I am as a person.
2. Narrating my story.
3. Sharing my story.
4. Introducing the balance between grief work and play.

Interventions

1. The children created nametags or T-shirts that stated 'Who I am'. There were no rules associated with this activity; rather, the campers were encouraged to interpret the challenge in their own way. The art therapist and counsellors encouraged discussion throughout that activity to begin opening the lines of communication. The campers then introduced themselves and their nametag or T-shirt to the group at large. Again, the counsellors and therapists encouraged dialogue as a signal that the camp was a safe place to talk about their loved ones and their death.
2. The campers spent a good portion of the first day realizing and voicing their story. The idea of a personal narrative was introduced through a bibliotherapy session (see Appendix). Campers then began working on their own personal narrative through the creation of a binder that would hold all of their creations and therefore their story as the week progressed. They also created a picture that told their story of loss.
3. After making their individual pictures, the children came together as a group and told their story of loss by explaining the picture they had drawn. They then weaved their individual pictures together with yarn to make a group quilt to underscore the idea that though the stories were different, they shared a similar experience that united them.
4. The first day was particularly difficult, as many kids had never verbalized their story. In anticipation of this, frequent breaks and a challenge activity were scheduled into the day. The frequent breaks allowed children to play and re-energize. It also showed them that it is ok to have fun amidst their grief work. The challenge activity was an important aspect, for when conquered, it affirmed a sense of control and autonomy. The challenge activity showed them that they can face a challenge such as grieving and come out successful and in control.

Day 2: Identification of feelings in a healthy way

As implied, day 2 focused on the myriad of emotions associated with the death of a loved one. Adults often do not acknowledge the breadth of emotions experienced by bereaved children, for they either do not realize that children can experience them or they do not wish children to be experiencing difficult emotions. However, children do have these emotions, and in order to perpetuate healthy grief and development they need to recognize these feelings and develop skills of coping with them throughout their development.

Objectives

1. Identifying and understanding feelings.
2. Recognizing stress as a consequence of emotions.
3. Recognizing anger.
4. Remembering the emotion of fun.

Interventions

1. The second day started with children identifying their feelings and the creation of a feelings chart as described by Figure 5.1. Emphasis is placed on the highs and lows associated with various feelings and the goal of preserving the emotions but diminishing their intensity. Art therapy involved the creation of life-sized paper dolls of the children labeled with the various parts of their body that felt emotions. They then discussed these dolls in front of the group. Small group activities echoed this with a discussion of mixed-up emotions. Finally, music therapy and bibliotherapy sessions (see Appendix) concentrated on the normalcy of emotions and how to have them in your life without them controlling your life.
2. During the discussions of emotions, stress was discussed as a consequence of the highs and lows associated with emotions. During a small group activity, healthy demonstrations and resolutions of stress were discussed such as writing, singing, and exercising. One active demonstration involved the use of clay as a vehicle of expression.
3. Children are often told to not be angry. However, it is a natural and common emotion. It is also an intense emotion that can lead to stress when ignored or mishandled. Campers began exploring concepts of anger and its management through a purchased board game named 'The Angry Monster Machine' (Childswork/ Childsplay, 1992). By using the game, the difficult emotion of being angry at the deceased was gently introduced.
4. Happiness should remain amongst a grieving child's emotional range. Thus, the camp continued to focus on joy by providing structured play sessions. Additionally, the day's challenge activity was a scavenger hunt that allowed children to forget their work and discover happiness as they sought the hidden treasure.

Day 3: Coping and identification of harder emotions

This day's theme focused on the darker feelings of grief – stress and anger. These emotions play an integral role in a bereaved child's life and therefore need to be acknowledged and accepted. Moreover, a child must learn the correct coping tools so that he can learn how to live effectively with these emotions. Thus, day 3 was devoted to stress and anger. Activities and discussions were designed to allow the campers to acknowledge and cope with these negative emotions.

Objectives

1. Dealing with anger.
2. Stress management.
3. Learning relaxation techniques.

Interventions

1. The day started with a dialogue between the children and a priest. He acknowledged that he had gotten upset by his God before; by doing so, he permitted the children to admit similar feelings toward their God, their loved ones, and even the one who died. This candid discussion allowed children to voice their ambivalence and anger in an arena where such emotions are not typically allowed. The priest reassured the children that despite having those emotions, they were good people and that no one was upset with them. More importantly, the priest stressed that these feelings exist but cannot be allowed to overwhelm the daily activities of living. He stressed that good people experience anger but redirect it into meaningful and productive ways.
2. Several small and large group activities focused on stress during day 3. During art therapy, the campers' most stressful days were discussed. Then, artworks of a safe haven during times of stress were drawn and discussed with the group. Small group leaders also taught stress management and relaxation techniques. The large group challenge activity was impromptu skits. Here the children were placed in a stressful situation, but it was enveloped in a spirit of fun. This challenge activity reinforced a sense of mastery over stress and encouraged their resiliency skills.

Day 4: Need to say goodbye in meaningful and personal ways

Bereaved children are often shielded from the death and funeral of a loved one. The grieving adult is often overwhelmed with his or her own emotions and wants to shield their child by keeping him or her away from the hospital or funeral. However, as previously stated in this chapter, many children are concrete thinkers with a limited ability to comprehend death. Therefore, many benefit by tangible evidence such as a funeral. Funerals can also reveal how to have a meaningful goodbye. Day 4 of the camp focused on demystifying the funeral process and learning how to say goodbye in meaningful ways.

Objectives

1. Understanding a funeral.
2. Creating a meaningful goodbye.
3. Reassurance that it is ok to cry and then laugh while dealing with difficult tasks like grief.

Interventions

1. Day 4 began with a field trip to a funeral home. Children were encouraged to bring a safe object such as a stuffed animal and/or a parent. When the children arrived at

the funeral home, they were introduced to the funeral director and then taken on a tour. Children learned how coffins are chosen, how someone fixes their loved one's hair, make-up, and clothes, and what happens after a funeral ceremony. Children were encouraged to ask questions and the funeral director answered in developmentally appropriate terms. Afterwards, the children discussed their feelings about going to the funeral home. Of note, the only families with regrets were those that chose not to attend.

2. After the funeral, the children explored and designed meaningful ways to say goodbye. Bibliotherapy focused on the different ways cultures say goodbye to the deceased through the book *Ethnic, Cultural, and Religious Observances at the Time of Death and Dying* (Ryan, 1986). Individuality and personal meaning were stressed throughout the activity. During art therapy, the children were then asked to design, draw, and discuss their own personal funeral ritual.

3. Day 4 was emotional and risked leaving the children vulnerable and overwhelmed. The challenge activity, an obstacle course, was purposely selected to help the children regain a sense of control and accomplishment. Like other days, the goal was to highlight and strengthen the resiliency skills that the participants could use in their daily lives.

Day 5: Remember always and go on living

The difficulty of saying goodbye during day 4 was complemented by day 5's theme – always remembering. Adopting Silverman and Nickman's concepts (1996b) that healthy grief is to accommodate the loss in meaningful ways, the goal of day 5 was to discover ways to go on remembering their loved ones on a daily basis.

Objectives

1. Remembering through objects.
2. Learning to be an individual within the group.
3. Going forth loving and living.

Interventions

1. The children brought in objects to display and discuss their loved ones with the group. The goal was to show the children how to continue having a meaningful relationship with the loved one. The 'show and tell' gave the campers a safe place to explore this relationship and the words to begin a lifelong conversation about and with the deceased. Parents were also present to witness and learn the power of a continued relationship with the loved one. Similarly, the last art project was sidewalk art. Given only chalk and no instructions, the children were encouraged to draw. Out of this came many murals of remembrance and continued relationships.

2. As the week came to an end, the children had come to identify themselves as members of a unique group and had gained strength from it. With the ending of the camp, the campers now needed to learn how to internalize the spirit of the group and go back to their lives. This was a risky endeavor as the separation could easily echo that surrounding the campers' losses. One activity to initiate this transition was the disassembly of the group quilt. The staff emphasized to the campers that they were not simply taking home their own stories; rather, they took a piece of the group

story home with them. Counsellors also stressed the group's continuity in the future by relaying the anticipated monthly meetings. Through these activities, the camp taught the children how to internalize the group and to go forth living.

3. Armed with coping and resiliency skills and a sense of belonging, the children were encouraged to go forth loving and living. A graduation ceremony complete with cake and certificates gave credence to all that the children had accomplished during the camp and all they were capable of handling in the future. Similarly, the challenge activity of the day was the 'Goofy Olympics', where the children celebrated their ability to laugh and have fun. The camp then ended with a balloon celebration. The children released a balloon with an attached message to their loved ones. Just as the day celebrated the continuation of the group, so too it celebrated the continued relationship with the deceased.

Camp Lost and Found follow-up

Though the camp ended, the relationships formed during the week did not. The Grief Support and Education Center held monthly meetings for each of the campers and their families. These meetings had four major focuses:

1. To re-affirm the identity of the group.
2. To provide a safe haven for the children and their families.
3. To provide further education and encouragement to go on living amidst their bereavement.
4. To assess the 'red flag' behaviour by its participants.

The meetings were held at restaurants to encourage a sense of fun and sociality. Similarly, families were encouraged to make additional play dates amongst themselves to re-enforce the identity of the group and the sense of a safe haven. During the meetings, activities were designed to reinforce resiliency and other coping skills. Finally, the grief director and counsellors were present to assess each participant's mood and state. If concerns arose, the participant was encouraged to have individual counselling sessions.

Summary

Through Camp Lost and Found and its follow-up, the children learned how to grieve and go on living. The program, like Winston's Wish, utilized a working knowledge of how children comprehend death and their unique challenges when grieving to create an age-appropriate microsystem that taught the tools for self-empowerment, resiliency, and effective coping skills. Through this, Camp Lost and Found fostered resilient children that have the capability to face the difficult emotions of grief while also living rewarding, full lives. A living example of this is Frank:

Frank was 11 when he participated in Camp Lost and Found. His father had been diagnosed with an incurable illness, but withheld the information from his children. He also chose not to undergo treatment; instead he received palliative care. After his father's death, Frank's mother sought support from The Center for Grief Counselling and Education. She was concerned that his father's reticence during his illness had left Frank with many unanswered questions and emotions. Frank was encouraged to participate in Camp Lost and Found.

At the beginning of the camp, Frank was shy and somewhat withdrawn. However, as the week progressed, he became a natural leader of the group. He was vocal in his emotions and an active participant in the sharing of stories. After the camp was over, he continued to attend monthly meetings. In the years that followed, he also became involved in his high-school's task force for grief intervention and was actively involved in the consolation of classmates who lost a loved one. He graduated high school in the spring of 2006 as the lead scorer of the state runner-up soccer team and is currently attending college on a full-ride athletic scholarship. More importantly, his mother describes him as a self-assured, caring person who has learned how to balance the loss of his father with enjoying life.

Note: Camp Lost and Found (1998–2000) was a path of the center's 'Seven-week support group for children' (1986–2000). Although some funding was provided for Camp Lost and Found by a charitable foundation, the center itself was never funded and had to close May 2000. As a result, the camp could not continue. Geraldine Humphrey PhD was the director and counsellor for 15 years. The majority of the services offered were without charge.

7 Anticipatory Grief

Anticipatory grief is a term that is most often associated with a terminal illness, with a prognosis of impending death within a stated time period. However, anticipatory grief can refer to a process for any loss that is expected in the future. Many illnesses that are not terminal have characteristics of significant change for the individuals and others involved with them. Heart disease, arthritis, and cancer are only a few of the medical conditions that alter lifestyles and have significant personal losses involved. Geographical moves, job changes, and retirement are also significant losses that are not often recognized as such, but require anticipatory work. The list is extensive, and as mentioned in Chapter 1, losses occur from the time one is born until one dies. Many of these losses could be more satisfactorily resolved if time was spent understanding what has already changed and anticipating what is going to be lost, what the potential effects of this loss are, and what one might do to prepare for this event. Anticipatory grief does not mean that one can avoid the pain of grief after a loss; it means that the defenses can somehow be better prepared to cope with the full bereavement experience. Without an awareness of a future loss or preparation for it, individuals are more likely to feel as if they have been assaulted and experience being out of control.

Definitions and Conceptions

Rando (1986) discussed the fact that there are no precise and consistent definitions of this type of grief. Acknowledging this, she first outlined what it is not. One error is to assume that because a person is terminally ill, anticipatory grief is present. Many patients and families in hospice programs continue to deny the impending death or to hope that a recovery might yet be possible. Another is that anticipatory grief is post-death grief begun earlier, or that there is a fixed volume of grief to be experienced and that anticipatory grief will reduce the amount necessary to be experienced after the loss. Findings from Glick et al. (1974) have validated that grief after an unanticipated loss differs in form and duration from one that is anticipated. The reason for this is that a loss that is unexpected has the potential to overwhelm the individual's adaptive capacities to accommodate, thus affecting abilities to function and recover. With sudden loss, the bereaved are often left on their own to understand what has happened to them. Individuals express more anxiety and lack of personal control when they have had no time to prepare. Many express being longer in a state of shock, and remember the need to retell the event several times in order to reconstruct it and attempt to make some sense of it. Lastly, there are more expressions of preventability and feelings of guilt, i.e., the belief that one could have done something to prevent it if he or she had only known about it. A common reaction by family members after a death following a heart attack is that they could have called an ambulance and saved the person if only they had been there at the right time.

With anticipatory grief, the time factor involved is an important variable. Lack of time to prepare adequately or too much time to anticipate can be non-productive also. Rando's (1993b) study with parents whose children died of cancer showed that less than six months did not allow enough time to prepare, and longer than 18 months resulted in an experience that compromised and depleted the parents' abilities to cope with the illness and the demands of being caretakers.

Rando acknowledged the difficulties in defining anticipatory grief. One reason for this difficulty is that previous researchers have viewed this concept as being unitary and evolving in a linear fashion. She views it in a multidimensional way and conceives the processes across two perspectives, three time foci, and three classes of influencing variables. The various processes of anticipatory grief are defined as:

> ... the phenomenon encompassing the processes of mourning, coping, interaction, planning, and psychosocial reorganization that are stimulated and begun in part in response to the awareness of the impending loss of a loved one and the recognition of associated losses in the past, present, and future. It is seldom explicitly recognized, but the truly therapeutic experience of anticipatory grief mandates a delicate balance among the mutually conflicting demands of simultaneously holding onto, letting go of, and drawing closer to the dying patient. (Rando, 1986: 24)

The two perspectives are the dying patient and the family or those emotionally close to the dying patient. For each, the experience will be somewhat different.

The three time foci that Rando (1986) uses demonstrate that the grief is not just for a future event; rather, it includes part of the past which has had to have been let go of, and the present which involves ongoing changes to grieve. Lastly, the influencing variables on the experience involve psychological, emotional, and physiological components.

For those who are emotionally involved with a dying person, the process is demanding, with conflicting pulls. Rando (1986) described this conflict as simultaneously having to come to terms with the prognosis both cognitively and affectively; staying involved with the dying person on a daily basis; and addressing family reorganization issues, which requires adaptation to new roles and responsibilities. Many who have difficulty managing these processes and coping with the time foci and interrelated variables attempt to disengage emotionally from the dying person while he or she is still alive. This premature emotional disengagement has negative effects both on the patient and after the death on the bereaved, who must come to terms with guilt and other difficult emotions.

Issues Related to Anticipated Losses Other than Impending Death

As discussed in the beginning of this chapter, there are many other types of losses that necessitate a process of anticipation and sadness for some part of life that is changing and for a future that might be less meaningful or rich because of loss and change. Gestalt theory addresses this need to pay attention to that which is changing and to grieve it before the new can be embraced. Grief is one of the primary emotions within Gestalt theory, as it is viewed as 'the emotion necessary to the process of destructuring within the gestalt cycle. Grief is necessary to living, as it is the emotional reaction to the losses we know during times of change' (Clark, 1985: 50).

Consider the example of retirement. Most people plan when they will retire; however, often little is done in preparation, and little is done to anticipate this event as a major loss of roles and identity in their lives. Often these individuals never seek counselling, but those who do reflect unresolved issues, psychosomatic and psychiatric symptoms, and an inability to reinvest in meaningful living.

Coping with illness, especially that which is chronic or life-threatening, has several aspects of loss to address, including one's eventual mortality. Even before a medical diagnosis is made, individuals have experienced some unwanted changes in their lives. After the diagnosis is made, the prognosis often includes physical, mental, and other lifestyle changes that need to be anticipated and prepared for. For those who have heart disease, the underlying grief is the fact that the heart is no longer reliable. When the heart can no longer be depended upon to perform its function, it is a loss experience that needs to be grieved in order to reinvest in meaningful living. This includes grieving for the loss of functioning, but also includes anticipatory grief for necessary changes that accompany heart disease. However, what often happens is a stubbornness and a denial by holding fast to former lifestyles, with a determination to prove that nothing has changed. Anticipatory grief would serve to address normal emotions that need validation and expression, and to help plan for future changes, with individuals participating in decision-making for alternative choices. As with other losses, life will never be the same again, and how one viewed him or herself needs to be changed. This cannot occur in a linear manner. As with other issues that necessitate a bereavement experience, coping with heart disease is a cyclical process that often involves setbacks.

Models of Intervention

Hospice programs

Hospice programs are among the most widely known approaches to caring for dying patients and those who will be involved with them during their last days. Dr Cicely Saunders, a British physician, began the modern hospice movement when she opened St Christopher's Hospice near London in 1967. The first hospice in the United States began in 1974 in New Haven, Connecticut. In the United States individuals are eligible for hospice care when a prognosis has been determined that cure is no longer viable, and that there are six months or less to live. Hospice care is palliative, with pain control as a primary goal of medical intervention. In addition to the medical professionals, a hospice program usually includes a team of mental health caregivers: counsellors, social workers, clergy, and volunteers for respite care. Most hospice care programs in the United States take place within the home environment of the patient and family. At least one person must assume the responsibility of being the primary caretaker. Some programs also have physical facilities for the patient and family members. Hospice programs vary, and often the services offered depend upon local resources, funding and reimbursement from third parties. Their philosophy is rooted in the belief that a person is important until he or she dies, and that there is still life to be lived in a quality manner. In its ideal form, the intention is for the patient to be given voice in his or her treatment within the home environment. Buchwald (2006), referring to his own hospice experience, wrote that it provided him with the opportunity to die with dignity. The goal of his final writings was to make 'hospice' a household word, as he believed that it remained a mystery to most people. His book *Too Soon to Say Goodbye* stands as his personal testimony to the benefits of hospice care.

Corr (1991) proposed four primary dimensions of personhood: physical, psychological, social, and spiritual. The physical dimensions of hospice care are usually addressed by the medical staff, with the other helping professions (e.g., clergy, counsellors, and social workers) intervening for the last three. Discussing the psychological tasks, Corr emphasized the importance of maximizing the psychological security, autonomy and richness of living one's life and being in control as much as possible. Among the social tasks is the need to sustain and enhance the interpersonal attachments which are significant to the dying person. Many do not understand that there are a number of social implications of dying. The dying person has had a life membership in his or her social environment; thus dying should not take place in isolation. Society often does not recognize the dying person. Often their names are dropped from conversations before they die. They have lost their past roles in that society; thus society does not know what to do with them in this final process of living. Professionals may need to be advocates to facilitate a process of integration between the dying person and his or her social environment.

Spiritually, it is important to identify, develop, or reaffirm sources of spiritual energy, and in doing so foster hope for some type of continued (though compromised) meaning in this life, and some type of existence after physical life has ended. Corr's (1991) approach is to assess a patient and those involved, determine areas of task work (based on the four dimensions of personhood), and design interventions from the assessment. His model emphasizes the need for professional caregivers of every discipline to enhance their understanding of their patients as unique individuals, to foster empowerment on the part of the patients, to emphasize participation (i.e., shared aspects of dying that require interpersonal communication and interactions with others), and to guide helping (i.e., professionals should not dictate treatment plans).

Whatever intervention model is used, it must address the patients and those involved, and understand ways of effectively supporting and intervening. Many professionals, especially the medically oriented ones, direct attention towards physical cures. Using the perspectives (Chapter 1 and 2) allows for more in-depth assessment, resulting in more effective treatment plans. Those with a terminal illness can no longer hope for a cure; however, they have expectations, wishes, and fears. Table 7.1 illustrates many of these that have been expressed over time by those who are dying.

Palliative care programs

Since the first edition, palliative care programs have emerged and extended services for a population that do not meet the criteria for hospice services. These programs were intended to medically treat and offer bereavement services to those who have illnesses (not only cancer) that are chronic and incurable. To date, the goal to offer care for all incurable illnesses has not been fully realized and services are still

Table 7.1   Dying patients

Expectations and wishes of a dying person

1. To be treated as a living human being (body, mind, and spirit) until death.
2. To maintain hope and have those who care for me remain hopeful.
3. To have my questions answered honestly, and not to be deceived.
4. To participate in decisions concerning my care, allowing me as much control over my life as possible.
5. To be able to express my experiences of this living-dying interval of life.
6. To have others respect my choices concerning the way that I prefer to die and the disposition of my body.
7. To be alleviated from my pain as much as is humanly possible.
8. To provide support for my loved ones (if needed).
9. To share my spirituality with others and to receive spiritual nurturance from others.
10. To not die alone.

Fears of the dying patient

1. The fear of being alone.
2. The fear of the unknown.
3. The fear of regression.
4. The fear of losing self-identity and meaningful roles.

primarily organized within cancer networks. Moreover, there are wide differences in the organization and delivery of services within palliative care programs. Most services provided have depended on clinical judgment and not on standardized measurements that identify needed interventions (Quinn, 2005).

In the United Kingdom, the United States, and other countries in Europe there is evidence of continued efforts to develop comprehensive palliative care programs that are available on the basis of need, not diagnosis. In the United Kingdom there has been ongoing discussions regarding the need for organizational change and policy innovation. Despite these attempts, funding remains a major problem. There is a persistent fear that monies funded by the government will have strings attached, distort care, and result in the 'medicalization' of dying (Clayson, 2003).

Similar organizational efforts and concerns exist in the United States. Despite some difficulties, the number of hospital-owned palliative care programs has increased by 75 percent between 2000 and 2004. Physicians have become comfortable including a palliative care consultant as part of the interdisciplinary treatment team. The focus now is on assuring consistently high standards in these programs. As a result, the National Consensus Project for quality palliative care has issued guidelines for having interdisciplinary teams, making grief and bereavement services available, and providing evidence-based pain and symptom relief services. However, similar to the United Kingdom and other countries, funding is a major problem in the United States. Insurance companies do not see palliative care services (in the home) as reimbursable, many hospitals do not see any financial benefits for these services, and programs of medical fellowships do not offer funding for training. Palliative care fellowships are currently funded by philanthropy (Schneider, 2006).

Hospice and palliative care programs are conceptually similar, yet different in the consideration of the life expectancy for the patient and the possible services needed for care and support. Hospice criteria require that patients and those close to them acknowledge that they have six months or less to live. Palliative care services medically and emotionally support patients and their significant others in their efforts to cope with issues of mortality and evaluation of lifestyle and change. Although some funding sources have not been able to appreciate differences in the two programs, palliative care proponents continue to emphasize that their approach to life-threatening and incurable illnesses encompasses a wider diversity in the experiences of the patients and families that differentiates them from those receiving hospice care.

Previous models of bereavement did not address issues of palliative care. Thus, the dual process model (Stroebe and Schut, 1999, 2001) was welcomed by palliative care practitioners (in the United Kingdom) who believed that there were distinct differences in their subspecialty and treatment of patients. This model addressed diversity, not only in patterns of oscillation, gender and cultural differences, but also offered a perspective that allowed practitioners to value diversity in each individual's response to their illness. Based on notions of oscillation inherent in the DPM, practitioners are able to address issues of emotional loss and practical tasks as patients continue to undertake life alterations and changing social roles and relationships (Quinn, 2005).

In addition to the usefulness of newer models, there are several practical considerations within the practice of palliative care. Purposeful communication can facilitate the transition from curative to comfort care. Some discussions address the patient's prognosis and their wishes for possible interventions such as resuscitation. Other conversations encourage patients to reintegrate into past activities (within current realities) that were meaningful to them before the onset of their illness. This type of discussion also allows them to reframe their goals in the time that remains (Abrahm, 2006). A 'new to do list' is another type of conversation to facilitate. Questions include: What do you wish to accomplish during your life? What might be left undone if you were to die today? What legacy do you want to leave your family? What do you want your children and grandchildren to remember about you (Lo et al., 1999)?

Treatment plans for patients, as discussed above, should not exclude significant others. These individuals are an integral part of the patients' lives and should be included in ongoing conversations. Most likely they have supported their loved ones throughout the illness and may eventually be involved in end of life decisions. The emotional needs for these individuals are often overlooked, as the patients are the primary focus of attention. Ongoing support for them must also be provided.

The Cancer Counselling Center of Ohio

The Cancer Counselling Center of Ohio has worked mainly with persons who have a life-threatening or chronic illness. Loss (of job, of money, of physical mobility, etc.) and possible death are constants in the treatment process. Zimpfer's (1992) holistic model includes perspectives that focus on the body, mind, spirit, and emotions. A spirit of harmony among these dimensions is sought, whether one strives to maintain a life amid losses, or whether one anticipates death. The model is based on the concept of wellness:

> ... wellness refers to positioning all the resources of the self so that they are neither competitive among themselves nor interfering ... In short the patient allows his or her body

the full use of its capacities for healing by removing impediments and by optimizing its innate tendencies towards health. Healing in this instance implies not merely bodily recovery but also inner harmony and fullest use of personal potential. (1992: 205)

In the situation of life-threatening illness, anticipatory grief is compounded by uncertainty. At the Center, many clients have a disease which is potentially lethal. They face, as if this threat were not bad enough, the incursions and perhaps the worsening of bodily illness, the difficult treatments and their often debilitating side-effects, and the loss of many aspects of their customary daily life. The possibility of dying is just one facet of a much greater complex of issues. Treatment in these cases often calls for unique methods. We routinely use tools which can access the internal states – the subliminal message systems – that lie beneath the surface of conscious awareness. It is our belief that where denial, doubt, and ambivalence prevail, clearer messages can often be obtained from the 'inner self'. We begin with relaxation, brainwave biofeedback, or other calming techniques to create a disposition of openness. Then, mental imagery, searching for internal direction (i.e., intuition, what my 'heart' or my 'gut' tells me), and hypnosis are often used to facilitate clarity on the issue of living or dying. Many concerns must be dealt with: the fundamental orientation to live or die; the will to persist or to give up; the desire to fight the illness using the standard medical treatments or to use alternative treatments or to let the body do its own work; and the reliance on God, on cosmic energy, or on some other higher power. Issues such as these are addressed as part of the fullness of the person, and to prevent such concerns from becoming impediments. Clients are involved in both the recovering and the dying process. Doubt about whether one is going to live or die, or even whether one wants to live or die, is tremendously complicating to the grief resolution process. Counselling involves evaluation of current lifestyle for modifications that are more consistent with physical abilities; attention to psychodynamics that allow for the release of past resentments, guilts, and emotional pain; and resolving old interpersonal conflicts that may be interfering with inner peace.

Our experience with persons who have cancer is that they are often isolated. Their associates at work, their neighbors, relatives, even fellow churchgoers, will 'write them off' as already dead and interact with them no longer. A spouse may abandon the ill one on the premise that he/she didn't get married to take care of an invalid. Sometimes spouses or friends exert pressure to 'get well', or accuse the ill one of not trying hard enough. This only compounds the desolation, the seriousness of their awareness of vulnerability, and the physical toll of the disease itself.

In dealing with life-threatening illness, the practitioner treads a narrow line between counselling for living or counselling for dying. In our own experience we 'go with the flow' of the client, picking up on his or her basic direction. It is after all not our choice but that of the client. This may be at odds with those medical practitioners whose viewpoint is that once their patient has invoked their help, their duty is to preserve life no matter what. The counselling process may alienate such a physician and in the process even compound the client's dilemma. If a client has resigned him/herself to the inevitability of dying, the counselling task is to help with reconciliation with the others in one's life, with living as physically and spiritually at ease as possible, and finishing any life tasks that may be still incomplete. For some there may even be a renascence of energy to pursue unfulfilled dreams.

Occasionally a client will present what appears to be continual denial of the possibility of death, even in the face of worsening symptoms and physical decline and the ineffectiveness of medical treatments. This person's focus may be entirely on restoring a former way of life, returning to their job, and maintaining friendships. Saying the unsayable may be appropriate in this event (namely, introducing the possibility of death to the client); it many unleash a cascade of fears and other emotions heretofore bound up in stoic silence. The counsellor must be cautious, however, that his or her own expectations or conclusions (namely, about the inevitability of death) do not become prophecies to be imposed on the ill one. And the reverse is true also, i.e., that the counsellor not impose a desire to live at all costs. It is, after all, the client's life to live. As helpers we can nudge and challenge a client's expectations, but we cannot prod or push toward what we consider is 'best' for the client.

Counselling for the dying involves a reinstatement of harmony of body, mind, spirit, and emotion. In the final stages of dying, the mind cognitively accepts the likelihood or inevitability of death; the emotions have resolved quarrels and guilts with other people living or dead, and have moved beyond the anger of perhaps being cheated of a more productive life; the spirit has accepted whatever sense of immortality or nothingness, welcome or anonymity that may come after death; and the body prepares itself for dying, perhaps even by ceasing to fight with its own resources any longer.

Anticipating death, as it is seen in this chapter, is a property of both the dying person and the significant others (particularly the family) around him or her. We have worked with families who were all present during the dying hours or days, who by turns held or caressed or breathed in unison with the ill person, who reminisced together, who cried and laughed together, and who in general turned what is often a solitary event into a loving community experience.

Additional tools for assessment and intervention

The psychological needs assessment, referred to in previous chapters, helps patients and those involved understand the importance of these needs, and how they have been greatly altered; it initiates a process of compromise and setting goals for the attainment of meeting these needs now and in the time that is still to be. Table 7.2 illustrates how this chart may be used with this population. For each need a different patient is used to show the variety of possible responses and goals. Designing goals for the future is done on a day-to-day or week-to-week basis. As mentioned in the other chapters, the goals must be realistic, meaningful to the person (not the counsellor), and attainable.

Another strategy to consider is the life review. Butler (1963) believed that this review was an integral part of normal development and a final reorganization and integration of the personality. He viewed the process as more than reminiscence; he considered it an opportunity to understand and resolve the conflicts of earlier life. The experience could be silent or oral, conscious or unconscious, nostalgic or painful. This therapeutic tool can be used with the elderly, the terminally ill, or anyone with a life-threatening illness. Working through earlier conflicts, integrating a life of meaningfulness, and accommodating to current realities are a therapeutic goal that encourages meaningful investment in the present life and the creation of future legacies.

Table 7.2   Psychological needs of dying patients

Needs	Past	Present	Future
Love: Case example of a patient with a brain tumour who is aware, but unable to talk.			
Who are the people whom I can trust and who love me and I can love in return? (family, friends).	Many friends. Husband. Children.	Friends no longer stop by. Unable to verbally communicate. Husband can't tolerate changes in wife – gone all day and evening. Paid professional caregivers.	Transfers trust and caring to hospice staff.
Belonging: Case example of a patient in end-stages of breast cancer.			
What do you belong to/feel comfortable with/feel part of and contribute to?	Family, friends, church, work, community.	Treatments create negative side-effects – prevent active involvement in most of her past activities.	Compromises and prioritizes – chooses 2–3 activities to remain minimally involved in. Does phone support for others.
Worth: Case example of a patient with a brain tumour, bedridden, and able to talk.			
What do I do/or like about myself, that makes me feel good about myself?	Based on performance as a top salesman.	Unable to see any self-worth outside of work roles. Has packed away awards – can't tolerate the sight of them – memories too painful.	Compromises – re-establishes a relationship with grandson – tells him stories of his days as 'top salesman'.
Recognition: Case example of a patient bedridden with end-stages of prostate cancer.			
Who appreciates me and gives me recognition? What do I do that I feel is worthwhile and is important to me?	Previous role of 'head of house-hold' and 'decision-maker'.	Wife is now primary financial head of the household.	Wife reinstates his power as 'head of the household' – sets up bed table as his desk to conduct the finances and make family decisions.
Fun: Case example of a patient who is in the end-stages of lung cancer.			
What do I do for fun – alone/with others? How much does it cost? How much of my fun is free?	Outdoor activities: hunting, fishing, camping.	Bedridden – refuses hospital bed– sets up 'quarters' on family room couch. Irritable – sullen – uncommunicative.	Compromises – night before he dies – requests all of family to have a 'camping trip' in family room. Reminisces about past fun together.
Freedom: Case example of a patient with lung cancer who is in transition to loss of mobility.			
What does freedom mean to me? Time, money, what I eat? Activities, what I say? Other choices?	Had been an independent, travelling salesman – in total control of his time, money, decisions. Always had multiple choices.	Stumbles – increased inability to move around. Family insists on a wheelchair. He refuses and continues to fall. Activities restricted to his living-room chair.	Accepts wheel-chair – sees it as a solution for more mobility and activities outside the living room and the house.

Lester (2005) offered a life review questionnaire that practitioners may find useful in their attempts to operationalize the concepts of Butler's therapeutic tool. Questions are organized under three categories:

1. Childhood/family life.
2. Adulthood/work life.
3. Here and now.

Practitioners may formulate their own questions based on the knowledge of their individual patients/clients, or refer to her chapter 'Life review with the terminally ill – narrative therapies' (Lester, 2005: 66–79).

A final strategy to consider with this population is music therapy. The goals of this therapy are physiological, psychological, and spiritual. Research has shown evidence of the positive effects of music therapy: distraction from pain, symptom management, ability to relax, and an overall improvement in the quality of life. Music therapists offer a creative approach that allows individuals to explore their inner states and transcend their present experience of time and space (Hanser, 2006).

Issues for Children and Adolescents who have Life-threatening, Chronic, or Terminal Illnesses

Some young children and adolescents will not have the advantage of growing up without the burden of serious illnesses. For this population, ongoing tasks of development will still need to be addressed; however, these tasks will often be disregarded if medical care becomes dominant.

Fox (1991) discussed various issues and concerns with this population and suggested methods of intervention. She proposed that pre-school age children would be concerned with four anticipatory grief issues: causality of their illness, concerns regarding their bodies, anxieties over treatments, and a pervasive fear of dying.

Young children have self-focused ideas about the cause of their illness and often blame themselves for having done something wrong to cause it. Counsellors need to be aware of this and understand that thoughts such as these are most likely present, even if not verbalized. As children ask questions, reverse the queries and ask them why they believe that they are ill. Directly answering questions often results in missed opportunities to understand the fears and self-imposed blame behind questions that appear straight-forward. Another major concern for this age group is on the physical aspects of what is happening to their bodies. As they endure multiple treatments with various side-effects, they often feel that their body belongs to the medical professions. Treatments often do not produce the desired effects, and relapses or negative side-effects result. Most pre-school age children do not understand how their bodies function; thus, these treatments and side-effects often evoke anxieties that professionals are not aware of. A common fear for a child is to see big tubes of blood drawn from his or her small body, and to worry if there is enough blood left inside to live. They are unable to conceptualize the body's ability to continue to produce blood.

An even greater concern is for those children who become too passive to treatment. It is psychologically healthier for children to fight treatment from time to time than to become overly conformative, with feelings of helplessness. Interventions must address the need for offering a child some control and decision in the treatment. Practitioners must assess the possibilities of choices they can give children. For example, they can give a treatment in the bed or on someone's lap where they might feel more secure. In-patient programs for children address many of these needs and provide secure environments for hospitalized children.

Lastly, this age group is very aware of the fact that they might die; and although they do not communicate this fear openly, they often express it in their actions. Spontaneous artwork can offer important non-verbal, symbolic clues to the inner world and fears of acutely ill and/or dying children.

Many of the same issues apply to school-age children (kindergarten through grade 8). Techniques such as art and play are also used for this age group. A major difference is the fact that this group can communicate better, and they are capable of past and future cognitions. Future concerns often are verbalized or apparent in acting-out behaviours during times of initial diagnosis or relapse. This is often difficult to address directly because well-meaning adults fear reprimanding children who are seriously ill. Often this becomes a focus of interventions: acknowledging the distress that the child is experiencing, and at the same time setting needed behavioural boundaries. Relapses often mean additional hospitalizations and disruptions in their school and social environments. Since school-age children are mature enough to be aware of their future, adults need to be honest about potential future treatments and hospitalizations. This age group needs a considerable amount of time to ask questions and to attempt to regain a sense of personal control.

Interventions must focus on more listening than talking. Counsellors must continue to ask themselves: 'What is this child really saying, and what is he or she internally working on?' Some helpers become overly concerned before meeting a child regarding what to say, what tools to use, etc. The primary intention should be to listen and to gain entry into the internal world of a child who has lost control of his or her own body. Often it might be more appropriate to meet with the parents first, especially if there is some uncertainty about how much the child understands about the illness. No matter what approach is chosen, the goals must include honesty, providing a safe environment, and listening. Interventions should include the provision of a network of supportive friends, family, and staff; flexible hospital policy; and creative strategies that provide opportunities for therapeutic play through different mediums (e.g., art, sand, and water).

Adolescents who are seriously ill present a different challenge for professional caregivers. Simultaneously they are working on issues of development as well as fears of their non-being. Adolescents with life-threatening illnesses have a unique developmental confrontation:

Tim, age 17, was diagnosed with Hodgkin's disease following a car accident. He had always been active: track, the school band, swimming, and so on. He had shortness of breath after track practice, but thought nothing of it. It was the summer of his junior year and he was looking forward to all the promises of his senior year. The car accident was not life-threatening; however, complications that resulted led to the above diagnosis. The medical plan included surgery, then chemotherapy and radiation, with a prognosis of a cure before Christmas of his senior year. He just had to get through all the treatments and the lifestyle adjustments, and life would be the same again. Tim smiled during the sessions and talked a good story: sure, he didn't like the treatments, and he certainly didn't like his early summer evening curfews. He had a girlfriend who had stayed by him during all this, and he wanted to have a good time with her. He felt fine three days after the chemotherapy, and believed he should be able to do what he wanted to do with his friends. His friends had been great. They continued to visit, and they talked about shaving their hair as a sign of support when Tim lost his from the treatments.

So, what was wrong? What were his anxieties that made it impossible for him to cope at times? With all this reassurance, positive prognosis, a semi-return to normalcy, and support, no one could assure him that he was not going to die. Exclusive focus on thoughts of the future and the normal dreams of adolescence were not a reality for Tim. He was confronted with the developmental tasks of planning for his future and contemplating his non-being at the same time. Control and choice are two important variables in treatment plans. Moreover, where they are with specific developmental issues and simultaneously where they are in the cycle of their illness (e.g., diagnosis, treatment, relapse) needs to be part of the ongoing assessments and interventions.

Krementz (1989) has raised awareness of adolescent issues from her interviews with teenagers with life-threatening illnesses:

> One female, age 15, was coping with lupus since age 8. She talked about the physical effects of this illness, and also the developmental ones of an adolescent. She expressed a desire to be less dependent upon her mother in many areas that she lacks control in because of the illness. A major concern was her inability to take part in normal activities and her mother's overprotectiveness of her, resulting in an inability to go new places and experience a fuller life. (p. 90)

Working with children and adolescents who have life-threatening, chronic, or terminal illnesses presents numerous challenges that are unique to their age and developmental level. Often the task of a developmental level (e.g., adolescent tasks) will take precedence (in the mind of the patient) over medical concerns and advice. Children who require extensive medical treatment also need to attend to their childhood needs for play and socialization, and the development of trust, initiative, and autonomy. Professionals must be aware of these needs and assure that there is opportunity for children to develop and enjoy life as much as possible within their medical condition. They cannot be treated as fragile and incompetent, nor denied opportunities to experience life. On the other hand, medical interventions cannot be ignored, nor can the child or adolescent be allowed to be irresponsible because he/she is ill.

This chapter has highlighted issues that those with life-threatening and terminal illnesses must face. Existential suffering, inherent in their conditions, forces them to question the meaninglessness of their current lives and the nature of their suffering. Programs and strategies have been discussed that offer therapeutic solutions for more effective coping and enhancement of the present quality of life.

8 Special Issues

Every loss has special features, and for each individual experiencing a loss, there are unique issues. While this chapter cannot address the numerous issues or the variety of hardships that must be endured after every loss, it will focus on certain special losses wherein resolution of grief can be more difficult. Included will be trauma in general, murder, suicide, AIDS, and perinatal/neonatal loss.

Inherent in these types of loss is the concept of disenfranchised grief. Disenfranchised grief, as defined by Doka, is the 'grief that persons experience when they incur a loss that is not or can not be openly acknowledged, publicly mourned, or socially supported' (1989: 4). He has proposed three possible reasons for this occurrence: the relationship is not recognized; the loss is not recognized; or the griever is not recognized. This type of grief is often more intense because of situations surrounding the loss. Moreover, these situations frequently cut off sources of needed emotional support. AIDS is a good example of disenfranchised grief in which non-traditional relationships are often not recognized or socially sanctioned, nor is the griever recognized as a legitimate griever. Often early pregnancy loss is not recognized as a legitimate loss, and there are hidden issues of intense loss and grief to cope with for those family members and friends who survive a death by suicide or murder. In addition to the griever not being recognized as a legitimate griever, there are often characteristics about the griever that discount their status as legitimate grievers. Young children, the elderly, and the developmentally disabled are frequently ignored in their grief. Work with the developmentally disabled has increased our awareness about the variety of losses that this population has experienced without social support or recognition. This group is often viewed as not having the same psychological and human needs as the rest of the population.

Trauma

Many losses occur within what would be considered traumatic events. Trauma, however, is not just loss. It involves dealing with circumstances that have catastrophic components. Some type of violence occurs at the same time as the loss. Earthquakes, fires, and floods are examples of natural disasters that are considered traumatic. Initially individuals experiencing such disasters are involved with the major ordeal of surviving the event, and then immediately are forced to face the reality that loved ones may not have survived. Multiple losses may follow natural disasters: loss of homes and contents within, a sense of personal control and security, loss of a past lifestyle, and so forth. The Indian Ocean Tsunamis (12/04) and Hurricane Katrina (8/05) are examples that attracted world-wide attention.

The world's most powerful earthquake in the last 40 years struck deep under the Indian Ocean, triggering massive tsunamis that obliterated areas from Thailand to Somalia and claimed over 240,000 lives. This trauma created additional losses in a population that was already over-burdened. These countries were all too familiar with war, death, and poverty. Many of the children were already living in orphanages, as their parents had been killed in ongoing civil wars, and this disaster had a major effect on its young. Children were reported to have made up 30 percent of the death toll, and they were at higher risk than adults to suffer post-traumatic stress disorder in the future.

Hurricane Katrina was reported to be costliest and one of the deadliest in the history of the United States. Although it was categorized as a natural disaster, similar to the tsunamis, there were some major differences. Loss is more difficult to come to terms with when there is a perception that the event could have been prevented. In these situations there is a greater sense of loss of control, hostility, and long-lasting bitterness. There was a belief by many that this disaster could have been prevented. Supporting this belief was an independent investigation (April 2006) that demonstrated that the levee failures were not caused by natural forces. Moreover, there was major criticism and condemnation directed at the Federal, State, and local governments on their delayed response to the floods, failure to implement an effective evacuation plan, and mismanagement and lack of leadership in the response and relocation efforts. Although Congress did initiate public policy about emergency management and investigated the issues of contention, they were not successful in lessening hostility or restoring faith in the American public. There were additional allegations that race, class, and other factors could have contributed to delays in the government's response. Whether or not there is truth in these allegations, these are perceptions that create realities for the victims and the nation. Thus the losses are not just as a result of floods, loss of homes and lives, there are major losses that a society must deal with regarding beliefs in their government to protect and be honest. Losses here are symbolic as well as concrete. And some of the losses will linger and fester and create a sense of victimization for survivors and the entire nation. Loss of faith, hope, and perceived values about one's country constitute major and long-lasting issues.

Trauma can also be experienced through violent acts such as murder, rape, war, hijackings, and varied forms of attack and destruction. Since the first edition of this book in 1997, the world has witnessed and experienced severe violence and loss. For the United States (September 11, 2001), Madrid (March 11, 2004), and Great Britain (July 7 and 21, 2005), the terrorists' attacks that killed thousands of innocent people resulted in profound changes in each of these countries and led to a mixture of political, social, and economic reactions around the world.

Concerns of future terrorism and fear of violence have led to, and will continue to incur, more violence. Although the purpose now and in the future will be to defeat violent extremism, protect the innocent, and help countries rebuild, history shows little evidence that these goals can be achieved. These attempts often have only resulted in more losses: loss of lives, loss of hope for peaceful solutions, and loss of confidence in national leaders. Changes in values and belief systems challenge individuals' and nations' assumptive world, and this is an integral part of the grief process. Losses must be addressed on all levels and across all perspectives.

Special considerations

Raphael (1992) discussed concepts and manifestations of trauma. The traumatized individual is often dealing with a double psychological burden: a post-traumatic reaction (PTR) and a bereavement response. Both may occur concurrently, or the PTR may override the loss. It will be important for the counsellor to assess which process should be responded to first. In any case, the trauma of the loss must always be dealt with; and if it has not been addressed prior to professional intervention, counselling must begin here. This initial acknowledgment may include a verbal and detailed repetition of the event, looking at pictures and objects, or a return to the scene of the crisis. Not to address trauma first opens the possibility that an individual will become 'locked in time' and not move past the event psychologically.

The emotional stress of trauma includes a sense of powerlessness, the horror of having witnessed suffering, identification with the victims (e.g., same age), over-involvement in efforts to save individuals, and lastly, the experience of grief associated with the loss. Trauma leaves an imprint cognitively and visually, and reminders are usually present in the survivor's environment. Behavioural responses may include denial, disassociation, arousal, repression, and/or splitting.

Raphael (1992) further proposed some patterns that could occur over time with various risks for pathology. She stated that a post-traumatic reaction (PTR) could evolve into a disorder (PTSD), and that pathological grief could develop if the issues involved with the crisis are overlooked or avoided. As previously mentioned, there are risks that individuals can become fixated to the trauma. There remains personal vulnerability well past the traumatic experience, and often there is a failure of needed support to help work through the multiple issues involved. As with other types of losses, once the event has occurred, initial support has been offered, and some time has passed, most people external to the loss do not perceive any additional problems or need for support. Moreover, just as every loss has secondary losses, trauma includes secondary or symbolic losses and secondary traumatic reactions, especially when it becomes drawn out in legal processes.

Interventions

1. Support individuals through shock, horror, and numbness. Deal with the needs as they are presented.
2. Review the circumstances of the event. Many try to avoid this because of the recall of the horror and the violence associated with it.
3. Intervene to help the client deal with the effect resulting from the event: fear, helplessness, shock, anxiety, anger, guilt. Address these effects in manageable amounts.
4. Assist the individual to gain mastery and control over the trauma through review, release of effective responses, and working through whatever needs to be addressed. People have to work through what they think they could have done differently. It is important to help clients reconstruct what has occurred.

Suicide

Suicide is an unspeakable loss. People in the Western culture do not want to listen to survivors talk. A survivor's legacy is shame, fear, guilt, rejection, anger, and distorted thinking, in addition to their sense of loss. Suicide puts psychological skeletons in the closets of survivors.

Special considerations

Suicide presents a triple threat. It is usually a sudden death that happens without any time to prepare for it. It means a loss of a significant person in the lives of many. And it is an action loaded with emotional content. Survivors may become preoccupied that perhaps they were to blame or that they could have done something to have prevented the outcome. The presumption of guilt runs as a thread through the whole bereavement process.

Suicide leaves a stigma on individuals and on families as a whole. Families develop conspiracies of silence, and often fail to talk to each other about the event and issues underlying it. Family members take on different roles after a suicide. Some play the role of detective and want to track down clues. Others try to quiet the whole matter. The emotional impact on the family centers on denial (disguising the cause of the death), anger (focus on one cause or person as 'scapegoat'), and guilt (moral failure or self-blame). Survivors ask value questions of themselves and others. They seldom answer the whys satisfactorily and often fear most what they understand the least about. The impact upon the survivors leaves great emotional suffering. Day (1992), after the suicide of her husband, described this loss as 'the ultimate abandonment', with anger being her greatest emotion. The social impact is one of social awkwardness, as there are no explicit rules or guidelines after a suicide. Survivors often retreat into themselves and experience feelings of rejection and abandonment (i.e., 'he or she chose to leave me'). These feelings in turn lead to a sense of hopelessness. At other times there are feelings of relief if the person had caused difficulties for some time and had emotionally drained those around him/her. This feeling is later replaced with guilt.

Interventions

1. When appropriate, follow the interventions suggested for dealing with trauma.
2. Address the major emotions (Humphrey et al., 1990):

   - **Shame** is a predominant effect for suicide survivors, because suicide is a stigma within the Western societies. Encourage clients to talk about the event openly. Help conduct a psychological autopsy. Review the events leading up to the death, but help them understand suicide as a long-term process and not just a singular event. Using the term 'completed' instead of 'committed' helps facilitate an understanding of suicide occurring over time, with the death as the completion.

     Encourage families to talk about it together. Suicide often involves two or more survivors. Break a family's conspiracy of silence by encouraging family sessions. Counsellors should address the family as a system (Chapter 4). If the counsellor is the only outlet for the client, he/she may get pulled in as part of the problem. The client will find talking to the counsellor safer and more comfortable, thus avoiding important family discussions.
   - **Guilt** is often manifested in self-punishing behaviours, such as over-eating, drugs, or alcohol. Help the client reality-test his or her guilt. Advise that most guilt is irrational. Ask clients: 'Exactly what could you have done differently? What did

you do? What else did you do? Whom did you tell'? Questions such as these assist individuals in processing their guilt, testing the appropriateness of it, and then reframing their understanding of the death.

- **Anger** is frequently misdirected. Assist clients in understanding that their anger is with the deceased. Help them identify what they do not miss about their loved one. This facilitates the necessary process of building a balanced picture, and helps the release of anger to be properly directed.
- **Fear** underlies the entire bereavement experience of the survivor. Assure clients that suicide is not hereditary. Educate clients about the signs of depression and suicide.

3. Use cognitive interventions to address distorted thoughts that often predominate. Help the client get accurate information before rumors about the death get started. Address cognitive distortions as they arise.

Murder

The unexpected, sudden death of a significant other in one's life through murder violates an individual's sense of security and control. Grief reactions are usually severe and intense. They are often exaggerated, with numerous complications. Support will be needed, at various levels, and for a longer period of time. Survivors of homicides often need additional coping mechanisms (Humphrey et al., 1990).

Special considerations

Redmond (1989) discussed several characteristics of issues underlying a homicide that must be understood and considered in assessment and interventions:

1. Cognitive dissonance refers to the inability of the mind to comprehend something that does not match one's perception of reality as it had been previously known. The violent act of murder is difficult to comprehend and place within one's framework of personal reality and understanding. It goes beyond the normal coping mechanisms of shock, numbness, denial, and disbelief. It is often beyond human comprehension, and requires additional cognitive and effective mechanisms in order to adequately process the experience.
2. Revengeful impulses on the part of homicide survivors involve normal anger compounded by rage. Many fantasize acting out this rage, and it is important to validate this feeling as normal. One mother fantasized cutting off the head of her daughter's murderer with the lawn mower. Mowing the lawn facilitated an expression of this impulse and provided an emotional outlet for the intensity of her feelings.
3. Fear and vulnerability are an integral part of the bereavement experience. Families fear further harm to themselves, family members, and friends. The same mother could not stay alone in her home, and went to a neighbor's house at 5.30 a.m. when her husband had left for work. She feared that the friends of the murderer would return to harm her, as he had threatened this after he had been arrested.
4. Coping as a survivor of a murder involves a conflict of values and belief systems. As discussed in Chapters 1 and 2, loss and the experience of grief are influenced by a number of perspectives, including the philosophical and spiritual ones. The difference after a murder is that the influence of these two perspectives is more intense, with little positive influence being contributed from past losses. For example, if the spiritual perspective had previously contributed a positive influence that

allowed individuals to cope more effectively with loss, in the case of murder it may not offer any support, and may exert a negative influence instead. Anger may be directed at God, as the bereaved experience a severe loss of faith and trust in a higher power.

5. In many communities, murder carries a stigma. Some blame the survivors or the victim for somehow 'allowing it to happen'. Ascribing blame allows others to hide behind a false sense of security (i.e., 'This will never happen to me').

6. In addition to the grief, survivors also have to contend with systems that they have little knowledge or understanding about, such as law enforcement, the courts, and the media. The survivors become victims because of these intrusions. 'Secondary victimization' has been described by homicide survivors and often described to be more severe than the trauma of the murder itself. Secondary victimization corresponds to a number of the characteristics defined in the concepts of disenfranchised grief: the type of grief is more intense because of situations surrounding the loss, secondary victimization is not identified or understood as a loss, and an individual who is forced to cope with various systems in society after a murder is not recognized as bereaved. Often they are subtly accused as participants or contributors to the death or even perpetrators.

Interventions

1. Address issues of trauma as needed.
2. Offer a full range of supportive services over an extended time period. This enables survivors to address pertinent issues as they arise, develop effective coping behaviours, and integrate the experience in order to rebuild their lives.
3. Educate clients regarding the various systems that they will have to deal with (e.g., terminology, policies, and procedures).
4. Provide an environment that validates and encourages a full range of emotional expression in order to gain a sense of empowerment.
5. Use cognitive methods to address distorted thinking, guilt and self-blame. Encourage ongoing and honest communication among family members.

AIDS

Doka (1989) stated that there are relatively few other areas in the field of loss where the concept of disenfranchised grief is more powerfully demonstrated. He has outlined unique aspects of AIDS grief, giving the practitioner a basis for assessment and intervention:

1. There is a powerful social stigma associated with this illness and death. Individuals have reported an intense experience of alienation and rejection.
2. There is a lack of social sanctions, especially when the relationship was a homosexual one.
3. There is a concern and a fear on the part of survivors for their own physical health.
4. There is an inordinate need for secrecy on the part of families, coupled with shame and guilt.

Special considerations

Those with AIDS and families of victims are likely to be morally judged by society and deemed unworthy of inclusion in daily activities. Support is virtually non-existent, and those involved are left on their own to cope with a long-term and devastating illness, death, and intense and far-reaching repercussions. Much of the stigma originates from the past reality that this was an illness that was almost exclusive to the gay community or to those involved in the drug culture (two segments of society already alienated and disenfranchised). Although the facts are rapidly changing, attitudes and needed support fall far behind. Lack of knowledge regarding transmission of AIDS is another factor that influences many to keep their distance. Examples of this have been observed in the alienation of school-age children who have family members with AIDS, or who have been diagnosed as HIV-positive.

Other factors influencing alienation often come from within the victim's family of origin, especially if the illness was a result of an alternative lifestyle. Some families cannot accept these differences in each other, and often reject those members who have chosen a homosexual relationship. The patient is not socially sanctioned in society, nor is he or she sanctioned as a family member. Closing the patient out often results in the family becoming isolated from prior community involvements and potential support. They create part of their own alienation, and they move back and forth between blaming the patient and self-blame and guilt. Parents have difficulty not being able to answer certain questions, and subsequently continue to ask each other 'Where did we go wrong?' Shame and guilt predominate, and fear that their secret (a family member with AIDS) will become known is a driving influence. One example is a family who moved to another part of the country where no one knew them prior to the terminal stages of their son's illness and subsequent death. Even after death they continued patterns of avoidance and secrecy, making it difficult to take advantage of professional services.

Lastly, for those who do belong to the gay community, in some cases, there has been a perceived sense of alienation from friends who they expected to offer support. Part of this is because this community has been overwhelmed with loss from AIDS, and may be lacking needed emotional resources necessary for support over extended periods. Others have declared in counselling sessions that they have pulled back on their involvement as supporters because they are dealing with conflicted and ambivalent emotions towards friends who are infected, and towards the significant others who have been left to grieve alone. They have expressed that they need time to process these feelings and integrate the illness/dying experience of so many, and to reflect on how they have been affected.

Although the above considerations are part of other loss experiences, they appear to be more intense in this type of illness and death. AIDS, in many respects, can be termed the modern-day leprosy, carrying with it the stigma, fears, alienation, and issues of disenfranchisement.

Interventions

AIDS calls for interventions both during the illness and after the death; however, the following will only address those bereaved following the death of a loved one.

1. Identify and address issues of grief that have not been socially recognized or sanctioned.
2. Validate the relationship and loss as legitimate and important to the bereaved.
3. Explore areas of guilt, anger, and ambivalence, or unfinished business with the deceased that may not be recognized or verbalized by the bereaved.

4. Explore concerns of health and future well-being on the part of the bereaved.
5. Assess current and future social supports, and address real or perceived alienation. Assess current family support.
6. Encourage demoralization, especially if the bereaved was denied participation in a funeral rite.
7. Support and become actively involved in helping the client regain a sense of personal control and power.
8. Identify and assist the client to address any issues related to AIDS that need clarification, correct information, education, or professional involvement.

Early Loss of a Child: Miscarriage and Perinatal Deaths

Parental loss of a child, as discussed in Chapter 4, is one of the most difficult and intense losses to cope with. The age of the child will bring unique issues along with it; however, one of the most unrecognized losses within the broader category of parental loss is miscarriage, stillborns, and other early deaths following childbirth. These losses have been called 'lonely' because often the mother has been left to grieve the death of her child alone. Often parents must say goodbye to their child before they even say hello. If the father has not bonded with the child during pregnancy, it is often difficult for him to grieve, or to understand what his wife is experiencing. For all, the grief process is more difficult because what is being grieved often is a dream. How one grieves and the specific issues to be addressed will relate strongly to how the parents had fantasized the child. A wished-for child may have represented various hopes and expectations. Many pregnancies are replacements for former losses; many have been planned to save the marriage, and many are planned with the expectation of giving one's life meaning and purpose. The experience and resolution are more difficult, and much of the healing process takes place on a symbolic level.

Special considerations

In order to understand and effectively intervene, it is first necessary to understand the concept of attachment with regard to pregnancy. Kennell and Klaus (1976) have proposed nine steps that occur in this process:

1. Planning the pregnancy.
2. Confirming the pregnancy.
3. Accepting the pregnancy.
4. Feeling fetal movement.
5. Accepting the fetus as an individual.
6. Giving birth.
7. Hearing and seeing the infant.
8. Touching and holding the infant.
9. Caring for the infant.

Note that the first five steps occur before the birth. Understanding that the greater part of the attachment process is completed before the birth helps bring into focus the nature of the human attachment, and the need to validate and support the difficult issues of grief and resolution.

Nichols (1986) discussed specific grief symptoms associated with this loss:

Physical: Emptiness, aching arms, slight sense of unreality, body tension, lack of strength, blurred vision and palpitations.
Emotional: Sadness, anger, guilt, depression, death-related anxiety, pining for what 'might have been', sense of failure, and inability to accept reality.
Mental: Preoccupation with thoughts of the baby, hallucinations, fantasies or dreams about the baby; fear of going crazy; and confusion/preoccupation of thoughts and memories of the deceased.
Social: Desire to be left alone; difficulty planning for the future; and social distance from, and problems communicating with, one's mate.

Mothers often carry the burden of the grief alone and lack adequate support systems. There are no stories or memories to share about this child, and significant others have not had a relationship with this child. Pictures are often few, and taken by hospital personnel after the infant's death. Memorabilia are usually a foot or hand print and a small lock of hair. For the parents, these items are treasures, but for well-meaning sources of support, they have little meaning and are an inadequate basis for remembering and memorializing, two important components of grief work and resolution.

Some of the common characteristics of grieving mothers include the fact that most women remember the specific details surrounding the loss for many years. Many women have reported some distance or discomfort with their physicians. They felt that the physician was too busy to answer additional questions as they arose months after the death. Many report strained marital relationships. The major source of this problem is that the husband has not had the opportunity to develop a strong emotional attachment with the deceased infant.

Interventions

1. If possible, help the parents complete the last three steps of attachment by providing the opportunity to see the infant, hold the infant, and to care for the child as if he/she were alive. This would include dressing the baby, caressing him/her, rocking him/her, and selecting clothing for the funeral.
2. Facilitate the process of assisting parents to plan the funeral and meaningful rituals.
3. Encourage memorialization. Many give gifts at Christmas to those less fortunate, in the name of their deceased infants.
4. Encourage parents to look at whatever pictures or objects that they have and tell the stories of their hopes, dreams, and expectations of this wished-for child.
5. Encourage journal writing. Reflect upon and write about any aspects of the pregnancy, birth, and death that they can remember.
6. Address difficult feelings associated with this loss:

- **Guilt:** A constructive and positive way to handle guilt is to find out everything possible about what happened. Prompt clients to ask direct questions and ask for honest answers. Encourage them to risk asking if anything that they had done made a difference. Advise them that sometimes there are no answers.
- **Fear**: Encourage parents to list their fears. Listing them allows individuals to look at them one by one, and not feel so overwhelmed. Many fear future pregnancies and losses. Sharing fears with another can help diminish them. Everyone will have a different perspective and this allows for re-evaluation and new integration and meaning.
- **Anger**: Anger is almost a universal grief reaction. Anger in this loss is more difficult because it often lacks a focus. Often the medical staff become a focus of parental anger. As with other clients in grief, help these clients find healthy outlets. If their anger is justifiable, the counsellor is often put in the position of becoming an advocate for this individual within the medical system. Advocacy is an important component of the counselling profession. It includes getting information, connecting clients to resources, and representing clients as needed in various decisions and negotiations that might affect their welfare and future.

7. Encourage clients to re-evaluate their environment and what they are doing, or not doing. A bedroom decorated as a nursery in anticipation of the birth should not become a shrine.
8. Advise against a pregnancy in the near future that is an effort to replace the deceased child before the grief has been fully experienced.

Other Losses

There are other unique, difficult, or horrendous losses that many are forced to cope with, resolve, and find reasons to reinvest in life again. There are losses that many are forced to live with that can make death appear to be the better alternative. These include floods and other natural disasters, fire, industrial injuries, chronic illnesses, job loss, rape, assault, robbery, random violence, forced relocation, and other circumstances in which loss and grief are key components. These examples have been intended to raise an awareness that different losses may appear similar yet at the same time raise unique issues. This awareness is intended to remind the practitioner of the need to explore all areas of a client's loss, and build interventions to meet the idiosyncrasies of each case.

9 When Grief is Not Resolved

The nature and symptoms of unresolved grief have been discussed and debated over the past several decades. Many who have contributed to general models of loss and bereavement have also laid foundations for the conceptualization of unresolved/abnormal grief. The focus of this book is on mental health services for uncomplicated grief, yet it is important to understand the limits of one's competence. Therefore, the purpose of this chapter is to broaden an understanding of potential problem areas within the realm of unresolved grief, but not to deal with it in depth.

A familiar question that we are asked is 'When is grief not normal?' As a practitioner, it is important to know the boundaries of normalcy, since the manifestations of normal grief often appear to be abnormal. It is important to have relevant criteria for assessment and to understand the limits of interventions. Moreover, counsellors need to know when a client's issues are beyond their professional scope, and a referral is indicated. Despite disagreement in some areas, there is general agreement that unresolved grief which becomes diagnosable as a syndrome or as a mental or physical disorder can have social, psychological, and medical implications for the larger society, and warrants intensive professional intervention. Many who have had multiple admissions and confinements on psychiatric wards and to mental institutions have been diagnosed with multiple losses, never resolved, from childhood on up.

Definitions

The *Diagnostic and Statistical Manual of Mental Disorders* (DSM-IV) (American Psychiatric Association, 1994) defines unresolved grief in terms of symptoms that can be identified as not being characteristic of a normal grief response. Moreover, these bereavement symptoms can be differentiated from symptoms of a major depression. The symptoms of unresolved grief include:

- Guilt about things other than actions taken or not taken by the survivor at the time of death.
- Thoughts of death other than the survivor feeling that he or she would be better off dead or should have died with the deceased person.
- Morbid preoccupation with worthlessness.
- Marked psychomotor retardation.
- Prolonged and marked functional impairment.
- Hallucinatory experiences other than thinking that he or she hears the voice of, or transiently sees the image of, the deceased person. (1994: 684)

Horowitz et al. used the terms 'pathological grief' and 'mourning' to describe problems in grief resolution:

> Pathological grief is the intensification of grief to the level where the person is overwhelmed, resorts to maladaptive behaviour, or remains interminably in the state of grief without progression of the mourning process toward completion. Pathological mourning involves processes that do not move progressively toward assimilation or accommodation but, instead, lead to stereotyped repetitions or extensive interruptions of healing. (1980: 1157)

Brayer (1977) used the term 'pathological grief' and defined it in relation to Freud's theory of mourning: a manifestation (on the part of the bereaved) of self-reproach and self-reviling that lead to delusional expectations of punishment.

Parkes and Weiss (1983) defined unresolved grief as abnormal, and stated that this occurs when recovery fails to take place. Recovery was then defined as the ability to replan one's life and to achieve an independent level of functioning.

Stephenson defined unresolved grief as 'exceptional grief'. He stated that grief can be labeled exceptional when there has been a 'lack of recognition of a significant loss, an extreme reaction far in excess of normative cultural expectations, and a lack of movement through the grief process' (1985: 151).

Demi and Miles (1987) delineated 31 manifestations of normal grief, but only define them as pathological when any one of the manifestations is five years post-bereavement.

Rando (1993a) defined this phenomenon of pathological, abnormal, or unresolved grief as complicated mourning. Her definition allows for personal involvement and choice. This term does not pathologize grief, as do other definitions.

Referring to the bereavement models of the theorists in Chapter 1, unresolved grief is a consideration of each one, with similarities and variations in each conceptualization.

Reference to Theoretical Models Introduced in Chapter 1

Freud's conceptualization of loss, grief, and resolution focused on the acknowledgment and acceptance by the ego that the object had been lost, that the energy that had been used to maintain the attachment had been withdrawn, and that energy to make new attachments had been mobilized. He stated that grief is hard work and takes a considerable amount of time; however, unresolved grief is a different issue. He did not base his theory of unresolved or pathological grief on the amount of time it took to complete the process; instead, in *Mourning and Melancholia* (1914/1957) he proposed that ambivalence in a relationship can be the root cause of unresolved grief and mourning. 'Melancholia' was a term that he used for psychiatric depression, and he stated that this condition may be caused by the real or symbolic loss of a person. According to his theory, the lost person is incorporated in some manner within the bereaved individual. Once this has been accomplished, the bereaved can then persecute and punish the lost figure for having abandoned him or her. The lost person is very much alive in the unconscious and the bereaved does not withdraw energy from what has been lost to make new attachments. This theory is not accepted by practitioners today, as further research has provided better explanations of pathological guilt after ambivalent relationships.

Lindemann (1944) was one of the first theorists to offer an application of his concepts to assessment and intervention. From his study of the survivors of the Coconut Grove fire in Boston, he proposed that there can be distorted manifestations of the normal expressions of grief. During his clinical interventions he observed a tendency on the part of his clients to resist the pain of grief and the bereavement process. This denial or avoidance seemed to be the most significant contributor to distorted manifestations of grief and potential problems in resolution. There is a period of avoidance that is psychologically therapeutic. To feel numb or to initially deny that a loss has occurred allows needed time for the mind to adjust to the full impact of the loss event. According to Fulton, implicit in Lindemann's work is the

> ... assumption that 'normal' people will, under 'normal' circumstances, experience a 'normal' grief reaction and ultimately return to a 'normal' state of well-being. Researchers have observed that when this pattern is upset in any way, such as the lack of conclusive or persuasive evidence that a death has occurred, or when an initial denial reaction is not overcome, maladaptive responses to loss may occur. (1977: 7)

The major criticism of Lindemann's work is that he gave no indication of the frequency of these distortions over a time period, and that he led practitioners to believe that interventions could be used to resolve these distortions in four to six weeks (Parkes and Weiss, 1983). Research since his study has indicated that resolution involves a more arduous and cyclical process, and that it is difficult to predetermine the number of weeks needed. Lindemann, despite some of the shortcomings in his study, was one of the first to describe specific symptoms that were characteristic of complicated grief. In addition to denial, he proposed that over-activity without a sense of loss, acquisition of the symptoms of the deceased or development of some other medical disease, severe alterations in relationships with family and friends, schizophreniform behaviour, abnormal hostility toward specific persons, self-destructive behaviour, and agitated depression were all indicative of potential distortions and maladaptive adjustment after loss.

Kübler-Ross (1975), in *Death: The Final Stage of Growth*, addressed philosophical, spiritual, and sociological/cultural perspectives that influence various cultures' difficulties with the death and dying experience. She stated that cultures that have prescribed rituals for bereavement resolve loss and grief more readily. Resolution is more likely to be achieved with a sense of transpersonal growth when there are prescribed ways of experiencing the process, and when there is validation and permission to grieve within a close supportive community. In these types of cultures, loss, especially death, is integrated into their understanding of life. Unresolved grief is often the product of cultures that deny or avoid death.

Bowlby's (1969, 1973, 1980) studies provided an understanding of human attachment and a framework for understanding the potential for complicated grief when these attachments are threatened or broken. Bowlby made it clear that the early loss of a significant attachment figure is not necessarily the root cause of future pathology; however, depending upon a number of different factors, early loss can predispose an individual to adult problems. One reason is that the normal process of searching for what has been lost is often hastened to the point of being negated. Time may not be taken to go through this painful process of searching, with subsequent anger when the lost person cannot be found or retrieved. Children often have the tendency to resist this search, and to prematurely state that the loss has been accepted. What happens psychologically is that the lost object (not searched for and eventually relinquished) is kept alive in the unconscious. Thus the child without awareness keeps the search alive, and this influences future losses and personality development. Fixation, repression, and splitting of the ego are common defense mechanisms involved, with pathological mourning and future psychiatric illnesses occurring as typical outcomes of this type of early childhood experience with loss. Another contributing factor is the type of relationship and the personality characteristics of the bereaved. As noted by other theorists, ambivalent relationships and characteristics such as dependency and compulsive caregiving often are indicators for problems with resolution after loss.

Bowlby (1980) also proposed that how one has experienced early relationships and the roles of early attachment figures can greatly influence bereavement. What he has called 'cognitive biases' are important determinants of reactions to future losses and attachments. Unhealthy and unfulfilling early attachments influence the loss experience, as the bereaved views the present based on cognitions and beliefs developed early in life.

Worden (2002) listed five factors regarding failure to grieve: relational (e.g., ambivalent or narcissistic relationships); circumstantial (e.g., uncertainties regarding death or multiple losses); historical (e.g., past complicated losses such as early loss of parent); personality (e.g., how one copes, or how well one is integrated); and social (e.g., socially unspeakable death or lack of support systems). He further discussed types of complicated grief and showed the relationship of each complication to his 'tasks of grief' work. He suggested that assessment identifies which tasks have not been completed, and that intervention begins at this point of immobility before attempting to continue through the normal tasks of grief counselling. One example would be delayed or inhibited grief, in which the bereaved has not been able to get in touch with or express the emotions involved. Although there may be various reasons for this difficulty, Worden suggests that the counsellor view the client as having a problem addressing Task II, and proceed to focus assessment and intervention on this task: namely, 'To experience the pain'. He or she would explore the nature of the relationship and the details of the death. Focusing on assessed problems at Task II will help the client experience the pain that is necessary for eventual healing. Other examples are those who have had highly conflicted or ambivalent relationships, and hesitate to discuss negative aspects. These situations and others can cause problems for resolution and promote delayed or inhibited grief. 'Grief therapy' is a term he or she uses to describe the idea that there is an area of complication in the individual's experience that needs to be addressed initially and resolved before the normal task work can be completed.

Rando in *Treatment of Complicated Mourning*, acknowledged and incorporated theories and terms used over the last few decades into her conceptualizations of complicated mourning. She states that '*complicated mourning* means that given the amount of time since the death, there is some compromise, distortion, or failure of one or more of the six "R" processes' (1993: 149). Her belief is that in all forms of complicated mourning there is an attempt to either 'deny, repress, or avoid aspects of the loss, its pain, and the full realization of its implications for the mourner; or to hold onto and avoid relinquishing the lost loved one' (1993: 149). Rando then further delineated two levels of potential responses when the process becomes complicated: symptoms and syndromes. Symptoms are indicators that there are definite problems in the process of bereavement; however, they do not meet the criteria for diagnosable disorders or syndromes as specified in the DSM-IV. Symptoms can be severe and usually appear in the psychological, behavioural, social, and physical areas of functioning. They must be assessed and understood in relationship to an individual's unique grief experience. Interventions are needed, but care must be taken not to quickly diagnose them as a syndrome or a mental or physical disorder.

Rando (1993) organizes syndromes under three headings:

- Problems in expression
  - absent mourning
  - delayed mourning
  - inhibited mourning
- Skewed aspects
  - distorted mourning
  - conflicted mourning
  - unanticipated mourning
- Problems with closure
  - chronic mourning. (1993: 156)

Diagnosis of a syndrome follows the definitions given in the DSM-IV. Under each of these syndromes, she relates a problem area in one of the 'R' processes of mourning. For example, delayed mourning would be represented by an inability to react to the separation, which is the second 'R' process. As with Worden's concept of tasks, Rando believes that it is necessary to locate the difficulty or impasse in one of the six 'R' processes, identify the complications and work that process through before moving on to the next process. Impasses and interferences may occur more than once and at any point. None of the processes can be avoided or severely compromised if healthy resolution is to occur. Details of Rando's work with complicated mourning are available in her writings (1993).

Types of Syndrome

Absence, inhibition, or delay of bereavement

Definitions and examples will be given for the types of distorted manifestations, using the works of a number of theorists.

Raphael (1983) stated that absence, inhibition, or delay of bereavement have similar characteristics when considered on a continuum of avoidance of the pain of loss. 'True absent mourning is rare because it requires that the mourner either maintain complete denial of the death or remain in a total state of shock – two quite difficult feats' (Rando, 1993: 155). Usually what is observed is extremely inhibited grief. Delayed grief is grief which is not manifested at the time of loss. When it emerges, sometimes years later, it is as fresh and intense as if the loss had just occurred. An example of this is when a loss, such as a death, occurs in the life of a child and well-meaning adults attempt to protect the child from pain and never discuss the death. Some time later, an unrelated event can trigger the memory of the death, and the grief emerges as if the loss is presently happening. Inhibited mourning has some similarities to delayed grief. However, unique to inhibited mourning is the avoidance of particular issues associated with the loss, and selective attention to others.

In addition to Raphael's work, significant contributions have been made by Deutsch (1937) and Bowlby (1980). These theorists agree that these manifestations of inappropriate mourning are often a result of negative and highly ambivalent relationships. A typical example is the adult child idealizing the abusive parent upon his or her death because the painful issues of abuse cannot be acknowledged. Attention must be paid to both the positive and negative aspects of relationships in order to integrate the full meaning of a relationship in healthy and realistic memory. Worden (2002) further discusses the possibilities of inhibited grief being manifested in physical and psychiatric symptoms. He terms this 'masked grief'; the physical signs (e.g., chest pains) or the psychiatric symptoms (e.g., panic attacks) may be real and diagnosable, but they cover up the reality of the avoided grief.

Distorted and conflicted mourning

Distorted and conflicted mourning have similarities. Conflicted mourning is highlighted by ambivalence in a relationship. Distorted grief also involves ambivalence; however, what differentiates the two is the intensity of specific emotions in the latter. Intense manifestations of guilt and anger are the primary grief responses in distorted grief. Research from Parkes and Weiss (1983) and Rando (1993) offers insight into these mourning responses. All human relationships have ambivalence (i.e., love, hate features). Bereaved individuals often have to deal with feelings of guilt after a death because they loved the person who died, but also disliked him or her at times. In conflicted grief the degree or intensity of ambivalence is much stronger and more difficult to resolve.

The death of a child is an example when both conflicted and distorted grief can occur. Parents invest a great degree of themselves in their children. Children represent the best and the worst features of the parents. These relationships are ripe for high degrees of ambivalence. Most parents have at least some negative thoughts and feelings about their children, and it is this reality of the normal parental relationship that can cause difficulty in grief resolution. In instances where children suffer untimely deaths, distorted and intense expressions of guilt and/or anger are often the main features of parental grief. Before normal grief work can be addressed, these emotions need attention. An example of a loss that manifested both distorted and conflicted grief was the murder of an adolescent female by her boyfriend on the porch of her home while her parents watched.

> The girl's death was an assault and an outrage in every respect. For almost two years it involved every segment of the community, the legal system, and a network of

counselling and medical professionals. Aspects of distorted grief were the first dimensions that had to be addressed. Nine months were needed just to address the extreme feelings and manifestations of anger. As noted above, the hallmark of distorted grief is anger or guilt that becomes extreme and goes beyond the normal response. Intentional murder of one's child highly predisposes parents to distorted manifestations of grief. Following the conviction of the perpetrator, the anger was somewhat dissipated; however, grief manifestations moved immediately to distorted feelings of guilt. The murder had happened quickly, and with little warning; yet, as parents, they tormented themselves with questions of why they could not have protected their daughter on their own property. The guilt was never resolved, and the anger continued to surface each time parole was considered for the convicted murderer. In addition to distorted manifestations, conflicted guilt was also part of the experience. As discussed, ambivalence in a relationship is a hallmark feature of conflicted grief. This was a highly ambivalent relationship. Developmentally their daughter was involved in a period of normal rebellion, and there were many volatile disagreements that had never been resolved. One of the major sources of tension had been her relationship with the boy who murdered her. For two years her parents had fought to keep her away from him, as his reputation for 'trouble' was well known. She had defied her parents on many occasions and met with him behind their backs. When she finally decided she did not want to be associated with him any more, he could not tolerate the rejection and killed her.

From this example, it is possible to understand the difficulties certain persons may have resolving grief or having a normal experience with it. For some the distortions can be addressed and resolved, and a normal process of bereavement facilitated; yet for others, the distortions continue to emerge for an indefinite period, hindering healthy resolution and reinvestment into meaningful living.

Unanticipated mourning

Unanticipated mourning predisposes individuals to difficulties because they have had no opportunity to prepare mentally or psychologically for the loss; thus their adaptive defenses have not been mobilized. Examples include losses such as sudden deaths and natural disasters – assaults that affect every perspective discussed in Chapter 1. Many affirm the effects of the assault and devastation but do not understand the psychological demands thrust upon them by these events. Often disasters have forced individuals to question the meaning and fairness of life, and to assimilate and accommodate to new environments or lifestyles that they had not been prepared for. The nature of the crisis can be of such a magnitude that it takes some time beyond the event to process and assimilate the full extent of the destruction that has occurred. And often, the additional losses that emerge as a result create ongoing demands for psychological coping and readjustment. The bombings in numerous countries over the last several years have created global awareness of the impact and far-reaching psychological effects of trauma and human destruction.

Chronic mourning

Chronic mourning is another category of potential concern for healthy grief resolution. This type of grief never seems to cease, as, for example, the client who continues to display signs of acute grief years beyond the loss. Counsellors who have assessed this syndrome are struck by the intensity of the grief, and state that the grief appeared to be so acute and fresh that they would have expected the loss to have just recently occurred. Moreover, there has never been a hiatus in the emotions. That is, there was never a period in which the bereaved experienced some relief from pain or some return to equilibrium. Bowlby (1980), Parkes and Weiss (1983), Raphael (1983), Rynearson (1990), and Rando (1993) have offered valuable contributions to this concept.

New Perspectives

Since the first edition of this book, there have been different theories proposed that challenge prior concepts of pathology and grief resolution. The new models discussed in Chapter 1 have suggested a need for different perspectives and language when considering the bereavement process. Continuing bonds, meaning reconstruction, and the dual process model all propose less emphasis on syndromes of grieving and more attention to an accommodation of changing realities. Addressing the need to revise assumptive worlds and to restore a sense of coherence to life narratives is thought to be an important area of focus when working with bereaved individuals (Neimeyer, 2001).

Moreover, these models do not presume that the bereaved must withdraw psychic energy from the deceased. They challenge former definitions of pathological grief that emphasized an inability to sever ties. Newer constructs propose that healthy grieving includes continued symbolic bonds with the deceased (Neimeyer, 2001). The focus for professionals should not be on helping the bereaved separate from their loved ones; rather, on how to change past connections while maintaining former relationships within new perspectives (Silverman and Klass, 1996).

Furthermore, these theorists do not view bereavement as a psychological state that ends and from which one recovers. Previously *grief resolution* was associated with notions of closure. Concepts of *resolution and closure* may need to be revisited in order to help grievers come to appreciate a more appropriate understanding of resolution that supports the notion that their process is more of an ongoing accommodation to changed realities. The bereaved are forever changed by their experiences of loss; they do not simply 'get over it'. The process of accommodation facilitates an incorporation of an individual's past relationships into a larger part of their total reality in order to reconstruct meaningful future identities. Thus, the emphasis should be on negotiating and renegotiating the meaning of a loss over time. Grief resolution, as conceptualized by *continuing bonds,* states that the meaning of grief resolution is inherent in the meaningfulness of the bonds that human beings have with significant others (Silverman and Klass, 1996).

Reasons for Problems with Grief Resolution

Numerous reasons have been proposed as to why grief becomes complicated or unresolved. Often the risk of developing complications during bereavement depends on both the immediate circumstances of the death and the background against which it occurs. For example, PTSD is more likely to occur following a loss that is traumatic. However, complications can also occur following losses that are not traumatic. Often grief becomes complicated based on how an individual copes with their loss. Those who have not been able to cope with prior losses become more vulnerable to complications with future losses. Thus an individual with a history of inability to cope, emotional difficulties, or a personality disorder is more likely to suffer complicated grief after their bereavement experience ('Complicated Grief', 2006).

In addition to the awareness that past difficulties and premorbid issues of personality and functioning can affect present accommodation to loss, bereavement difficulties can also stem from society and the types of loss incurred. Society often dictates the specific rituals for mourning and prescribes a timetable for their completion. Often the funeral is the only recognized and accepted ritual. After the funeral, the bereaved feel abandoned in their grief because the support systems vanish and they are left on their own to comply with an expected timetable. Society's push for a quick resolution often sets the stage for complications and difficulties in healing. Moreover, certain deaths and losses have potential to activate complications and unresolvable issues. Suicide, homicide, AIDS, death of a child, and various types of losses that receive no social validation are examples that provide a basis for unresolved grief or complications in the normal grief process, as discussed in Chapter 8.

Since the first edition, concepts of forgiveness have been explored as a meaningful component of the healing process. Forgiveness involves the willingness and ability to let go of past resentments and resist the tendency to become victimized. The energy that is needed to reconstruct one's life is often consumed by resentments, and the bereaved remain frozen in the role of *victim*. Statements such as 'If this had not happened to me, I would have a better life … ' or 'He stole my ability to love again by what he did to me …' allow individuals to blame others and not assume personal responsibility to rebuild meaningful futures.

As it has been suggested in earlier chapters, the bereaved are often dealing with memories of past losses simultaneously with current grief. In a similar manner, a present experience of loss often reopens past unresolved resentments that have been repressed. Time alone may not have healed grief or resentments. Rather, time and lack of attention to painful issues often become the underpinnings for complications in the grieving process. It is often at this point, after sufficient time has passed and there is an internalized awareness that their coping abilities are no longer effective, that bereaved individuals initiate counselling. Their inability to reconstruct personal identities, along with intensified emotions, ongoing intrusive thoughts, and impaired functioning are finally acknowledged as symptoms that require professional intervention.

In addition to other strategies suggested, professionals are encouraged to foster forgiveness in their interventions with the bereaved, not as an acceptance for their perceived violations but as a gift that they can give to themselves. Past losses and wrongs can never be righted and violators may never be punished. Only the bereaved can make the choice to let go of past issues and put their energy to better use.

Intervention

When clients present issues that reflect unresolved areas of grief, counsellors must make a decision regarding their expertise and scope of practice. A referral at this point of assessment might be the most appropriate decision. However, it is very likely that most counsellors will have clients who come for one reason, and later on in sessions realize that unresolved losses from the clients' past are contributing to present difficulties. Loss is an integral part of life and will, in some way, contribute to most issues presented in counselling. We are not suggesting that the mental health practitioner refer every case of complicated grief; we are suggesting that mental health practitioners have an understanding and awareness of symptoms and syndromes so that they will be able to assess and rule them out. Most complications can be handled, especially under supervision. One reason to have this knowledge is to avoid the neophyte's error of quickly addressing the presenting loss at face value, without taking into consideration any complicating factors that might be underneath and eventually hinder resolution. From our experience, we have learned that it is not possible to address the current loss if past, unresolved issues have emerged. Moreover, experience in this field has verified our view that many who present themselves in counselling have issues of loss that go beyond the present situation. Many have past losses representing repressed or unfinished business that need to be addressed, often before the current loss can be processed. If these issues go beyond the counsellor's skill or available time, a referral may be in order.

The following case example represents a client who had been treated for PTSD in various settings for the past 20 years.

Bob: Loss and Grief Masked in Symptoms of PTSD and Vietnam

I now remember certain things about my childhood. I was five and playing with my marbles on my bed. My baby brother Matt was there with me. The marbles were great colors, and had been a gift from my uncle who had come to visit that day. All of a sudden dad grabbed Matt off the bed and ran from the house. Now I remember the scene. I know that he died because he swallowed one of the marbles. I realize that I have lived with shame and guilt all these years. (45-year-old Vietnam Veteran presenting for symptoms of PTSD 20 years later)

Presenting issues for counselling were centered around symptoms of PTSD, violent headaches, flashbacks from the war, survival guilt, unrelenting anniversary reactions, and periods of deep depression. He had spent a short time in a veterans' hospital about seven years prior, with minimal benefit from the interventions offered. He had recently been hospitalized for depression and became a patient of a local psychiatrist who referred him for counselling, but followed him for his medications. In addition to the multiple medicines prescribed by the psychiatrist, a local family physician was administering morphine shots on a weekly basis for his headaches.

For two years, sessions focused on the above symptoms and recurring episodes of PTSD and depression. On one occasion, he related that a man had called him

(Continued)

claiming to be a cousin whom he had not seen since age five. Bob said he was skeptical and had refused to continue the conversation. Trust was a difficult issue for Bob. After this statement, it became apparent that Bob was not mentally present. He had done this before when flashbacks occurred, or when he decided it was too painful to continue talking. The routine had come to be to ask him where he was mentally. Usually he would reply that the walls had just gone up and this would be the signal to back off. However, this time he continued and said he was on a bed playing with his marbles. His baby brother was there with him. All of a sudden his father grabbed the baby and ran. The baby died; subsequently, dad abandoned the family, resulting in mom's decision to take Bob and his sister to Ohio to live with his grandmother. His grandmother raised him, as his mother was not emotionally healthy. Until this time, he had never allowed this reality into conscious awareness. He now recognized that the baby had swallowed one of the marbles. In his young mind he had imagined that it had been his fault. The guilt was understandable and the confusion became apparent: the gift had been transformed into an object of shame and guilt that influenced daily life and carried a powerful message of negativity into the present. Vietnam was an event that many survived with minimal scars; however, for those who came from childhood backgrounds such as Bob's, Vietnam had more deleterious and long-lasting effects. Over the following decades Bob had come to mistrust gifts and good feelings, as they seemed to represent pain and negativity.

It was a few weeks after this that Bob experienced the flashback that had never been clearly defined, but one that connected the war experience with his childhood experience. He was in the streambed. Eleven men had been assigned to this combat mission. The attack came. His captain abandoned them; several buddies were killed instantly. (His father had abandoned him also after his baby brother died, and his wife had left him after he was in Vietnam for a year.) He believed that he was the only one left in the streambed, about to die. He crawled under a pile of dead bodies to hide. Some days later another American unit found him. Only three of the 11 survived. The captain was never seen again. Two days later Vietnam was evacuated. He returned to the States, but not as a hero. He was a reject and felt abandoned by his own country. For many years he coped by using alcohol. He then married his present wife, and his long search for who he was and his journey to mental health began.

Issues of loss and grief from the war, the end of his first marriage, and the recent death of his grandmother were obvious issues of loss to address. The deeper, hidden losses of childhood, the death of his brother, the abandonment by his father, a dysfunctional mother, and multiple intangible losses were buried. Eventually the focus of intervention shifted. PTSD and depression were symptoms masking deeper issues. Strategies switched to interventions based on theories of loss and grief, which address core issues of guilt and shame that were rooted in early childhood. Today he understands the connectedness of his past to his present. He continues to gain awareness into issues that have been repressed. From this awareness, he has also grieved past losses and has relinquished their tenacious hold. Emotionally he has been freed to explore fuller dimensions of himself and begin the journey toward self-actualization.

Bob could not begin a normal grief process until he had addressed the issues that were preventing the completion of this process. Issues such as these are often at the root of unresolved grief and may be present in many counselling sessions.

Within the professional literature there are a number of terms defining unresolved grief. Although these terms are often synonymous with patterns of emotional disorder, it is questionable if there is ever a pure manifestation of a specific syndrome. Rather, it appears that within specific cases of unresolved grief, there are manifestations of components of various syndromes. Bob's situation exemplifies this. The extreme guilt that dictated his present life mirrored concepts of distorted grief. Distorted mourning is manifested by either extreme guilt or extreme anger (Raphael, 1983). Although Bob had periods of uncontrollable anger, guilt seemed to predominate, with strong roots in early childhood. For various reasons, Bob's grief was also delayed, laying the foundation for complications. There was not just one loss event, but multiple losses over decades that were never addressed, grieved, or resolved.

It is probable that counsellors in any part of the world today will have multiple issues of grief to address with their clients. It is predicted that there will be significantly more clients predisposed to complications, pathology, or inability to resolve grief. Increase in violence and more conflicted social relationships are only two indicators of future concerns.

Counsellors have the responsibility to know the limitations of their professional abilities, training, and experience. After several sessions, practitioners must reflect back on their professional role with each client and what has been achieved in terms of identified goals and needs. It is often at this time that pre-morbid issues of personality, mental disorders, and past losses have emerged and are exerting a powerful influence on the process. Counsellors who are not trained or licensed to diagnose and treat mental disorders must seek supervision at this point to determine what is in the best interest for their client. Competent counsellors are aware of issues beyond the scope of their education and practice, they seek supervision as needed, and refer when appropriate.

Appendix: Resources on Dying, Death, and Grieving

Books for Professionals

Cook, A.S. and Dworkin, D.S. (1992). *Helping the Bereaved: Therapeutic interventions for children, adolescents, and adults*. New York: Basic Books.
The authors present examples of working with the bereaved. They stress the need for clinicians to individualize intervention, especially for non-whites, who may have differing values about death. They also expect self-awareness on the part of the therapist. Assessment methods, the process of intervention, and recommendations for considering group or individual therapy are provided.

Cox, G.R. and Fundis, R.J. (eds). (1992). *Spiritual, Ethical, and Pastoral Aspects of Death and Bereavement*. Amityville, NY: Baywood.
This volume assists caregivers in arriving at acceptable ethical positions in their pastoral, counselling, medical, and mortician roles. Spiritual and ethical aspects are considered. Attention is given to ministry for people with AIDS, to children's experience with death, and to spiritual care in hospices. Discussion includes euthanasia, organ transplants, neonatal death, and other issues.

Dunne, E.J., McIntosh, J.L. and Maxim, K.D. (eds). (1987). *Suicide and its Aftermath: Understanding and counseling the survivors*. Dunmore, PA: Norton.
Hope and compassion for suicide survivors are offered, and specific ideas for caregivers on how to understand and respond to families in the aftermath of suicide.

Dyregrov, A. (1991). *Grief in Children: A handbook for adults*. Bristol, PA and London: Jessica Kingsley.
This is useful for teachers, counsellors, pastoral workers, parents, and others faced with the task of understanding children in grief and trying to help them.

Fitzgerald, H. (2000). *The Grieving Teen: A guide for teenagers and their friends*. Concord, MA and London: Simon and Schuster.
Devotes attention to special needs of adolescents struggling with the loss of a peer or an other person in their life whether through violence, illness, or suicide.

Haasl, B. and Marnocha, J. (1990). *Bereavement Support Group Program for Children*. Muncie, IN: Accelerated Development.

Presents a five-session bereavement support program to use with children, with details of purposes, materials, and specific activities. The leader manual contains rationale, objectives, and procedures. The participant workbook includes fill-in activities and information for the children.

Heegard, M.E. (1992). *Facilitator Guide for Drawing Out Feelings*. Minneapolis, MN: Woodland Press.
This guide offers suggestions for developing grief support groups, and also gives directions for using the art process to help children (ages 6–12). Can be used individually or in groups dealing with loss and change. Curriculums are provided to use with four workbooks in the series: 'When someone very special dies', 'When something terrible happens', 'When mom and dad separate', and 'When someone has a very serious illness'.

Hendriks, J.H., Black, D. and Kaplan, T. (1993). *When Father Kills Mother: Guiding children through trauma and grief*. London: Routledge.
This is a sensitive reading to help professionals work with one who endures the impact of a simultaneous murder and parental loss. Trauma and confusion are compounded by fear, guilt, and/or anger.

Jarratt, C.J. (1994). *Helping Children Cope with Separation and Loss* (Rev. edn). Boston, MA: Harvard Common Press.
Death, adoption, foster care, abandonment, and divorce have great impact on children. This book shows the child's grief process. Counsellors learn how to tell a child about a loss, how to understand and support grief, how to help children respond to their emotions, how to deal with problems of self-esteem and control, and how to help the child eventually to let go and move on. Activities and props such as puppets, drawings, journals, and rituals are included. Issues such as getting stuck in mourning and recycling loss are discussed.

Kübler-Ross, E. (1973). *On Death and Dying*. London: Routledge.
A classic text for nurses, doctors, clergy, and others working with the dying.

LaGrand, L.E. (1986). *Coping with Separation and Loss as a Young Adult*. Springfield, IL: Charles Thomas.
Covers major types of loss in the lives of young adults, coping mechanisms, managing grief, and interventions. Based on the author's research with young adults.

Lendrum, S. and Syme, G. (1992). *The Gift of Tears*. London: Routledge.
Designed to help people who find that they have to cope, in the course of their work or daily lives, with the grief of others. The authors use theory, accessible case histories, and exercises to involve the reader.

Levine, S. (2005). *Unattended Sorrow: Recovering from loss and reviving the heart*. Emmaus, PA: Rodale.
Spiritual approach offering a series of techniques to help heal the pain. Addresses present loss as well as the impact of earlier losses through childhood abuse, teen rape, early divorce, or loss of a loved one.

Locke, S.A. (1990). *Coping with Loss: A guide for caregivers.* Springfield, IL: Charles Thomas.
This volume focuses on loss in the health-care setting: trauma or death in the emergency room, life-threatening illness, loss associated with reproduction, children and loss, the elderly and loss.

Miller, S. (2002). *Finding Hope when a Child Dies: What other cultures can teach us.* Concord, MA and London: Simon and Schuster.
Responds to questions like 'Why did my child die?' in order to seek meaning and to offer possibilities for returning to wholeness.

Mogenson, G. (1992). *Greeting the Angels: An imaginal view of the mourning process.* Amityville, NY: Baywood.
This book, in the genre of Imaginal Psychology, introduces 'angels', the interior figures who greet the bereaved during the mourning process in reverie and dream. As the bereaved person enters into a relationship with these images, grief becomes individualized. In a process which may become spiritual (but not necessarily religious), the therapist draws on dreams, biographical fragments, poetry, psychoanalysis, and Jungian psychology.

Murray Parkes, C. (1996). *Bereavement: Studies of grief in adult life* (3rd edn). London: Routledge.
A seminal study into the effects and scientific understanding of bereavement based on 12 years of work with widows.

Oates, M.D. (1993). *Death in the School Community: A handbook for counselors, teachers and administrators.* Alexandria, VA: American Counselling Association.
For counsellors, teachers, and administrators who must be prepared to respond to tragedy in their school, this book provides a step-by-step action plan and techniques for coping with post-traumatic stress disorder. It also explains the grief process in children and adolescents, healthy grief responses, and how to lead loss and grief groups. Case studies, various materials, and forms are provided.

O'Toole, D. (1988). *Bridging the Bereavement Gap* (2nd edn). Burnsville, NC: Rainbow Connection.
A comprehensive manual for preparing and programming hospice bereavement services.

Parkes, C.M., Laungani, P. and Young, B. (1997). *Death and Bereavement Across Cultures.* London: Routledge.
A cross-cultural perspective of issues related to death, dying, and the bereaved. Explores mourning traditions, rituals and beliefs of major world religions, with psychological and historical context.

Pennells, M. and Smith, S.C. (1995). *The Forgotten Mourners: Guidelines for working with bereaved children.* London: Jessica Kingsley.
This volume helpfully addresses the specific issues and methods that relate to younger bereaved.

Rosen, E.J. (1990). *Families Facing Death: Family dynamics of terminal illness.* Lexington, MA: Lexington Books.
This is a guide for those who are trying to help families through the struggle of living with dying. The purpose is to find principles for understanding why families behave as they do and how they can be helped. Examples are offered of families who confronted loss successfully as well as some that did not. It doesn't moralize, nor does it merely present sterile data.

Roth, D. and LeVier, E. (eds). (1990). *Being Human in the Face of Death.* Santa Monica, CA: IBS.
This book can help caregivers who work with dying people unlock one of the best resources they have: their humanness. The focus is on the dying process, and on the function that caregivers can play in being present for a dying person and in being able to facilitate communication between patient and family members. Includes training resources for caregivers.

Staudacher, C. (1991). *Men and Grief: A guide for men surviving the death of a loved one.* Oakland, CA: New Harbinger.
This volume explores the unique patterns of male bereavement. Based on extensive interviews with male survivors, it describes the characteristics of male grief, explains the forces that influence it, and provides step-by-step help for the male survivor. It is presented both as a guide for men surviving the death of a loved one and a resource for caregivers and mental health professionals.

Wolfelt, A. (1988). *Death and Grief: A guide for clergy.* Muncie, IN: Accelerated Development.
Focuses on adult grief, with special emphasis on the role of clergy in bereavement care.

Woznick, L.A. and Goodheart, C.D. (2002). *Living with Childhood Cancer: A practical guide to help* families. Washington, DC: American Psychological Association.
Professionals will be able to help families address the impact of pediatric cancer. This book offers emotional guidance, useful information, and practical advice.

Books on Loss Including Death

Aiken, L.R. (1994). *Dying, Death, and Bereavement* (3rd edn). Boston, MA: Allyn and Bacon.
A comprehensive and interdisciplinary survey of research, theory, and professional practices concerned with death and dying. It is a review of thanatology, including cultural beliefs and practices, human development and death, moral and legal issues, treatment of the dying and the dead, and bereavement and widowhood. Contains material on abortion, euthanasia, and AIDS.

Corless, I.B., Germino, B.B. and Pittman, M. (1994). *Dying, Death, and Bereavement: Theoretical perspectives and other ways of knowing.* Boston, MA: Jones and Bartlett.

Presents six chapters on aspects of death and dying, and 11 chapters on thanatology. A unique section gives a critical interpretation of several images of death from the literary and visual arts in an effort to explore the universal experience that underlies both traditional and non-traditional forms of mourning.

Counts, D.R. and Counts, D.A. (eds). (1991). *Coping with the Final Tragedy: Cultural variation in dying and grieving*. Amityville, NY: Baywood.
This book emphasizes common concerns shared by all humanity while at the same time emphasizing cultural differences and the variety in the ways that people experience death and grief.

DeSpelder, L.A. and Strickland, A.L. (1992). *The Last Dance: Encountering death and dying* (3rd edn). Mountain View, CA: Mayfield.
Diverse points of view on death and dying are presented to examine the assumptions, orientations, and predispositions that have limited or inhibited discussion for decades. The book's theme is that unbiased investigation will make choices available which otherwise might be neglected due to prejudice or ignorance.

Dickinson, D. and Johnson, M. (1993). *Death, Dying and Bereavement*. London: Sage.
A collection of separate writings expressing diverse viewpoints on the human issues surrounding death.

Leming, M.R. and Dickinson, G.E. (2005). *Understanding Death, Dying, and Bereavement*. Boston, MA: Wadsworth Thomson.
A social-psychological approach to theory and research, with an emphasis on the individual and coping with death and dying.

Littlewood, J. (1992). *Aspects of Grief: Bereavement in adult life*. London: Routledge.
Looks at the importance of support networks, both family and professional, and how society's attitudes affect our ability to cope.

Marris, P. (1986). *Loss and Change* (Rev. edn). London: Routledge.
Discusses social change and the diffusion of innovations that have influenced our lives. Bereavement is treated as a special form of loss.

Rickgarn, R.L.V. (1994). *Perspectives on College Suicide*. Amityville, NY: Baywood.
With the words of college students themselves about their suicidal experience, the reader learns the effect suicide has upon individuals and the campus as a whole. Information on suicide rate, suicide prevention programmes, antecedents and aetiology of suicide, and intervention procedures is offered, so that both paraprofessionals and professionals will gain insight and information on how to act appropriately to suicide incidence on campus.

Stroebe, M.S., Hansson, R.O., Stroebe, W. and Schut, H. (eds). (2001). *Handbook of Bereavement Research: Consequences, coping, and care*. Washington, DC: American Psychological Association.

Broad view of diverse contemporary approaches to bereavement, examining both normal adaptation and complicated manifestations of grief.

Wertheimer, A. (1986). *A Special Scar: The experiences of people bereaved by suicide.* London: Routledge.
This book places special emphasis on understanding family relationships as they have been affected by a loved one's self-inflicted death.

Zisook, S. (ed.). (1987). *Biopsychosocial Aspects of Bereavement.* Washington, DC: American Psychiatric Press.
This book distinguishes between 'normal' and pathological grief. Includes the varied reasons for an individual crossing the boundary, spousal grief and adjustment to widowhood, inventories and measures of grief and distress, and psychoendocrine and immune functions during bereavement.

Books Focused on Children

Carney, K.L. (2004). *Barklay and Eve: Explaining cancer to children of all ages.* Wethersfield, CT: Dragonfly (www.BarklayEve.com).
This book provides basic information that is needed to understand a cancer diagnosis. Barklay and Eve define cancer, explain radiation and chemotherapy, and emphasize that everyone's cancer is different.

Clifton, L. (1983). *Everett Anderson's Goodbye.* New York: Henry Holt.
Portrait of a little boy who is trying to come to grips with his father's death. (For ages 5–8.)

Cohn, J. (1987). *I Had a Friend Named Peter: Talking to children about the death of a friend.* New York: Morrow.
When a child learns about her friend's death, her parents and teacher answer questions about dying, funerals, and the burial process. (For ages 5–9.)

Gootman, M.E. (1994). *When a Friend Dies.* Minneapolis, MN: Free Spirit.
A self-help book for teens about grieving and healing. (For ages 11 and up.)

Hipp, E. (1995). *Help for the Hard Times.* Center City, MN: Hazelden.
This book is for adolescents experiencing losses of many kinds. It explains types and experiences of losses and ways to navigate through grief, grow through the hard times and heal.

Holmes, M.M. (2000). *A Terrible Thing Happened.* Washington, DC: Magination.
A gently-told and illustrated story for children ages 4–8 who have witnessed any kind of violent or traumatic episode, including physical abuse, accidents, homicide, suicide, and natural disasters such as fire and flood.

Krementz, J. (1981). *How it Feels when a Parent Dies.* New York: Knopf.
Youth of different religious and ethnic backgrounds tell of their experience and feelings upon loss of a parent. (For ages 8–16.)

LeShan, E. (1976). *Learning to Say Good-bye when a Parent Dies*. New York: Macmillan.
Through numerous case histories, the psychologist-author discusses the feelings, fears, fantasies, and questions children have when a parent dies. Topics range from fear of abandonment and guilt to recovery and meeting future challenges. (For ages 8+.)

Mills, J.C. (1992). *Little Tree: A story for children with serious medical problems*. Washington, DC: Magination.
Utilizing the healing metaphor of a tree, this book presents a powerful message of inspiration and hope. (For ages 4–8.)

Mills, J.C. (1993). *Gentle Willow: A story for children about dying*. Washington, DC: Magination.
This book is written for children ages 5–9 who may not survive their illness. The story will also help all children to deal with the death of family, friends, or even pets. It addresses feelings of sadness, love, disbelief, and anger. Ultimately it is one of hope.

Moser, A. (1996). *Don't Despair on Thursdays*. Kansas City, KS: Landmark.
The grief process is explained to children (ages 5–10) and helps them understand that grieving is a normal response. In addition, children learn that grief will last more than just a few days or weeks. The author offers practical approaches and easy-to-follow methods that children can use day by day to cope with the emotional pain they feel.

Oelhberg, B. (1996). *Making it Better: Activities for children living in a stressful world*. St Paul, MN: Redleaf.
This workbook is intended for classroom use in grades 1–8, but may also be used in counselling sessions. It offers 70+ practical activities based on sound research, and guidance on how to seize opportunities to reach children and help them survive, thrive, and heal.

O'Toole. D. (1989). *Aarvy Aardvark Finds Hope*. Burnsville, NC: Rainbow Connection.
A story for all ages about loving and losing, friendship and hope.

Shuman, C. (2003). *Jenny is Scared: When sad things happen in the world*. Washington, DC: Magination.
This book explores children's fears and reactions surrounding terrorism, war, and other violent events. (For ages 4–8.)

Traisman, E.S. (1992). *Fire in My Heart, Ice in My Veins*. Omaha, NE: Centering Corporation.
A creative journal for adolescents that encourages them to honor, record, and experience their many feelings and questions related to their loss and memories.

Wolfelt, A.D. (1996). *How I Feel: A coloring book for grieving children*. Batesville, IN: Batesville Management Services.

A coloring book designed for children ages 3–8 that presents many of the feelings that grieving children experience. The book can also be used by adults to read, explain, and color along with their grieving child.

Organizations

American Academy of Grief Counselors, American Institute for Health Care Professionals, 2400 Niles-Cortland Rd SE, Suite #3, Warren, OH 44484, USA. Tel: (330) 652–7776; www.aihcp.org/aagc.htm.
Offers certification and fellowship programs for professionals who practice grief counselling.

American Association of Suicidology, 5221 Wisconsin Ave NW, Washington, DC 20015, USA. Tel: (202) 237-2280; www.suicidology.org.
Education organization that serves as a national clearing house on suicide.

American Sudden Infant Death Syndrome (SIDS) Institute, 509 Augusta Dr, Marietta, GA 30067, USA. Tel: (800) 232-SIDS (7437); www.sids.org.
Offers support and crisis counselling to persons who have lost a child to SIDS. Also provides grief literature and referral information.

Association for Death Education and Counseling, 60 Revere Dr, Suite 500, Northbrook, IL 60062. Tel: (847) 509-0403; www.adec.org.
A nonprofit educational, professional, and scientific organization devoted to the promotion and upgrading of the quality of death education and death-related counselling. Annual conference.

Befrienders Worldwide, www.befrienders.org. Website lists contact information in many countries worldwide. Helpline offers support for people in distress and those who may be considering suicide.

Childhood Bereavement Network UK, www.childhoodbereavementnetwork. org.uk.
CBN works in partnership with service providers to support bereaved children throughout the UK and to increase access to information, guidance, and support.

Child Death Helpline (UK), Tel: 0808-808-1677; www.childdeathhelpline.org.uk.
Helpline for anyone affected by the death of a child.

Children's Hospice International, 1101 King Street, #131, Alexandria, VA 22314, USA. Tel: (800) 24-CHILD; www.chionline.org.
CHI provides a support system and resource bank for health-care professionals, families, and organizations that offer hospice care to terminally ill children.

CLIMB, Inc. (Center for Loss in Multiple Birth), P.O. Box 3696, Oak Brook, IL 60522, USA. Tel: (907) 222-5321; www.climb-support.org.

International network. Support by and for parents who have experienced the death of one or more of their children during a multiple pregnancy, at birth, or in infancy or childhood. Telephone support, information on the grieving process, monthly chapter meetings. National newsletter and sibling newsletter. Chapter leader's manual. Resource library.

Compassionate Friends, Box 3696, Oak Brook, IL 60522, USA. Tel: (877) 969-0010; www.compassionatefriends.org.
Nationwide (in USA) self-help support groups for parents who have experienced the death of a child from any cause at any age. Newsletter. In the UK: www.tcf.org.uk.

Cot Death Research and Support for Bereaved Parents, c/o Jim McDonald, 117 High Street, Worle, Weston-super-Mare, BS22 0EM, UK. Tel: 0468-525525.
A full counselling service to newly bereaved parents following the unexpected death of their baby.

CRUSE-Bereavement Care, Cruse House, Unit 0.1, One Victoria Villas, Richmond, Surrey, TW9 2GW, UK. Tel: 020-8939-9530; www.crusebereavementcare. org.uk.
A registered charity offering counselling, information and support through nearly 200 branches in the UK.

Lesbian and Gay Bereavement Project, Counsellling Department, Lighthouse West London, 111-117 Lancaster Road, London, W11 1QT, UK. Tel: 020-7403-5969.
Telephone counselling giving support and counselling for those bereaved by death of same-sex life partner. Helpline volunteer can help locate suitable religious leaders or secular officiants for the funeral, and suggest solicitors and funeral directors.

National Association of Parents of Murdered Children, 100 E. Eighth Street, Room B-41, Cincinnati, OH 45202, USA. Tel: (888) 818-POMC (7662); www.pomc.com.
Self-help group helps families and friends of those who have lost their lives through violence. Offers resources and referral support to parents.

National Hospice and Palliative Care Organization, 1700 Diagonal Rd, Suite 625, Alexandria, VA 22314, USA. Tel: (703) 516-4928; www.nhpco.org.
Maintains resource and referral information for persons who are dying. Strives to help make appropriate choices, and for highest quality patient care using hospices, with dignity and freedom from pain.

The Rainbow Centre, 27 Lilymead Avenue, Bristol, B54 2BY, UK. Tel: 0117-985-3354; www.rainbowcentre.org.
Free and professional support for children and families affected by cancer, life-threatening illness, and bereavement.

Rainbows for All God's Children, 1111 Tower Road, Schaumburg, IL 60173, USA. Tel: (841) 310-1880.
International organization with 4,000 affiliated groups. Establishes peer support groups in churches, schools or social agencies for children and adults who are grieving a death, divorce, or other painful transition in their family. Groups are led by trained adults. Newsletter, information, and referrals.

Samaritans, c/o Chris, P.O. Box 9090, Stirling, FK8 2SA, UK. Tel: 08457-909090; www.samaritans.org.uk.
Offers emotional support and befriending to the lonely, suicidal, and despairing in complete confidence at any time of the day or night.

Share, St Elizabeth's Hospital, 211 S. 3rd Street, Belleville, IL 62222, USA. Tel: (618) 234-2120.
International support groups for parents who have lost a child, particularly (but not exclusively) through miscarriage, stillbirth, or newborn death.

Society of Military Widows, National Association of Uniformed Services, 5535 Hempstead Way, Springfield, VA 22151, USA. Tel: (703) 750-1342; www. militarywidows.org.
National nonpartisan group of widows and widowers of career members of the uniformed services whose purpose is to provide companionship, sympathetic understanding, referral services, and helpful advice.

St Francis Center, 1768 Church St NW, Washington, DC 20036, USA. Tel: (202) 363-8500.
This nonsectarian organization counsells and supports adults, children, and families; offers guidance to schools, religious institutions, and workplaces; and helps the community to respond better to those affected by loss. A significant service is the offering of training workshops on thanatology for professional and volunteer caregivers, clergy, and mental health workers.

Stillbirth and Neonatal Death Society (SANDS), 28 Portland Place, London, WIN 4DE, UK. Tel: 020-7436-7940; www.uksands.org.
Help to individuals or couples by way of befriending or group support from parents who have suffered a similar bereavement.

Tender Hearts, c/o Triplet Connection, P.O. Box 693392, Stockton, CA 95269, USA. Tel: (209) 474-0885; www.peacehealth.org.
International network of parents who have lost one or more children in multiple births. Newsletter information and referrals, phone support, penpals.

THEOS (They Help Each Other Spiritually), 717 Liberty Avenue, 1301 Clark Building, Pittsburgh, PA 15222, USA. Tel: (412) 471-7779.
International, over 100 chapters. Assists widowed persons of all ages and their families to rebuild their lives through mutual self-help. Network of local groups. Quarterly newsletter, chapter development guidelines.

Twinless Twin Support Group, P.O. Box 980481, Ypsilanti, MI 48198-0481. Tel: (888) 205-8962; www.twinlesstwins.org.
International network. Mutual support for twins and other multiples who have lost their twin through death or estrangement at any age. Provides information and referrals, phone support, penpals, conferences. Newsletter. Group development guidelines. Provides assistance in starting local groups. Annual meeting.

Victim Support, Cranmer House, 39 Brixton Road, Stockwell, London, SW9 5DZ, UK. Tel: 0845-3030-900; www.victimsupport.org.uk.
Practical help and advice and emotional support to victims following crime.

Winston's Wish, Clara Burgess Centre, Bayshill Road, Cheltham, GL50 3AW. Tel: 01242 515157; www.winstonswish.org.uk.
Supports bereaved children and young people up to age 18 after a family death. Offers programs of practical support and guidance to families, to professionals and to anyone concerned about a grieving child.

Websites

www.childrensgrief.net   offers information that is useful in helping children deal with grief. Grief therapist and educator, Linda Goldman, manages this site.

www.compassionatefriends.com   site whose mission is to assist families toward the positive resolution of grief following the death of a child and to provide information to help others be supportive.

www.healingheart.net   dedicated to providing grief support and services to parents whose child has died – includes information on sibling grief, parent and grandparent grief, and a section on infant loss.

www.journeyofhearts.org   site created by physicians for anyone who has previously or is now experiencing a loss. Contains information as well as stories and poetry.

www.kidshealth.org/parent/emotions/feelings/death.html   an article from kidshealth.org on how parents can help their child deal with death.

www.grievingchild.org   site sponsored by the Dougy Center for Grieving Children – includes sections for children and adults who have experienced the death of someone close to them.

www.kidsource.com/sids/childrensgrief.html   chart that discusses developmental considerations concerning children's grief, including their developmental stage, concept of death, grief response, signs of distress, and possible interventions.

Bibliographies and Publishing Houses

Taylor and Francis Group, 325 Chestnut St, Suite 800, Philadelphia, PA 19106, USA. Tel: (215) 625-2919; www.taylorandfrancisgroup.com.
Offers several books, video and audio tapes, and leader manuals for groups dealing with grief and loss.

Baywood Publishing Co., 26 Austin Avenue, Amityville, NY 11701, USA. Tel: (631) 691-1270; www.baywood.com.
Offers a large selection of publications on death, dying, and loss.

Compassionbooks, www.compassionbooks.com.
An internet website which offers over 400 books, videos, and audios to help children and adults through serious illness, death and dying, grief, bereavement, and losses of all kinds including divorce, suicide, trauma, and violence.

Rudman, M.K., Gagne, K.D. and Bernstein, J.E. (eds). (1994). *Books to Help Children Cope with Separation and Loss: An annotated bibliography*. New Providence, NJ: Bowker.
This volume includes over 740 recommended fiction and nonfiction 'real-life' situation books focusing on separation and loss experiences. For working with children aged 3–16.

Simon and Schuster, 30 Monument Square, Concord, MA 01742, USA; www.simonsays.com.
Handles a variety of books ranging from professional treatises to how-to guides on death and bereavement-related topics.

Sounds True Catalog, 413 S. Arthur Ave, Louisville, CO 80027, USA; www.soundstrue.com.
Offers video and audio tapes on dying, death, and mourning.

Magazines and Professional Journals

Bereavement: A magazine of hope and healing. Bereavement Publications, P.O. Box 61, Montrose, CO 81402, USA. Tel: (888) 604-4673; www.bereavementmag.com.

Bereavement Care. CRUSE, Cruse Bereavement Care, Unit 0.1, One Victoria Villas, Richmond, Surrey, TW9 2GW, UK. Tel: 020-8939-9530; www.crusebereavementcare.org.uk.

Death Studies. Taylor and Francis, 325 Chestnut St, Suite 800, Philadelphia, PA 19106, USA. Tel: (215) 625-2919. Also at Rankine Road, Basingstoke, Haugushire, RG24 8PR, UK. Tel: 01256-813000; www.taylorandfrancisgroup.com.

Omega: Journal of Death and Dying. Baywood Publishing Co., 26 Austin Avenue, Amityville, NY 11701, USA. Tel: (631) 691-1270; www.baywood.com.

References

Abrahm, J. (2006). 'Practical aspects of palliative medicine: Integrating palliative care into clinical practice'. Paper presented at the Harvard Medical School Center for Palliative Care, Boston, MA, October.

Ainsworth, M., Blehar, M., Waters, E. and Wall, S. (1978). *Patterns of Attachments: A psychological study of the strange situation*. Hillsdale, NJ: Erlbaum.

American Psychiatric Association (1994). *Diagnostic and Statistical Marmal of Mental Disorders* (4th edn). Washington, DC: APA.

Attig, T. (1992). 'Relearning the world'. Paper presented at the annual bereavement seminar of the Grief Support and Education Center, Canton, Ohio, October.

Augsburger, D.W. (1981). *Caring Enough to Forgive*. Ventura, CA: Regal.

Beck, A.T. (1978). *Beck Depression Inventory*. Philadelphia, PA: Centre for Cognitive Therapy.

Becker, E. (1973). *The Denial of Death*. New York: The Free Press.

Benard, B. (1991). *Fostering Resiliency in Kids: Protective factors in the family, school, and community*. Minneapolis, MN: National Resilience Resource Center, University of Minnesota.

Bending, M. (1993). *Caring for Bereaved Children*. Richmond, Surrey: CRUSE-Bereavement Care.

Black, D. (2002). 'Bereavement'. In M. Rutter and E. Taylor (eds.), *Child Psychiatry: Modern approaches* (4th edn). Oxford: Blackwells. pp. 299–308.

Bowen, M. (1974). 'Toward the differentiation of self in one's family of origin'. In F. Andres and J. Lorio (eds.), *Georgetown Family Symposium*, Vol. 1. Washington, DC: Department of Psychiatry, Georgetown University Medical Center.

Bowlby, J. (1969). *Attachment and Loss, Vol. 1: Attachment*. New York: Basic Books.

Bowlby, J. (1973). *Attachment and Loss, Vol. 2: Separation: Anxiety and anger*. New York: Basic Books.

Bowlby, J. (1980). *Attachment and Loss, Vol 3: Loss: Sadness and depression*. New York: Basic Books.

Bowlby-West, L. (1983). 'The impact of death on the family system'. *Journal of Family Therapy*, 5: 279–94.

Brayer, M.M. (1977). 'The spiritual component'. In N. Linzer (ed.), *Understanding Bereavement and Grief*. New York: Yeshiva University Press. pp. 47–72.

Bronfenbrenner, U. (1979). *The Ecology of Human Development*. Cambridge, MA: Harvard University Press.

Buchwald, A. (2006). *Too Soon to Say Goodbye*. New York: Random House.

Butler, R.N. (1963). 'The life review: An interpretation of reminiscence in the aged'. *Psychiatry*, 26, 65–75.

Cattell, R.B., Krug, S.E. and Sheier, I.H. (1957/1976). *IPAT Anxiety Scale Questionnaire: Handbook*. Champaign, IL: Institute for Personality and Ability Testing.

Childsworks/Childsplay, LLC, subsidiary Genesis Direct, Inc. (Manufacturer). (1992). *The Angry Monster Machine: A game to teach kids how to express anger* (game, available from Childworks/Childsplay, LLC, Secaucus, NJ).

Clark, A. (1985). 'Grief and gestalt therapy', *The Gestalt Journal*, 1, 49–63.

Clayson, H. (2003). 'Hospices to fortune', (*BMA News*, 22 February, 13–14).

'Complicated grief'. (2006). *Harvard Mental Health Letter*, 23, 1–3.

Corr, C.A. (1991). 'Care of the terminally ill'. Paper presented at the Association of Death Education and Counseling 13th Annual Conference, Duluth, MN.

Corr, C.A. (1995). 'Children's understanding of death'. In K.J. Doka (ed.), *Children Mourning Children*. Washington, DC: Hospice Foundation of America. pp. 3–16.

Couldrick, A. (1991). *Grief and Bereavement: Understanding children*. Oxford: Sobell.

Cullinan, A. (1989). 'Challenges counseling children in grief'. *The Forum Newsletter*, 13 (5), 4, 14.

Davidson, M. (1983). *Uncommon Sense: The life and thought of Ludwig von Bertalanffy*. Los Angeles, CA: Tarcher.

Davies, B. (1990). 'Long-term follow-up of bereaved siblings'. In J.D. Morgan (ed.), *The Dying and the Bereaved Teenager*. Philadelphia, PA: The Charles Press. pp. 78–9.

Day, B. (1992). 'Suicide: The ultimate abandonment'. Paper presented at the Association of Death Education and Counseling 14th Annual Conference, Boston, MA, March.

Demi, A.S. and Miles, M. (1987). 'Parameters of normal grief: A Delphi study'. *Death Studies*, 11, 397–412.

Dent, A. (2005). 'Theoretical perspectives: linking research and practice'. In B. Monroe and F. Kraus (eds.), *Brief Interventions with Bereaved Children*. London: Oxford University Press. pp.13–27.

Duffy, W. (1991). *The Bereaved Child*. Ongar: The National Society.

Deutsch, H. (1937). 'Absence of grief', *Psychoanalytic Quarterly*, 6, 12–22.

Doka, K. (ed.). (1989). *Disenfranchised Grief: Recognizing hidden sorrow*. Lexington, MA: Lexington Books.

Duvall, E.M. and Miller, B.C. (1985). *Marriage and Family Development* (6th edn). New York: Harper and Row.

Engel, G. (1961). 'Is grief a disease? A challenge for medical research'. *Psychosomatic Medicine*, 23, 18–22.

Erikson, E. (1980). *Identity and the Life Cycle*. New York: Norton.

Fox, S.S. (1988). *Good Grief: Helping groups of children when a friend dies*. Boston, MA: The New England Association for the Education of Young Children.

Fox, S.S (1991). 'Grieving children and adolescents'. Workshop presented by National Center for Death Education, Newton, MA, July.

Freud, S. (1914/1957). 'Mourning and melancholia'. In J. Strachey (ed. and trans.), *The Standard Edition of the Complete Psychological Works of Sigmund Freud*, Vol. 14. London: Hogarth.

Fulton, R.F. (1977). 'General aspects'. In N. Linzer (ed.), *Understanding Bereavement and Grief*. New York: Yeshiva University Press. pp. 3–9.

Glasser, W. (1990). *Control Theory*. New York: Harper and Row.

Glick, I.O., Weiss, R.S. and Parkes, C.M. (1974). *The First Year of Bereavement*. New York: Wiley.

Grotberg, E. (1995). *A Guide to Promoting Resiliency in Children: Strengthening the human spirit*. The Hague: The Bernard van Leer Foundation.

Guerin, P.J. and Pendagast, E.G. (1976). 'Evaluation of family system and Genogram'. In P.J. Guerin (ed.), *Family Therapy: Theory and Practice*. New York: Gardner Press.

Hanser, S. (2006). 'Music therapy in palliative care'. Paper presented at the Harvard Medical School Center for Palliative Care, Boston, MA, October.

Horowitz, M., Wiltier, N. and Alvarez, W. (1979). 'Impact of events scale: A measure of subjective stress'. *Psychosomatic Medicine*, 41 (3), 209–18.

Horowitz, M.J., Wilner, N., Marmar, C. and Krupnick. J. (1980). 'Pathological grief and the activation of latent self-images'. *American Journal of Psychiatry*, 137, 1157–62.

Humphrey, G.M., Harper, C.D. and Bridges, V. (1990). *Units on Loss and Grief for Use with Children and Adolescents in the School Setting*, Vol. 1, No. 2. North Canton, OH: The Grief Support and Education Center.

Ivey, A.E. (1986). *Developmental Therapy*. San Francisco, CA: Jossey-Bass.

Jackson, D.D. (1965). 'Family rules: Marital quid pro quo'. *Archives of General Psychiatry*, 12, 589–94.

Jackson, E. (1977). 'The spiritual component'. In N. Linzer (ed.), *Understanding Bereavement and Grief*. New York: Yeshiva University Press. pp. 78–9.

Jordan, J.R. (1992). 'Cumulative loss, current stress, and the family: A pilot investigation of individual and systemic effects'. *Omega*, 24 (4), 309–32.

Kennell, J.H. and Klaus, M.H. (1976). *Maternal Infant Bonding*. St Louis, KT: Mosby.

Kenyon, B. (2001). 'Current research in children's conceptions of death: A critical review'. *Omega*, 43 (1), 63–91.

Kissane, D.W. and Bloch, S. (1994) 'Family grief'. *British Journal of Psychiatry*, 164: 728–40.

Kissane, D.W. and Bloch, S. (2002). *Family-focused Grief Therapy*. Milton Keynes: Open University Press, McGraw-Hill Education.

Krementz, J. (1989). 'You always have to have hope: How it feels to fight for your life', *Family Circle*, September, 88–92.

Kübler-Ross, E. (1969). *On Death and Dying*. New York: Macmillan.

Kübler-Ross, E. (1975). *Death: The final stage of growth*. New York: Macmillan.

Lazarus, R.S. and Folkman, S. (1984). *Stress, Appraisal, and Coping*. New York: Springer.

Lester, J. (2005). 'Life review with the terminally ill-narrative therapies'. In P. Firth, G. Luff and D. Oliviere (eds), *Loss, Change and Bereavement in Palliative Care*. Milton Keynes: Open University Press, McGraw-Hill Education. pp. 66–79.

Lieberman, S. and Black, D. (1982). 'Loss, mourning and grief'. In A. Bentovim, G.G. Barnes and A. Cooklin (eds), *Family Therapy: Complementary frameworks of theory and practice*. New York: Grune and Stratton. pp. 373–87.

Lifton, R. (1994). *The Protean Self: Human resilience in an age of fragmentation*. New York: Basic Books.

Lindemann, E. (1944). 'Symptomatology and management of acute grief'. *American Journal of Psychiatry*, 101, 141–8.

Lo, B., Quill, T. and Tulsky, J. (1999). 'Discussing palliative care with patients'. *Annals of Internal Medicine*, 130: 744–9.

Marwit, S.J. and Klass, D. (1996). 'Grief and the role of the inner representation of the deceased'. In D. Klass, P.R. Silverman and S.L. Nickman (eds), *Continuing Bonds*. Washington, DC: Taylor and Francis. pp. 297–309.

Minuchin, S. (1974). *Families and Family Therapy*. Cambridge, MA: Harvard University Press.

Multicultural Family Institute (2006). 'Geneograms'. Accessed January 2007 from www.multiculturalfamily.org/geneograms.

Nadeau, J.W. (1998). *Families Making Sense of Death*. Thousand Oaks, CA: Sage.

Nagy, M.A. (1948). 'The child's theories concerning death'. *Journal of Genetic Psychology*, 73, 3–27.

Neimeyer, R.A. (1998) *Lessons of Loss: A guide to coping*. New York: McGraw-Hill.

Neimeyer, R.A. (2001a). 'Introduction: Meaning reconstruction and loss'. In R.A. Neimeyer (ed.), *Meaning Reconstruction and the Experience of Loss*. Washington, DC: American Psychological Association. pp. 1–9.

Neimeyer, R.A. (2001b). 'The language of loss: Therapy as a process of meaning reconstruction'. In R.A. Neimeyer (ed.), *Meaning Reconstruction and the Experience of Loss*. Washington, DC: American Psychological Association. pp. 261–92.

Nelson, M.K. (1992). 'A new theory of forgiveness'. Unpublished doctoral dissertation, Purdue University, West LaFayette, IN.

Nichols, J.A. (1986). 'Newborn death'. In T. Rando (ed.), *Parental Loss of a Child*. Champaign, IL: Research Press. pp. 145–57.

Nichols, M.P. and Schwartz, R.C. (1991). *Family Therapy: Concepts and methods* (2nd edn). Boston: Allyn and Bacon.

Noppe, I. and Noppe, L. (2004). 'Adolescent experiences with death: Letting go of immortality'. *Journal of Mental Health Counselling*, 26 (2), 146–67.

Parkes, C.M. and Weiss, R.S. (1983) *Recovery from Bereavement*. New York: Basic Books.

Quinn, A. (2005). 'The context of loss, change and bereavement in palliative care'. In P. Firth, G. Luff and D. Oliviere (eds), *Loss, Change and Bereavement in Palliative Care*. Berkshire, England: Open University Press, McGraw-Hill Education. pp. 1–17.

Rando, T.A. (ed.). (1986). *Loss and Anticipatory Grief*. Lexington, MA: Lexington Books.

Rando, T.A. (1988). *Grieving: How to go on living when someone you love dies*. Lexington, MA: Lexington Books.

Rando, T.A. (1993a). *Treatment of Complicated Mourning*. Champaign, IL: Research Press.

Rando, T.A. (1993b). 'An investigation of grief and adaptation in parents whose children have died from cancer'. *Journal of Pediatric Psychology*, 8, 3–20.

Raphael, B. (1983). *The Anatomy of Bereavement*. New York: Basic Books.

Raphael, B. (1984). *The Anatomy of Bereavement*. London: Hutchinson.

Raphael, B. (1992). 'Counseling after catastrophic loss'. Paper presented at the Association of Death Education and Counseling 14th Annual Conference, Boston, MA, March.

Redmond, L. (1989). *Surviving: When someone you love was murdered*. Clearwater, FL: Psychological Consultation and Education Services.

Rose, A.M. (1962). *Human Behaviour and Social Processes*. Boston, MA: Houghton-Mifflin.

Rosenblatt, P.C. and Fischer, L.R. (1993). 'Qualitative family research'. In P.B. Boss, W.J. Doherty, R. La Rossa, W.R. Schumn and S.K. Steinmetz (eds), *Source Book of Family Theories and Methods: A contextual approach*. New York: Plenum. pp. 167–77.

Rotter, S.B. (1966). 'Generalized expectancies for internal vs. external control of reinforcement', *Psychological Monographs*, 80 (1), (Whole No. 609).

Rowling, L. (2003). *Grief in the School Communities: Effective support strategies*. Milton Keynes: Open University Press.

Rowling, L. (2005). 'Loss and grief in the school communities'. In B. Monroe and F. Kraus (eds), *Brief Interventions with Bereaved Children*. London: Oxford Press. pp. 159–73.

Rubin, S.S. (1996) 'The wounded family: Bereaved parents and the impact of adult child loss'. In D. Klass, P.R. Silverman and S.L. Nickman (eds), *Continuing Bonds*. Washington, DC: Taylor and Francis. pp. 217–32.

Ryan, J.A. (1986). *Ethnic, Cultural, and Religious Observances at the Time of Death and Dying*. Boston, MA: The Good Grief Program.

Rynearson, E. (1990). 'Pathological grief: The queen's croquet ground'. *Psychiatric Annals*, 20, 295–303.

Schneider, M.E. (2006). 'Palliative care to be recognized as a new subspecialty'. *Internal Medicine News*, 39 (20), 1–2.

Silverman, P.R. and Klass, D. (1996). 'Introduction: What's the problem?' In D. Klass, P.R. Silverman and S.L. Nickman (eds), *Continuing Bonds*. Washington, DC: Taylor and Francis. pp. 4–27.

Silverman, P.R. and Nickman, S.L. (1996a). 'Children's construction of their dead parent'. In D. Klass, P.R. Silverman and S.L. Nickman (eds), *Continuing Bonds*. Washington, DC: Taylor and Francis. pp. 73–86.

Silverman, P.R. and Nickman, S.L. (1996b). 'Concluding thoughts'. In D. Klass, P.R. Silverman and S.L. Nickman (eds), *Continuing Bonds*. Washington, DC: Taylor and Francis. pp. 349–55.

Smith, C.S. and Pennells, M. (1995). 'The grieving child: From grief to belief'. In S.C. Smith and M. Pennells (eds), *Interventions with Bereaved Children*. London and Bristol, PA: Jessica Kingsley. pp. 1–6.

Speece, M.W. and Brent, S.B (1984). 'Children's understanding of death: A review of three components of a death concept'. *Child Development*, 55, 1671–86.

Sprenkle, D.H. and Piercy, F.P. (1992). 'A family therapy informed view of the current state of the family in the United States'. *Family Relations*, 41, 404–408.

Stephenson, J.S. (1985). *Death, Grief, and Mourning*. New York: The Free Press.

Stokes, J.A. (2004). *Then, Now and Always.* Cheltenham, GL: Winston's Wish.

Stroebe, M.S. and Schut, H. (1999). 'The dual process model of coping with bereavement: Rationale and description'. *Death Studies*, 23, 197–211.

Stroebe, M.S. and Schut, H. (2001). 'Meaning making in the dual process model of coping with bereavement'. In R.A. Neimeyer (ed.), *Meaning Reconstruction and the Experience of Loss.* Washington, DC: American Psychological Association. pp. 55–73.

Thomas, W.I. (1923). 'William I. Thomas on the definition of the situation'. In N. Rousseau (ed.), *Self, Symbols, and Society.* Oxford: Rowman and Littlefield. pp. 103–15.

Thoresen, C.E., Harris, A.H.S. and Luskin, F. (2000). 'Forgiveness and health: An unanswered question'. In M.E. McCullough, K.I. Pargament and C.E. Thoresen (eds), *Forgiveness.* New York: The Guilford Press. pp. 254–80.

Walsh, F. and McGoldrick, M. (1988). 'Loss and the family cycle'. In C.J. Falicou (ed.), *Family Transitions: Continuity and change over the life cycle.* New York: Guilford Press. pp. 311–36.

Wisensale, S.K. (1992). 'Toward the 21st century: Family change and public policy'. *Family Relations*, 199, 141, 417–22.

Wolin, S. and Wolin, S. (1993). *The Resilient Self.* New York: Villiard.

Worden, J.W. (1996). *Children and Grief: When a parent dies.* New York: Guilford Press.

Worden, J.W. (2002). *Grief Counseling and Grief Therapy: A handbook for the mental health practitioner* (3rd edn). New York: Springer.

Yalom, I.D. (1995). *The Theory and Practice of Group Psychotherapy* (5th edn). New York: Basic Books.

Zimmerman, S.L. (1992). 'Family trends: What implications for family policy?'. *Family Relations*, 41, 423–9.

Zimpfer, D.G. (1992). 'Psychosocial treatment of life-threatening disease: A wellness model'. *Journal of Counseling and Development*, 71, 203–9.

Index

Abrahm, J., 130
Accommodation, 15, 44
AIDS, 142–4
Ainsworth, M., 63
American Psychiatric Association, 147
Anticipated loss
  definitions/conceptions, 125–6
  illness, 126
  retirement, 126
Assessment, pre-counsellling, 19–20
Attachment
  theory, 6–7, 62–3, 149–50
  styles, 62–3
Attig, T., 49
Augsburger, D., 16

Beck, A.T., 34
Becker, E., 13
Benard, B., 112–14, 116
Bending, M., 107
Bereavement, 3–4
Black, D., 111
Bowen, M., 59, 67
Bowlby-West, L., 61
Bowlby, J., 6–7, 62, 149–50, 152, 154
Brayer, M.M., 148
Bronfenbrenner, U., 113–14
Buchwald, A., 128
Butler, R., 132

Cancer Counselling Center, 130–2
Case vignettes
  Ann: suicide of husband and chronic
    illness, 17–18, 51–2
  Arnie: suicide of a son, 73
  Bob: post-traumatic stress, 156–8
  George: War veteran with unresolved
    losses, 30–1
  Karen: death of son, 24–5, 41–4
  Katy: death of husband, 32
  Les: death of a partner in a gay/lesbian
    relationship, 76–7
  Marie: loss of identity after heart attacks,
    28, 48
  Marnie: Drowning death of a sibling, 61–2
  Pat: HIV Positive, 23–4,
  Pete: losses involved with adoption, 78
  Sam and Gina: life-threatening illness, 70–3
  Sid: death in the family, 60–1

Categories of loss, 9–12
Cattell, R.B., 34
Childhood Bereavement Study, 110
Children
  Death conceptualizations, 107–9
    age-based, 108–9
    stage-based, 107
    task-based, 107–8
  Death of, 144–6
  Grieving process, 109–12
    Complications, 111–12
    healthy responses, 109–11
  Illness in, 134–6
  Interventions in bereavement
    Bronfenbrenner model, 112–17
      Family, 114–16
      School, 116–17
      Community, 117–24
        Winston's Wish, 117–18
        Camp Lost and Found, 118–24
    Resiliency, 112–113
  Interventions in illness, 134–6
Childsworks/Childsplay, 120
Clark, A., 127
Clayson, H., 129
'Complicated grief', 155
Continuing bonds, 8, 25, 45, 101–2, 154
Coping
  definition, 8, 15, 42
  strategies, 15, 99–100
  styles, 97–8
Corr, C., 108, 128
Couldrick, A., 107
Cullinan, A., 11

Davidson, M., 77
Davies, B., 75
Day, B., 140
Death
  of a child, 75
  of a grandparent, 77
  of a parent, 74
  of a partner in a gay/lesbian
    relationship, 76
  of a sibling, 75
  of a spouse, 74
Demi, A.S., 148
Dent, A., 111
Deutsch, H., 152

Diagnostic and Statistical Manual
    (DSM M IV), 147, 151
Doka, K., 142
DPM, 8, 26, 110, 130
Duffy, W., 108
Duvall, E.M., 56–8
Dying person
    expectations of, 129
    fears of, 129
    life review, 132, 134
    psychological needs of, 132–3

Engel, G., 17
Erikson, E.H., 114

Family development, 56–8
Family patterns, 60–1
Family tasks, 56, 58
Family therapy, 58–73
    communications theory, 58–9
    constructivism, 63–4
    geneogram, 67–73
    meaning-making strategies, 65–7
    structural theory, 60
    systems theory, 59–60
    symbolic interaction, 59, 62
Feelings spiral, 92
Forgiveness, 15–16, 46, 155
Fox, S., 107, 109–11, 134
Freud, S., 4, 148
Fulton, R.F., 149
Funerals, 32–3

Gestalt theory, 127
Glasser, W., 27, 50
Glick, I., 125
Grief
    tasks of, 7
    unanticipated mourning, 153
    unresolved
        absence, inhibited, delay of
            grief, 151–2
        chronic mourning, 153–4
        definition, 147–8
        distorted or conflicted mourning, 152–3
        reasons for, 154–5
        unanticipated mourning, 153
Grief counselling, 35–6
    early sessions, 37, 41–5
    middle sessions, 45–9
    later sessions, 49–52
Grief issues in families: 74–9
    death of a child, 75
    death of a grandparent, 77
    death of a parent, 74
    death of a partner in a gay/lesbian
        relationship, 76
    death of a sibling, 75

Grief issues in families Cont
    death of a spouse, 74
    family losses other than death, 77–78
Group counselling
    adult ten-week support group, 83–106
    evaluation, 105
    group procedures and expectations, 85
    therapeutic factors, 80–2
Grotberg, E., 27
Guerin, P., 70

Hanser, S., 134
History of loss, 32–4
Horowitz, M., 40, 148
Hospice, 127–8
Humphrey, G.M., 9, 140

Intake, pre-counselling, 34–5
Ivey, A.E., 36

Jackson, D.D., 59
Jackson, E., 14
Jordan, J.R., 58

Kennell, J.H., 144–5
Kenyon, B., 108
Kissane, D.W., 60, 62–3
Krementz, J., 136
Kubler-Ross, E., 5, 149

Lazarus, R.S., 8, 15,
Lester, J., 134
Lieberman, S., 61
Life Review, 132, 134
Lifton, R., 27, 112
Lindemann, E., 4–5, 149
Lo, B., 130
Loss
    aspect of self, 10–11
    child, 144–6
    definition, 3
    developmental, 21–2
    models of, 4–9
    perspectives on, 12–17
    relationship, 19
    treasured object, 20–1

Marwit, S.J., 101–2
Memorialization, 100–3
Meaning-making strategies, 65–7
    characterization, 66–7
    coincidancing, 66
    comparison, 65–6
    dreaming, 65
    family speak, 67
    storytelling, 65
Meaning reconstruction, 9, 17, 23,
    93–5, 103–4

Minuchin, S., 60, 67
Models of loss, 49
Mourning, see grief
Multicultural Family Institute, 68–9, 71
Murder, 141–2

Nadeau, J.W., 59, 62, 65–6
Nagy, M.A., 107
Narrative, 9, 23, 43
Needs assessment, 28, 29
Neimeyer, R.A., 9, 18, 23, 43, 154
Nichols, J.A., 145
Nichols, M.P., 59–60, 63
Noppe, I., 109

Palliative care, 128–30
Paper plate exercise, 95
Parkes, C.M., 148–9, 152, 154
Perspectives on loss, 12–17
    philosophical, 13, 21, 23–4
    physical, 17
    psychological, 14–16, 25–9
    sociological/cultural, 16–17, 29–31
    spiritual, 13–14, 31–2
Post-traumatic stress, 139, 155, 156–8
Psychological needs, 27, 50, 132–3
Psychological tests, 34

Quinn, A., 129–30

Rando, T.A., 7, 10, 75, 101, 125–6, 148, 150–2, 154
Raphael, B., 3, 14, 60–1, 64, 139, 151–2, 154, 158
Redmond, L., 141–2
Reminiscing, 47, 88–90
Resiliency, 15, 26–7, 46, 93–4, 103–4, 112–13, 116
Resolution of grief, 3, 8, 52–4, 154
Rituals, 30, 100–2
Rose, A.M., 62
Rosenblatt, P.C., 62
Rotter, S.B., 34

Rowling, I., 116
Rubin, S.S., 53
Ryan, J.A., 122
Rynearson, E., 154

Schneider, M.E., 129
Silverman, P.R., 8, 25, 45, 53–4, 101, 110, 154
Six 'R' Processes of Mourning, 7, 150–1
Smith, C.S., 108
Speece, M.W., 107
Sprenkle, D.H., 55
Stephenson, J.S., 11, 148
Stokes, J.A., 117–18
Stress, 8, 15, 97–9
Stroebe, M.S., 8, 110, 119, 130
Suicide, 139–41
Support group design, 83–106

Tasks of grief, 7
Terminal illness, 125
Thomas, W.I., 62
Thoresen, C.E., 15–16
Traumatic loss, 137–9

Unresolved grief
    absence, inhibition, delay of grief, 151–2
    mourning, 153–4
    definition, 147–8
    distorted or conflicted mourning, 152–3
    reasons for, 154–5

Walsh, F., 58
Wisendale, S.K., 55
Wolin, S., 15,
Worden, J.W., 7, 110, 150, 152

Yalom, I.D., 80, 82

Zimmerman, S.L., 55
Zimpfer, D.G., 9, 130–2